THE
LONG
TAIL
OF
TRAUMA

THE
LONG
TAIL
OF
TRAUMA

ELIZABETH WILCOX

A memoir

GREEN PLACE BOOKS | *Brattleboro, Vermont*

Printed in the United States

10 9 8 7 6 5 4 3 2 1

Green Writers Press is a Vermont-based publisher whose mission is to spread a message of hope and renewal through the words and images we publish. Throughout we will adhere to our commitment to preserving and protecting the natural resources of the earth. To that end, a percentage of our proceeds will be donated to environmental activist groups and The Southern Poverty Law Foundation. Green Writers Press gratefully acknowledges support from individual donors, friends, and readers to help support the environment and our publishing initiative. Green Place Books curates books that tell literary and compelling stories with a focus on writing about place—these books are more personal stories, memoir, and biographies.

GREEN PLACE BOOKS · GREEN WRITERS PRESS

Giving Voice to Writers & Artists Who Will Make the World a Better Place
Green Writers Press | Brattleboro, Vermont
www.greenwriterspress.com

ISBN: 978-1-950584-62-8

COVER PHOTO BY JILL BATTAGLIA
COURTESY OF FINE ART AMERICA

In memory of my father who asked,
for my mother, that this story be told.

Simply put, a long-tail risk is one in which the manifestation of loss will occur far later than the behavior that led to the loss.[1]

FOREWORD

Now fifty-two years old, I began writing this book when I was only twenty-two. At that age, I understood little of childhood trauma and its impact on mental health. I did not know of the link between early childhood trauma and the chronic diseases people develop as adults, of the likelihood of young children who have experienced acute trauma to develop autoimmune disease, depression, PTSD, and suicidal thoughts. Few popular books at that time seemed to tackle that topic, particularly with the intention of fostering a deeper understanding among those who love and care for the people who struggle as adults.

I am one of seven children, a daughter of a mother who endured what is now known as adverse childhood experiences—more commonly called ACE. ACE is a label that I think no one, least of all my mother, would have conferred upon herself as a child and which carries an altogether different association in her adulthood: one of struggle and one of having to overcome.

My psychologist friend Beth was the first to help me to understand the implications of the term as it relates to my mother. I befriended Beth when our children were young and we both were in the throes of raising three children in the age of what was being called "curling" parenting: parents crouched on hands and knees attempting to create for their children the perfect patch of ice. In our many conversations, I shared with Beth not only my struggles in parenting but also with my mother. I told her my mother had mood swings and challenging behaviors and that I was often insensitive and impatient with her. I also explained how my mother was a displaced child of war, separated from her own mother and abused. Beth responded by telling me that, despite what my mother endured, how surprisingly well-adjusted me and my siblings were. To help, she gave me D. W. Winnicott's book *Deprivation and Delinquency*.

Beth sent me on a journey that became the foundation of this book. With further research, I discovered how Winnicott's fears and objections to separating young children from their parents were borne out in my mother. One study showed me that some forty-eight percent of four- to seven-year-olds evacuated out of London in Operation Pied Piper during World War II suffered a minimum of level-two depression in later life.[2] I learned this level of depression could manifest as anger, anxiety, sleep problems, repetitive thoughts, manic behavior, and even substance abuse.[3] Studies also suggested that extended duration of separation and poor quality of care could further impact future psychological well-being, and mid- or late-life crisis often proved a destabilizing force. Given that my mother was barely three when separated from her mother, who herself had been separated from her mother at birth and endured complex trauma of her own, I began to see how destabilizing her repeated separations were, how vulnerable my mother was in her later years, and how traumatizing those experiences remained.

It all may sound obvious now, and perhaps it always was, but through my work in communications—first for an organization that promotes the emotional competence of young children and then for Beth's organization, which supports emotional literacy among the underserved, my understanding of my mother deepened. I learned that the two most important windows for the development of what is called "self-regulation"—the regulation of emotion, behavior, and thought—are early childhood and adolescence, with early childhood being the foundational period during which mental health is built and adolescence being the time in which adjustments and repairs can be made.[4] My mother had both windows shut on her. I learned that our ability to self-regulate informs our ability to successfully manage our thoughts and our feelings; to deal with strong feelings so they don't overwhelm us;

to focus and control our behaviors; to negotiate challenges; and to be resilient in the face of adversity[5]—all of which my mother sometimes struggled with. In addition, our primary caregiver—our mother, our father, or the people who primarily care for us during this formative time—shapes and promotes these abilities in us, these skills and competencies so critical to our ability to cope and to our lifelong learning, mental health, well-being, and success[6]. Not only did my mother experience acute trauma in these years while lacking a consistent, loving primary caregiver, but the young life of my grandmother—her caregiver—also was beset by trauma, maternal separation, and a world war.

Not until Beth set me on this course of discovery and research did I begin to appreciate what my mother had to overcome in order to successfully raise my six siblings and me. In time, I began to understand the reason behind her behaviors in later life. Through my research, I learned that ACE has a strong association with PTSD, with which my mother was eventually diagnosed. I saw that childhood abuse and neglect have been shown to increase PTSD symptoms in adulthood. I discovered that more severe PTSD is reported for individuals, like my English mother, who have been exposed to ACE at 3–5 years old;[7] that women are more than twice as likely as men to suffer from PTSD;[8] and that one in three English women who experience severe trauma develop PTSD. I also discovered that there is a strong case for the role of genetics in PTSD. People with higher genetic risk for several mental disorders are at higher genetic risk for developing PTSD after a traumatic event,[9] and family linkage studies that investigate patterns of diseases within families provide good evidence for the heritability of PTSD.[10] Based on her own repeated trauma, my grandmother, I realized, no doubt suffered from PTSD as well, which made my mother more vulnerable from the outset.

This knowledge helped me. My mother's PTSD and her visible inability to self-regulate in her later years were in many ways outside her control. A mother now myself, I understand that what a mother wants above all is to lay a strong foundation for her child, but that given my mother's and grandmother's lack of a stable and secure foundation, my mother had to be very intentional in raising us. Through my own professional work in trauma-informed care and early childhood development, I also began to recognize the value, both for her and for me, of working to develop those competencies in myself—competencies that include empathy, emotional sensitivity, emotional awareness, and the ability to self-regulate—an ongoing process for me.

This book is the result of what I have learned and what I still do not know. It is an exploration of the inheritability of trauma and of maternal past and maternal present. It is a book that my own mother encouraged me to write—a book for her, for my children, and for all those families with histories of trauma, families separated at national borders, detained in refugee camps, or who, unlike my own family, still endure prejudice and structural racism. It represents a living autopsy of sorts, a dissection of the seen and unseen, of what lies beneath. It is memoir, but because experience of fact is subjective, it includes fictional narratives as well. We can listen to our mothers' stories, but to understand why those stories so visibly impact us and others, we have to use our imaginations. To be empathic and to try to understand how others feel, we have to try to take their perspectives, as hard as that effort may be. So here follows an imagined history of maternal memoir that is my attempt to find truth.

PROLOGUE

While tails are very rare in humans, temporary tail-like structures are found in the human embryo. Most people aren't born with a tail because the structure absorbs into the body during fetal development, forming the tailbone . . . Sometimes the tail remains due to a defect during the developmental stage.[II]

This is a story of mothers. This is a story of daughters. This is a story of the trauma we carry and the trauma we tend to.

This story begins long before me. It begins with the first trauma my ancestral mothers bore, something passed deep in our wombs, from one generation to the next.

I feel it lashing when I am changing the sheets on my elderly mother's bed and she tells me that she has decided I don't like her very much.

I don't disagree.

I love my mother but in that moment, as my mother leans against her rubber-capped cane beside a second-hand armoire, I do not like her. But then I am not sure at that moment, with my temper frayed, anyone particularly likes *me*—most of all me.

For three days, my mother has been complaining ceaselessly of a litany of health concerns, of her inability to pay for food, of the dangerous policies of this U.S. president. She has lived through Hitler. She knows the consequences of incendiary politics. She fears another war.

I am not empathetic. I am tired of tending to her, of being her caregiver, and of her enveloping despair.

My mother, Barbara, has had to overcome adverse childhood experiences. At the outbreak of World War II, when she was only three years old, she was placed alone on a train to Wales with her eighteen-month-old brother, Neville. Picked up by a stranger from a train platform with a number hanging around her neck, she spent her childhood in a succession of foster homes and boarding schools. She was abused.

I know these facts. I am aware that her own mother, my grandmother, also suffered through world wars and was separated from her own mother in early childhood. I know my grandmother Violet's physical and mental health also was impacted in later life. But when making my mother's bed after a long weekend of caring, this knowledge does not help me cope with her.

"I became a mother at the age of three," she often told my six siblings and me growing up. "I had no childhood at all."

My mother and grandmother never fully recovered from the trauma they endured. I, in contrast, had a happy, loving, and secure childhood. But even with this knowledge, I still struggle to manage the effects of my mother's trauma as they manifest in her and, by extension, me.

This story is an attempt to shed light on a narrative seldom found on teleprompters or in historical texts. It is a story of mothers whose voices we hear as we brush the knots in our daughters' hair. It is a story told in bathrooms and in kitchens, passed from one generation to the next, and carried in our DNA. It is our daughter's story, our mother's story, and our grandmother's story. It is a story of repeated childhood separation, complex trauma, and abiding maternal love.

This is a story that I first began to pursue when I was only twenty-two, inadvertently, at my mother's kitchen table, in her upscale London flat. It is a story to help me understand why my mother struggles so much, why she shakes and can be imbalanced in so many ways, why she is the way she increasingly has become: exhausted and manic, determined and struggling, physically fit and mentally unwell—pairings that can seem to me not meant to coexist but in my mother somehow do. It is a story buttressed by its psychological underpinnings, such as the importance of mother-child attachment and the ways in which separation and trauma can influence generations to come.[12] It is a story of the early childhood traumas that our mothers carry, evident in my own mother's later age as PTSD, as well as their remnants in us and in the children we bear. It is a story in which I have intentionally layered my voice with hers and with the imagined voices before us, unearthing a palimpsest of maternal history. It is what happens after the incidence of trauma has passed but its vestigial tail remains.

THE
LONG
TAIL
OF
TRAUMA

CHAPTER I

LONDON, ENGLAND — 1989

What cannot be communicated to the mother cannot be communicated to the self.[13]

My part of the story, I decide, begins here, the first night of my mother's visit, after I have abandoned counting sheep, after their fat bushy bodies have crumbed, their thin wobbly joints buckled before my imagined fence as I try in vain to sleep. It is several months after I have graduated from college. I am lying in bed listening to the high-pitched voice of a woman who is flirting on the fire escape below, her voice slipping through the crack of my bedroom window. Other noises are joining her voice: the rolling murmur of a waiting taxi and the exclamatory bursts of a man's mocking laughter. When the cries of a woken baby wail their way up, I push shut the window and smother my head with a pillow. Still unable to sleep, I get up and walk to the kitchen, passing my mother's closed bedroom door. I remove a painted mug from the cupboard and turn on the stove to heat a quart of vanilla milk dashed with an ample portion of scotch.

My mother emerges, beckoned by the tapping of a wooden spoon. In the light, her nightgown is translucent, her body a silhouetted ghost.

"What are you doing?" she asks as the milk is beginning to warm.

"Can't sleep," I say.

"I never can sleep."

I stir the milk to stop the thin skin from forming.

"That's why I take a pill every night," she says while I watch bubbles turn to froth. "My mother used to make scotch milk when she couldn't sleep. Just like her," she continues, eyeing the bottle on the countertop. "I'd take it off now," she says, taking hold of the pan's handle and filling my painted mug.

I watch my mother pour. I do not want to talk, not with my mother bent over my mug with puffy lids and bare toes and a worn nightgown that desperately needs a robe. The night prior, I had no patience for her. I did not want to hear that my nails needed a trim or that I had yet to thank her for another meal that she had gone out of her way to buy and cook. I did not want to be reminded of how she worked tirelessly for us growing up. I did not want to learn about her childhood and how difficult life was for her. So that night, without saying goodnight, I left. Like the self-absorbed adolescent child that at twenty-two I no longer should have been, I shut my bedroom door to her, as I so often did.

In the kitchen now, she is heating up my milk as if nothing has transpired between us and I still cannot stop myself from stone-walling her. I do not want to delve into the why behind our latest impasse. Silently, I watch her work.

"I'll just fill up your mug, darling, and then you can go and get some sleep," she tells me, gently kissing my cheek and pushing the bottle away.

She pours. I take the cup.

"I love you," she says.

"Me too," is a whisper as I walk to my room.

Propped against my pillow, sipping my warm milk, I think about the fact that gratitude does not come easily to daughters like me. I feel my belly's small bulge—a roll of taffy that one day might stretch. My mother's expanded seven times—so many years of stretching skin and needy children searching for a teat. Daughters never fully appreciate their mother until she dies, at least that's what my mother and allegedly her mother Violet always said. One of life's tragedies, they maintained. In the dark of that small room, I think about the fact that all too often I slip into this familiar pattern of serve and no return, incapable of absorbing my mother,

her requests and her concerns falling off me like beads of rain on water-resistant glass and which seem to me to emanate in her from such contradictory needs—to be close and to set boundaries, to be cared for and to care, to be acknowledged for what she has accomplished and to be recognized for what she has been deprived. Since I was a little girl, I have seen these needs expressed by my mother, but as I mature into adulthood, the expectation that I answer feels burdensome to me. She seems to me in want of so much, a void so deep that no amount of attention will ever satiate her, no matter how I try. So I do not.

But as her twenty-two-year-old daughter, I know that I could be providing more. I am here, living rent-free in my parents' apartment from which they have moved but not yet sold, despite the fact that my mother herself, having been separated from her parents at a very young age, was later again thrown out of her parents' home. I am here, with a mother who has ensured that all seven of her children have always had a secure home and were never in want of anything growing up, including a college education, despite the fact that her parents denied her one. I am here, knowing that she has an unwavering belief in what I can achieve, despite the lack of belief her parents had in her. I am here, sipping warm vanilla milk dashed with scotch that she has risen out of bed to pour in her beautifully appointed apartment in London's desirable West End, even after I have shut my bedroom door to her. I am here, knowing how much she lacked growing up. I am here, confident of the unconditional and unwavering love she and my father have provided me since birth. I should be offering her more in return. And yet, I do not. I do not want to be the one to provide the affirmation and the support that she, as a child, never had. I am here, believing I cannot give back to my mother what she never received but also knowing that as her child, I should at least try.

"I'm sorry if I was abrupt at dinner," I tentatively offer the next morning, placing a cup of Twining's English Breakfast Tea by her bed.

In response to my apology, my mother is seemingly unbothered, even nonchalant, telling me to forget it as she walks to the bathroom drugged with sleep, scratching her arms, every filed nail leaving a strip of red skin. When she returns, I watch as she folds herself against the pillow. Her skin is beginning to slip on her neck and the bones on her shoulders push up. She is beautiful, everyone says, but I do not want to imagine myself a middle-aged mother like her. She reaches for her cup, purses her lips, and sips. I take a deep breath.

"Mom. I'd like to learn about your mother and you," I begin. In the night, I have decided to invite her to record her story. I tell myself the offer is at least something. A step. Through the recording, I will provide her at last the chance to make her and her mother's story heard. By having her record it, the story also will be contained and I will not have to sit as she aimlessly wanders the recesses of a maternal past, as she so often does. I will not have to attend as her deep-set eyes move endlessly over her surroundings, the backs of her pupils skimming the recesses of her mind's eye like fingertips reading infinitely scrolling Braille.

"Why?" my mother asks as she notices a silk lampshade askew on the other side of her room. She gets out of bed, straightens it, and climbs back beneath the sheets.

"Maybe because you think I'm just like her?" I suggest, uncertain how to respond.

"Not just," she says, her blue eyes moving to the mold that climbs the brick wall outside her window in streams of green, spreading at the top into a big slippery fan. "I tell you things about her all the time." She sips her tea once again.

"I know," I say. "I just thought it might be interesting. You can get it all out at once. I can leave that Dictaphone out. It records your voice."

"I know what a Dictaphone is. I was secretary for the British Consulate in Germany, you'll recall."

"Yes, in Germany, I know," I say, showing her that I have been listening to what she says.

Again, my mother sips and carefully lays her teacup down on the glass-surfaced side table with the ruffled skirt of tailored chintz. "I'm very busy this visit but if I have time, I will," she offers, swiping her hand in the air as if pushing away a spider's web. Her past is like that, thin and delicate but stubbornly present in unreached corners and hidden undersides. "Maybe at some point," she continues, evasive still, reaching back for her tea and taking one more long, sustained slurp. "It is an interesting story," she says, before adding, "I did have a difficult childhood, you know. So did my mother. Unlike you. Unlike your siblings."

"Unlike us," I repeat.

"I did love those red shoes too," my mother continues, laughing.

"You did," I affirm. I motion to leave.

"Well doesn't your mother get a kiss before you leave for work?" she asks, chin tilted up, neck stretched.

"Okay."

"Elizabeth?"

I stop.

"I will do it. Just leave me a note on how to work that contraption. We didn't actually use those in Germany then."

"That's fine," I say.

"And by the way, what time are you due back this evening? Want to run? Could you take my tea? Remember, I'm only here for a short time. You can't just go running off all the time while I'm here. I need to talk to you about things. I expect you to eat with me properly while I'm here. And not to drink all the port, leaving your father to fill it up every time."

I do not reply. Instead I pick up her tea. I reenter the kitchen, rinse my mother's cup, and place the Dictaphone on the kitchen table with a few instructions scribbled on a frayed pad. I draw a diagram of the Start, Stop, and Record buttons on the pocket-sized machine. My mother has an aversion to anything that requires a battery. "I'm just not mechanical," she often tells my six siblings and me. "I sometimes see myself as Ferdinand the Bull, content to smell the flowers in the fields."

It is several days before I hear her voice on tape. The first few words are uttered tentatively. "Elizabeth, I'm not sure I'm doing this correctly, but here it goes: the story of my mother and me." In a few moments, her voice has the transfixed quality of a pianist lost in a movement. I listen to the tape early in the morning before my mother awakes.

"I never knew my mother was illegitimate. She never talked of her childhood. She kept many secrets. If it hadn't been for the letter that my brother, Neville, found in her drawer after she died, we wouldn't know still. It was a cold letter from her father in Canada, whom she had never met and who seemed to have dismissed her request to meet him. I must see if I can get a copy of that letter for you from my brother, Neville."

So the narration goes, retelling the stories that my six siblings and I experienced as countless and disconnected threads while growing up. The narration has many loose ends and that morning I can only begin to untangle them. But over the course of those ten days and what will be many more, the act of my mother's telling will often feel like the untwisting of a high-pressure valve to an all too capacious past. That past begins with a single event: the birth of my illegitimate grandmother, Violet Helene C. Bracker, née *filius populi*, in 1904. She was conceived by a German house servant Anna and the ignominious Jack in the home of his mother, Priscilla, who likely did not know that the withdrawal of maternal support early in a child's life can have consequences that contribute to a complex and changing pattern of vulnerability throughout a child's life.[14]

PRISCILLA

WHITCHURCH, ENGLAND, 1904

A bastard not yet crowning in this cold attic room. The midwife, Mrs. Baxter, in attendance, and a sixty-five-year-old woman Priscilla perched on a wicker-seated wooden chair, watching her cook and aging house girl, Anna, labor on a coil-spring bed.

Anna, pillows at her back, pushing on the horsehair mattress with those dark, forlorn eyes—anguished, unblinking, fixed. Beneath those eyes, a small nose and a pronounced Hapsburg chin, creating a countenance simultaneously resolute and resigned, surrendering and unflinching in the face of an inevitable fate. And that buxom chest of hers, slightly rising before every push, like the swell on a wave.

At first, Priscilla did not get up from her chair, as nothing was assured. This hidden thing with its speck of something, maybe bloodied hair, might not emerge into the cold, spring-evening damp. The midwife might fail. Anna might not prevail. How could Priscilla know? Yes, one might see this house servant pound veal, her back erect, her shoulders set, her wide hips aligned to the edge of a butcher block, and know that she could cook, that she was strong, that she had force. One might assume that when Priscilla's own black-sheep son had lain with her, the sperm would quickly take. But there was no guarantee that Anna would get the baby to emerge, and after each push, the bloodied speck retracted into its mother. No matter how strong, no mother could will her child to life (or for that matter, death), and sitting on her wooden chair by the window so that she could look away when it all got to be too much, Priscilla was not altogether dismayed by that fact.

"Push, love," pleaded the midwife, crouched at the foot of the bed. "Keep on, love. Very nearly," she implored, ignoring the presence of Priscilla behind her.

Priscilla did not react, knowing the baby wise to be afraid. Prescient perhaps. She wished her son, Jack, had had the same presence of mind. Instead he had not considered the implications of his little tryst, his clandestine fornication. This baby, should it live, would be parentless by law, the sin of its feckless father and wanton mother branded upon it, stigmatized, the incarnate of carnal, living the penance of its parents: this mother, Priscilla's employee, and this father, her son, Jack. Perhaps Priscilla should have seen it coming, Jack and his licentious behavior. She had failed in raising him.

Despite what appearances might suggest, Priscilla had helped, in her way. The circumstances were difficult, even the midwife had to concede that, though no doubt she had seen it all before. Engaging Mrs. Baxter had not been easy. Discretion was required, accommodations made. Priscilla had required that Anna stay homebound at the end, when she was unable to hide her girth. "She's very ill," Priscilla had explained to the butcher. "Can't get out of bed," she had told the milkman.

But Germany? Of all countries. If she only had known that she would have a grandchild by a German, Priscilla never would have hired Anna. France—why had Priscilla not thought about the French? Allies they were now. Friends. France would protect them from Germany, whom one could not trust, with her powerful army and aggressive ways. And that navy—her husband Frederick always went on about that German navy, growing so fast, threatening to take away England's dominance at sea. "Oh, those Germans," Frederick complained, "always testing," testing France in Morocco while good old England stood loyally by France's side. No, it would not be German, this baby. Priscilla would not abide that.

Priscilla sighed aloud, casting in vain for somewhere to look and somewhere to lay the blame. She turned to the garden below. She usually loved spring. Not today.

"It certainly is having a bit of a tough time of it," Priscilla remarked from her perch.

Mrs. Baxter did not reply.

The contractions had been occurring for most the day, the bloodied speck of a baby appearing but then fearfully retracting into its mother's womb. Strong though she began, Anna was now pale and exhausted, and Priscilla decided the chances of the baby living were beginning to wane. A part of Priscilla was concerned, but another part told her it was fine, that it would be easier if Anna gave up and the baby did not emerge. What kind of life would the child lead?

"It's okay, lass," Mrs. Baxter was assuring the girl. *No, a woman,* Priscilla thought, for Anna was thirty-four.

Priscilla remained in her chair, positioned six feet away. She no doubt was frustrating the midwife by not offering more, by sitting on her perch like some sort of visiting swallow who had dropped onto a nearby limb, curious and peering. But what did Mrs. Baxter expect? In a short time, Anna would have to learn to fend for herself. Priscilla had already raised seven children and given birth to an eighth, who sadly did not survive. She certainly did not need another one at this age, under these circumstances, and a half-German child at that. She had been generous enough to engage the experienced Mrs. Baxter here in Whitchurch, despite the damage such a birth could do to their family's reputation, even with the agreement by the reluctant midwife to register the birth in another town where the baby would be raised, if it indeed survived, which it might not. Poor little black lamb. No, no one could fault Priscilla at all. She had remained in this room all day.

The midwife interrupted Priscilla's thoughts. Was she asking for a quill?

"Sorry," Priscilla replied absentmindedly. "I didn't hear you quite."

"Pass me that quill, Mrs. Cross," Mrs. Baxter repeated with impatience.

"A quill?" Priscilla asked, perplexed.

"Yes, in my medical case, by the sill there. The quill," Mrs. Baxter repeated.

"Whatever for?"

"Please," she snapped.

She could be tough, this Mrs. Baxter, a bona fide midwife who prided herself on her success rate—fifty-nine babies, and all had survived.

"The quill." She was near yelling now.

"I'm coming," Priscilla replied. "No need to repeat." She reached down and handed the quill to her and, without so much as a word of acknowledgement, Mrs. Baxter took it. She then proceeded to clean the inside with alcohol and cut it on both ends as Priscilla watched with interest.

"That small packet of cayenne pepper as well," Mrs. Baxter said.

So Priscilla again obliged, and again she watched as Mrs. Baxter unfolded the small packet of cayenne and dipped one end of the quill into it. Then she put the quill into Anna's nose and blew. Anna started sneezing, not just once, but repeatedly.

"Well, I never," Priscilla said.

"Here we go," Mrs. Baxter said with a hint of pride. "See, the perineum is bulging now. Not long now."

"Not long," Priscilla said. But she was not at all sure. Her son, Jack, had claimed in his puerile defense that this child was not

Anna's first, that there was another bastard child before this one, but this labor did not support that defense at all.

"Mrs. Cross," Mrs. Baxter said.

"Yes."

"I am going to move Anna from the Sims position."

"The Sims position?" Priscilla asked.

"Yes," Mrs. Baxter snapped, and Priscilla, knowing better than to ask for an explanation, observed as Mrs. Baxter began to adjust the position of the cook on the bed. She unbent the knees from the chest and laboriously turned her from her side to her back.

"Could you please lay those pillows against the wall?" Mrs. Baxter asked, nodding to the pillows on the floor with only the back of her head.

Priscilla again complied, rising up and positioning the pillows as Mrs. Baxter asked. Mrs. Baxter then tied two belts to the foot of the bed.

"There now, scooch up a bit will you, lass." Anna nodded and shifted up the bed, wincing in pain as she did. "There now, try to sit and grab those belts, and next time the contraction comes, pull and push with all your might, alright?"

Anna nodded again. A contraction came, and Anna screamed in pain.

"Now, Mrs. Cross, would you give her another sip of that tea?" Mrs. Baxter asked, and Priscilla, who had obediently moved back to her perch, got up once again. She walked to the bureau with the uneven leg and took the cup of tea that Mrs. Baxter had earlier brewed from ginger wine and strained juniper and gently held it up to Anna's mouth without saying a word.

"Sip," Mrs. Baxter interjected from the foot of the bed when the contraction had passed.

Anna did, and Priscilla then obsequiously took the cup away, placing the cup back on the lace doily before shuffling back to her chair.

"Sit up more, please, and keep hold of those belts, Anna," Mrs. Baxter commanded. "There you go."

Another contraction came, and Anna pushed, breathing a German expletive as she did. This German language was so harsh, so hard to bear, Priscilla thought. But at least Anna's vomiting had ceased and the push seemed more forceful than before, she assured herself. Then the top of the head showed and this time it held.

"Well done, Anna. Getting closer now," Mrs. Baxter remarked encouragingly, and Priscilla told herself that she did not mind if the baby lived or died, despite the pluck of it.

But pluck it did have. In fact, in thinking about that very trait, Priscilla began to feel a slight affinity with this little thing. Perhaps, Priscilla thought, this baby even carried a little bit of her, some of her fortitude, some of her stubborn will. And as loath as Priscilla was to admit, sitting on her little wooden chair, she was beginning to feel a degree of sympathy for this woman, too, she on her coil-spring bed. She could not help that she was poor, that men were the way they were. Fornication had consequences for women but really not men. Anyway, Anna was stuck in this situation now, as were the rest of them, and she was carrying on, as women did. The pain of birth was inexorable, and this Anna was enduring that, too, without complaint. Priscilla knew that pain all too well, and all that pain the result of a few brief moments, which must have been for Anna a chore, though they were sheer pleasure, no doubt, for her son. As much as Jack suggested the contrary, Priscilla was quite certain that Jack was largely responsible. He had been a cad, just as Frederick had said. Women were too often forced. Even this *fräulein*, Priscilla decided, could have been coerced. What unmarried woman would want this? Yes, Priscilla thought to herself, if this baby lived, she hoped it, too, found the capacity to prevail, by whatever means it must.

"Stay strong. We're getting there, love," the midwife was saying, and Priscilla found herself no longer able to dispel this same hope.

She shifted on her chair. Anna was panting, breathing in tempo with her contractions as best she could. She was trying, this Anna, this earnest *Kraut*.

The midwife reached into a basin of warm water, squeezed the sponge, and wiped along Anna's inner thighs. "There, there, lass," she said, "another one should soon come."

Anna screamed and pushed again. The baby was definitely crowning now, and Priscilla surrendered to relief. The baby might live.

"Mrs. Cross, could you please put that blanket atop her?" Anna had started shaking. She was cold, it seemed. The pain, no doubt.

Priscilla hastily obliged. As she laid the blanket across Anna's torso, she noted the water dripping down the inside of Anna's thighs. If only a baby emerged like a drip, she thought. How simple that would be. Why had God made childbirth so hard? The curse of Eve was no explanation for it.

"Mrs. Cross, please straighten the blanket. It's all askew," Mrs. Baxter admonished.

Yes, she could have forced Jack to marry, Priscilla thought, tugging the corners of the blanket so that it was aligned over Anna's torso, but what would marriage to Jack provide? No, Priscilla had done right by insisting this baby be given up. Jack would be an absent father and Anna a poor mother with nothing to give. Love and milk did not pay the bills. They all were better off with him in Canada. Priscilla was certain of it. He was unlikely to strike gold, but there he could find steady work and a decent wife she hoped, and perhaps a more respectable life than the one he lived here. The Canadian government seemed to want men like him, God bless them. Anna was better off putting this whole thing behind them.

She leaned closer toward Anna. "Alright?" Priscilla asked, trying to be helpful, perhaps standing a little too near.

"Please go back to your window," Mrs. Baxter interjected.

Priscilla did. She sat down and smoothed out a wrinkle on the lap of her dress and wondered how this situation had come about. Well, of course she knew "the how" of it. Jack had always been mischievous, kicking about the place with that smug gigglemug of his. His sisters mollycoddled him too much. Priscilla had always told them that. And Jack had never carried his weight around the house. They had all seen the way his eyes lingered on Anna and that great chest of hers. Still, Priscilla had never anticipated that he would succumb to a working girl from Germany, who was quite plain and stolid, even if Frederick said he could see the appeal in her. Excuse me, Priscilla had said. I only speak as a man, he had said in response, and she had wanted to throw her glass of water at him. Men!

Anna was pushing again. "Almost there. Push, love," Mrs. Baxter said. "The head is fully out, staying now. You're almost there. Just a bit more."

Priscilla turned to watch the rest to emerge. The excrement was out. Anna's screams were turning to grunts and Priscilla anticipated that the baby's shoulders would soon come. And yes, the bastard probably would be a girl. Priscilla had intuitively known that. Anna had carried the child low and centered, and now with the shape of that head and the size of its ears, her earlier suspicions seemed confirmed. *Poor little bundle*, Priscilla thought.

Priscilla decided to get up to be certain. Leaving her chair, she clasped her hands behind her back so as not to mislead the midwife into thinking that she was venturing to assist. She leaned over the bastard's face and peered. The baby had dark hair like its mother, eyes that were deep set, a thin nose, lips that were tight though slightly fuller than Anna's, and that forthright chin, the obstinate streak. *Good for her*, Priscilla thought. She'd suspected as much. Hadn't she said so?

"Back," the midwife barked.

Priscilla flinched. She returned to her spot.

The contraction passed. "Stop pushing for a bit, please," Mrs. Baxter said, her attention back to the *fräulein*.

Anna obliged. She was quite good that way. A good *Kraut*. They had a good working relationship, the two of them. Neither beat around the bush. When Priscilla had had her suspicions that Anna was with child, when that girth of hers had started to expand beneath her tidy black uniform and when those white apron ties had became harder to twist into a bow above her rump, Priscilla had gone directly to Anna to confront her about the misbegotten development in their midst.

"Are you with child?" she had asked directly of Anna, and Anna, in her stern German way, had immediately nodded.

"And the father?" Priscilla had asked, knowing full well the answer before she asked.

Anna had remained mute.

"Anna, tell me the father or I will dismiss you right now."

Anna had chosen not to speak but instead had nodded toward the ceiling, toward the room where Jack, when he was home visiting, slept.

"Alright, then," Priscilla had said, not seeking further details at that point. "But you are keeping it?" she asked, aware by its size that the decision was made.

Anna nodded again.

When Priscilla later had confronted Jack, he, too, had eventually confessed but he required so much badgering and then once the confession came, he steadfastly had claimed that it was Anna who had propositioned him. "She is not my type of woman," he had said. As if that had anything to do with it at all.

In short order, Priscilla then had called the two of them into the salon and prescribed the outcome to them both. She had come to a solution quickly, as she usually did.

"Jack, you will move to Canada and support this child from abroad through me, provided it lives. Anna, if you reach full term, you will give birth to the child in this house, to ensure the birth is carried out properly, but we will register the baby in another town, where the child will be raised. We have many relatives in Rickmansworth, which is a day's ride from here, and you can bring it there. You yourself will then go to London, where you will forge your own independent life. We will provide additional financial support so long as the child remains in Rickmansworth. Mr. Cross has two spinster nieces there, who I'm sure could use the extra income. I have not yet written to them, though I'm quite sure they will say yes. If they say no, there are others I can approach. This way the child will not be known as a base-born child, and you can rest assured that it will be in good hands. All of this will be done on the condition that you say nothing of this incident to anyone at all."

Priscilla then had inquired whether Anna had any alternative solutions. She had given her that chance. She had not asked Jack.

Anna had replied, "No."

"Nothing at all?"

"No, ma'am," Anna had said.

And with that, Priscilla had dismissed them from the room.

When Priscilla received a response from Frederick's nieces, Edith Mary and May, it was exactly what she had expected. Under the proposed financial arrangement, the two spinsters had agreed to house and raise the child. Anna would stay with the infant in their home for a few nights, as soon after the birth as was possible, and they would register the child in their town as a *filius populi*, so as not to implicate Jack. If pressed, they would say that an unknown woman had been passing through town and that, on seeing she was in labor, they in their graciousness had offered her a bed. Nowhere would the name "Cross" appear on its birth certificate. "Bracker" it would be, the child of Anna. That was it and so it would be. The matter had been dispatched.

Priscilla looked back at Anna. She seemed in such pain. Childbirth was such hell.

"It's burning. So hot. A ring of fire," Anna blurted out from the bed.

"Sit up more, dear," Mrs. Baxter said. Priscilla heard a trace of impatience in Mrs. Baxter's voice. *A bit unfair*, Priscilla thought.

"Come assist me, Mrs. Cross. Light breathing now, Anna. Short, shallow breaths, in and out," Mrs. Baxter continued, modeling the breaths. "Like blowing out a candle. Don't bear down." She turned to Priscilla. "Mrs. Cross, kindly hand me that small mirror by my maternity case." Mrs. Baxter said the word kindly in a way that did not sound kindly at all but Priscilla obliged her nonetheless.

Mrs. Baxter positioned the mirror at an angle, up high, just beyond the vaginal area. "See the baby's head? It's there," she pointed out to Anna.

"Yes," Priscilla heard herself say, though Anna did not reply. "Push on," Priscilla said.

Had she been asked, Priscilla now would concede very much to wanting the baby out. The day had gone on so long, sitting all day, and she was getting tired of all this. And in addition to this birth, the pregnancy had been quite trying as well. Priscilla had had to go about finding a ship for Jack's passage to Canada, all the time saying nothing to anyone, except those spinster nieces and Frederick, who was sworn to secrecy as well. Meanwhile, Anna herself had ruled out abortion. "Keeping it," Anna had repeated whenever Priscilla approached her. If she changed her mind, Priscilla told her, there were of course ways to address the situation. Some mothers cut the throats of children like this one, or buried them alive, or drowned them like bunnies. But Anna had insisted on no such thing and so Priscilla had acquiesced. Of course, if the baby survived, they both knew Anna could not have possibly cared for an infant alone, penniless as she was, a German immigrant, a working-class girl with broken English and no spouse. *Crèches* closed their doors to children like Anna's and the parish authorities would offer no succor; they found all possible ways to avoid supporting an illegitimate. And yes, there were industrial schools, and private charities like the Waifs and Strays Society or the Salvation Army, but the wards of these charities lived such hard lives through no fault of their own. As for the crusaders, Heaven help the child. Those poor bastard children, wrenched from what family they had, their flesh raw from scrubbing workhouse floors. And when they weren't in the workhouse, the children looked so pathetic: hair cropped, dressed in thick clogs and caps with nearly all their hair shaved off, marching to school and to church in crocodile lines, and all the time wondering why their mothers didn't love them, why their mothers didn't get married like all the others. It was a terrible situation but there was no choice. *Yes*, Priscilla thought, dispatching with regret. She'd done what was best in the hope that they could get as quickly as they could past it.

But it was evening now. Priscilla had earlier positioned her wooden chair by the window so that she could look away when the day got to be too much. From that spot, she had believed she would be able to feel the warmth of the daylight and appreciate the garden below and not get too involved. It had not turned out that way, damp and gray as the day had been, and now the room was no longer warm and Priscilla was unable to see the garden due to the lack of light.

She looked at Anna—her walnut-shaped face (yes, a walnut shape it was) so drained, so white—and she found herself fully succumbing to the hope that this woman would prevail, that the baby would survive.

"Keep on. You're very close," Priscilla heard herself say. "Just get it out."

Anna glanced at her and then raised herself somewhat defiantly on the bed before giving another hard push. The baby seemed to respond, its head emerging further out from between its mother's legs. Emboldened, Priscilla leaned toward Anna more. "Come on, Anna, push on," she repeated "One, two, three." What were the German words? *"Eins, zwei, drei."*

"One, two, three," the midwife repeated, somewhat less animatedly.

"One, two, three," Priscilla repeated with conviction. This baby, after all, was going to speak English. She would start to hear it at birth.

With another strong grunt, the baby's shoulders appeared and started to slip out with no need for forceps, no umbilical cord wrapped around the infant's neck, no obstructions at all. She remembered what Jack had told her, that this baby was not the first, but then reprimanded herself.

The torso came, and then the hips, and then a pair of small bent legs with tiny feet curled in at the ends. The placenta followed, splattering onto the edge of the bed before tumbling onto the floor. Priscilla never could get used to that.

The scissors! Mrs. Baxter wanted the scissors. "Oh, yes. Of course." Where were they? On the hand towel, by the basin of warm water. "Oh goodness. Here they are," Priscilla said.

Mrs. Baxter dropped the baby onto Anna's chest without a word, though it was still covered in film and blood, with an umbilical cord trailing out.

"Hold it up," Mrs. Baxter instructed to an awestruck Anna, and Anna weakly raised the baby over her chest.

"Beautiful," Anna said.

"Yes, beautiful," Mrs. Baxter affirmed. Then she turned to Priscilla. "Mrs. Cross, I need you to cut."

Priscilla hesitated, confused.

"Cut, I said. The cord," Mrs. Baxter commanded.

Slowly, steadily, Priscilla moved toward the cord. The scissors opened, just beneath the pink baby's flailing hands. Snip. The umbilical cord dropped. Priscilla watched it fall.

"Hold her, dear, hold her close. Don't worry about the mess. I'll wipe it up," Mrs. Baxter said.

Anna clutched the child to her chest and cradled it close, unbothered by the slippery, bloody film. Anna looked as if she might cry. Priscilla placed the scissors on the ground. She too beheld the pointy head, the quivering pink lips, the fragile blue hands and delicate curved feet—a sweet pickled thing it was. She felt awe rise through her like a wave.

Mrs. Baxter began wiping the child down with a wet cloth as Anna clutched it.

"Beautiful baby," Mrs. Baxter said.

"Beautiful," Priscilla repeated.

"Healthy," Mrs. Baxter said. "That makes sixty for me. So what shall you name her?"

Anna studied the baby. "Violet," she said after a long pause, with her harsh German accent.

"Violet?" Priscilla asked, making sure she understood.

"*Ja,*" Anna said.

Violet Bracker, that is fine, Priscilla thought. But buried beneath that name was Cross, and Priscilla forced herself to silently repeat the name, *Violet Cross.* She shuddered. This tiny Violet with so much to withstand, but she did look at peace, attached closely to her mother's breast, however fleeting that attachment might be.

CHAPTER 2

LONDON, ENGLAND — 1990

Emotions are an indispensable part of our mental life. . . . There is a great variety of strategies to regulate emotion efficiently. Distraction guides attention to a secondary task. . . . Detachment refers to distancing oneself from an emotional stimulus, thereby reducing its personal relevance.[15]

On the last morning of my mother's latest visit, I find her lying in the tub. Her naked body is a relief map of her many births, with thick, branched varicose veins running down her thighs into her knees, where they split into little blue streams. She seems to me a seahorse in still water, her seven babies all popped out.

I am still only twenty-two. I do not want to look. At my mother's request, I have obediently gone into the bathroom and taken a seat on her scrubbed toilet lid. For some reason, she is in an uncharacteristically good mood. As I sit, she reassures me to pay no heed to how Angus, the son of my grandmother Violet's half-brother George, ignored me the night before. With my mother's encouragement, I went reluctantly to meet her half-cousin Angus. Angus was reticent, unwilling to talk much about his family. ("We had better be careful," he had reportedly said to my mother's brother, Uncle Neville, before my arrival. "Elizabeth might use what we say for a book.") I immediately wished that I had not gone. Angus did not talk to me, nor did I talk to him. I felt awkward pursuing a maternal story with him and now this morning, I question whether I should record this story at all, even if my mother tells me that I can, even if she believes in me, even if I have so long been aware of her need to air it. There seems now too much emotional complexity to it. I manage better when I am detached. When my mother loses her temper, I contain mine. When she becomes emotional, I disengage. I like to say that I am a cold fish. The comment makes people laugh. The cold fish in the room is acknowledged but she slips past, not revealing how close to the surface her emotion was.

"My mother and Angus's father, George, who was her half-brother, not to be confused with my father, George, had a falling out. No one has ever spoken of why," my mother is explaining from the tub. "Maybe it was too painful for Angus. Of course, my mother and I had differences too. She could turn on a dime. I wish we were closer. But don't worry about last night and the way Angus was. Elizabeth, it doesn't matter what other people think. I always told you that growing up. You had a good childhood. You can't deny that. Could you grab me that soap from the vanity, darling, while you're here? Can you see it?"

I tell her I cannot.

"Yes, you can. It's beneath there, under the vanity. I like the Basis soaps. They are the best. Dove is cheap. Maybe my brother, Neville, can tell you more. He and your father have always got along so well. My father always called your father a peach of a fellow. Make sure you include that in my book."

"Okay," I say flatly, wondering when I can leave this toilet lid.

"I have the most terrible eczema on my arm," my mother is continuing from the tub, punching her arm toward me. "I have so many problems. The doctors think I'm quite unique. Can you see the eczema, the way it pops up? I'm on all sorts of steroids. I hope you don't inherit this problem when you're my age. Everything is genetics, you know. And now I'm getting spots on my face. I never had them when I was young. I have special cream for it from the dermatologist here. Look. You had a few spots when you were young. This Basis soap is the least irritating for it."

"I can't see anything," I say. I lean over, see nothing, and turn away. "Looks fine," I say dismissively.

"Fine? Honestly? It's there. You are blind. Anyway, my mother never talked about her half-brother, so I'm not surprised that Angus did not talk to you about him. He would be your great half-uncle, right? I'm never sure how that all works. To be fair, my mother actually never talked about her childhood at all, not to me anyway. She did speak about that time in Rickmansworth with her two spinster aunts. She loved those aunts so dearly and her early life there so much. That was the one part of her childhood she would talk to me about, the only bit really. I have that memory at least. She'd tell me how she used to walk in crocodile lines and how she had to wear white gloves to her school and how much she loved those aunts. She said how in her early years in England she had led a privileged life. Then the war came. You children don't understand what it's like to grow up during wartime, as both she and I did. It's not good. It changed us both. Your generation does not understand. Could you get your mother that flannel by the vanity?"

"What?" She has lost me.

"The washcloth? Maybe you need to get your hearing checked. I get wax buildup in my ears. Maybe you have inherited that. I have to get my ears washed out every year. A real pain. They put tubes in your ear and squeeze water and it makes one feel so dizzy, one can barely stand afterward. Similar to when you stand in a field and twirl and twirl. Have you done that?"

"Yes, I've twirled."

"I know. I watched you spin endlessly in fields when you were young. I'm your mother. My question was did you get your ears checked?"

"No."

"Well, you should. Can you please get me that washcloth darling, as I asked? I'm waiting."

"Okay," I say, handing it to her. I hope that now at last maybe it is acceptable to leave. I motion toward the door.

My mother stops me. "Wait. Stay just a moment more. You're always running off. You can spare a few more moments for your old mother. It's my last day. Surely your boss will understand."

"Maybe," I say, though admittedly my boss will never know. My editor always arrives late, in her large black cape, dab, dab, dabbing concealer beneath her eyes. When my editor works, she holds her pen in her tiny fist, her thumb clicking, clicking, clicking as she proofs, moving her pen back and forth, back and forth, between the clutch of her glossed lips and the galleys strewn all over her desk. It drives me mad. Patience is not my forte. "I really should go," I say, though not with as much conviction as I decide I probably need in order to get away.

"Just a few moments. You're about to lose your dear Ma-Ma. Certainly you can stay a bit more. I have a few more things to ask."

"Like what?"

"Do you like your job?"

"Enough."

"And also how's your friend Lou? I love Lou. I feel so connected to her. She always puts herself together so well. She presents so well. When are you next getting your hair cut?"

"I don't know."

"Well don't leave it too long. Your father doesn't look after himself either when I'm not there. He does love Vermont. I just prefer London. 'When a man is tired of London, he is tired of life.' That is Samuel Johnson. Did you know that?" she asks, cleaning the underside of her arm.

"Sure," I say, turning my eyes away from my mother's sagging breast to focus on the fluffiness of the pink towels against the wall. The towels are folded lengthwise toward their center and in half on the heated rack. I am not a fan of pink.

"For there is in London all that life can afford. I believe that," my mother continues as I decide that actually maybe I do like the color of the towels as they are not quite pink, more salmon in fact, and they are really quite soft. No matter how much softener I add, I never can get them as soft as she can.

"Elizabeth, which do you prefer?"

"What?"

"Don't say what. Say 'excuse me.' I always have told you that."

"Excuse me," I repeat.

"That's better. England or Vermont?"

"They're both good."

"Good?"

"Yeah."

"*Yes.* I thought you were a writer."

I do not reply.

"You could be."

"Maybe."

"Yes, you can. Could you hand me a towel now too?"

"Okay," I respond, grabbing what I'm now calling the salmon towel from the rack. I feel better about salmon. "But I should go," I add, deciding it acceptable to leave.

"Thank you, my darling," my mother says, slowly lowering one foot out of the tub and reaching toward the towel in my hand. I avert my eyes so I do not have to look at her pubes. "And just wait one more moment while I dry," she adds, toweling one waxed leg and then the other. "Really, you can't say England or Vermont?"

"No," I reply, though we both know it isn't true. I love Vermont, just like my father. I love walking down the long path to our pond, with my curled toes sinking into the warm mud. I love listening to the crickets playing their wings and to the trees creaking like old rocking chairs. I love lying on the dock with Glebe Mountain hovering above. But such observations will only lead to remaining in the bathroom longer with my mother, and I don't want to slip into nostalgic sentiment about our past.

"Okay then," I say.

"One more thing," she continues, wrapping the towel around her torso. She tucks the corner of the towel above her left breast and walks to the dimly lit vanity. "Elizabeth?"

"Yeah?"

"*Yes.* You sound so American. What does your editor think of that?"

"She's American."

"Well, she can't like that."

"She says the same."

"Americans. Anyway, before you go, I wanted to tell you that those aunts who raised my mother, the cousins of her biological father, they were quite brave, bluestocking types. Feminists, similar to you and me. She remained very attached to them, even if she was later separated from them when she moved to Germany. But

I have to admit that I never actually asked my mother about those aunts. Not much anyway. I never explored that part of her youth with her and how that all must have felt. My brother will know more. My mother and he were very close. She shared so much more with him. I never asked her enough. I often think about that. Have I told you that?"

"Yes, Mom," I say.

"I didn't realize. I'm sorry," she replies, clearly hurt as she begins rubbing anti-aging cream into her wrinkles, the few cracks less visible with each stroke. "By the way, I would have preferred you all to call me Mum. As a Brit, I never did like Mom."

"Yeah, Mom."

She gives a small laugh to the mirror. "There you go again. It's because of me that you have your British citizenship. That was a lot of work. I had to wait for hours at the Home Office. It took a whole day to get there and back. My mother, you're aware, was half British and half German, but she hated England and really was a European at heart. And can't you be anything other than monosyllabic this morning?"

"Sorry. It's just that I probably should be on my way. I really should get to work. Thank you for coming to visit, but I really should go."

My mother sets the floss down. "Hurrah, multiple words with multiple syllables. The writer at last."

"Thanks, Mom."

"You're welcome. It's just sometimes, I feel as if I'm a burden to you, as if you don't want me around and you think you'd be better off if I were gone. I made that mistake with my own mother. And don't forget it was you who asked me to speak into that silly contraption of yours and tell you this story. I'm by no means trying to hold you up. I can tell you're impatient to go. I don't want to keep you."

"You're not keeping me."

"I am. It's fine. You go. I understand. You have to live your life. You're an adult now."

"I can stay."

"No, you can't."

"Yes, I can."

"Go. I'm fine. Really."

"Really?"

"Yes, go. I'm not some decrepit old woman. Give your mother a kiss."

I do, of sorts, brushing her cheek with mine, kissing the empty space behind her ear.

"I hate it when you kiss like that. You kiss the air, not my cheek. But go. I love you and don't forget to water the plants after I've left, and call me, anytime, with questions about my mother. It's quite a story. You should write it. You can. I love you very, very much."

I tell her I love her too and leave. But as I walk to work, I begin again to question my commitment to writing a maternal history. No doubt, there are elements that are worthy: persecution, wartime escapes, and thwarted suicide attempts. Dramatic and tearjerking events like that. My college English professor always told me that I wrote such damn good prose and that all I needed was a good story, one with a beginning, a middle, and an end, and to write what I knew, to connect. This story, I know, is a good one although in thinking about it, I tell myself that it does not have an arc in the traditional sense. It has a climax, maybe, yes, but it also carries a history of trauma that I fear will preclude any clear resolution at the end. Yes, I know I can toy with the story. Imagine back, invent, and play with voice, but there is no way I can sit with my mother for hours on end, exploring the deep crevices of a maternal past and discovering what is worthy to tell. I lack the disposition—the patience and the understanding—to delve into the emotional complexity of this story with her.

Admittedly, at that point in my life, I do not know how my mother's behaviors will manifest in her later adult years and how deeply they will affect us. Nor am I aware of how they already have. I do not yet know the extent of the trauma she endured. I do not yet know that when my mother was in foster care, she was locked in closets, given only bread and water for hours on end, and that similarly when we were young, she locked herself in closets after arguments with my father who, along with my eldest sister, would patiently coax her out. When we were young, she hid that from us. Blithely unaware, I continue in my tentative exploration of my mother's story for reasons I choose not to confront. At that point in my life, I do not know how palpable my mother's struggle will become when she and my father come under financial strain. I cannot know that my mother's voice will break, that the effects of her lack of a relationship with her own mother—or indeed any form of early childhood attachment to any adult at all—will surface at last, like frozen water expanding beneath untended road, rendering the route ahead difficult for her to cross or even impassable in the end. At twenty-two, I simply think I will try to record a maternal history and maybe, if I am lucky, it will lead to something publishable as well.

Half-heartedly, I set about imagining the next phase of Violet's youth: her adoption by those two spinster aunts in turn-of-the-century England. I have not yet read about the importance of attachment between a child and a caring, loving adult. Only later will I learn that what matters most in young children's relationships with their primary caregivers are such things as consistency, boundaries, and responsive, loving care. Only later will I begin to understand the repercussions of the unfortunate parallels in my maternal line. Unlike the mothers before me, I have never been severed from those people who cared for me when I was young and to whom I remain attached, even if when dealing with my mother, I often revert to being distant and distracted—a coping mechanism that reportedly can add additional stress.[16] I am still young, without children, and I do not yet understand so much. I do not yet recognize how important the skills of constructively expressing, understanding, and managing emotion play in our lifelong success and mental health and how foundational our early care is in that development and growth.[17] Even if that care is not from a biological parent, early attachment is a protective factor that provides reduction in exposure to family risks.[18] To sever it carries untold risk.

EDITH MARY

RICKMANSWORTH, ENGLAND, 1910

Do not judge us, nor the child. We are sisters, May and I, and with us lived the child, our ward, named Violet Bracker, though our name is Cross. We are of a "certain age," the age at which one passes from eligible to ineligible. But pity us not; we are not societal debris. We are entitled to the freedom of aging spinsters, and this has been in a measure true for some years now. We can judge what is right and honorable for ourselves, and we know when to shun the temptations of the world. We chose our life and abide by the prevailing rules of etiquette. We accompany one another when expedient, though that is infrequent now. We pay attention to our dress. We are seamstresses both and fashion a respectable income from that occupation. We sew all our family's clothing and the clothing for many in the town, and when our Uncle Frederick is in great need of haberdashery for his clients, we assist. We are very skilled and do quite well. Pray do not ask why we chose to be spinsters, but know that it takes honor to hold this status. Many women do, choosing not to embody what Queen Victoria decreed as God's intent for women—to be helpmates for man—but instead to take on different duties and vocations.

There is a newfound power in spinsterhood in these days that few outside our ranks are willing to acknowledge, much less proclaim. We are among the new women, the new spinsters, who need not be restrained by societal constraints. We reject the demands, the restrictions, and the inequalities of marriage, defining our own paradigm within the domestic sphere. Marriage is by no means an assured route to happiness, just as singledom is not without its blessedness. We are no worse off than our married sisters, many of whom are bound to men whom they neither love nor respect. We select for ourselves, buy for ourselves, provide for ourselves in every way. We seek the right to vote and to ride bicycles unaccompanied. We have one another's companionship to the grave. We are neither meek nor dried up nor sour, and we are no burden to any man. We are not pathetic old maids.

While we have not borne children of our own, May and I have nevertheless employed our female talents to assist in rearing our siblings' children and, of course, to care for Violet as well. Those inherent female talents, should you choose to believe them as defining or innate, we are actively employing.

In all candor, when Aunt Priscilla first proposed that Violet come to us, May was not receptive. The occasional tending of our nieces and nephews quite sufficed, she maintained. But May is nothing if not practical, and even she acknowledged that the prospect of a supplementary income was compelling. Also, for all her pragmatism, May is quite compassionate. When presented with the alternatives for the child—the horrors of the workhouse are well-known—she would not bear the thought of such a place for any child, let alone a child who bore the suggestion of the name Cross, if only as an afterthought, in an initial. With little argument, May, too, was therefore convinced.

Having completed the recommended post-birth convalescence without incident, Anna arrived at our house by carriage when Violet was only two weeks old. We were able to register her as Violet Helene C. Bracker in Watford in the same month in which she was born. The child was born without scrutiny, the midwife having accommodated Aunt Priscilla's requests in exchange for a small additional recompense. Violet's father, our cousin, agreed to pay us a stipend of five shillings a week through Priscilla. Priscilla was his guarantor and agreed, moreover, to match his sum, thus doubling our income. We were comfortably provided for as a result.

As anyone who has raised children knows, the demands of raising a child begin at infancy and are intensive from the start. And yet people speak so little of those demands, as if concerned that by speaking this universal secret aloud, they will put the reproduction of the human race at risk. Even those female writers who cause their heroines to fall victim to the dream of marriage and what ensues (for its realization is perceived as the epitome of female fulfillment) end their novels before the ensuing labor is exposed, the secret safe, the myth preserved. No suggestion of an alternate way is ever promulgated. The status quo remains intact.

We were not blind to the demands that awaited us in our decision to take on the girl, but we would be propagating that same myth were we not now to speak frankly of the extent of those demands. Despite our familiarity with children and our experience with our nieces and nephews, and with our own siblings when young, the arrival of Anna and Violet required an adjustment from us. Anna was of limited help in those first few weeks, nursing every two hours as she was. We cared for her, even with her bleeding nipples and her still-healing torn perineum. She was the food source for the child in those early weeks, and we tended to her in the interest of the small infant to whom we had committed ourselves.

We had many other tasks in those early days, and each was time-consuming in itself. Washing laundry for four, a newborn among them, took close to ten hours per week. Each load required water to be carried to the copper tub and heated beneath with a fire that frequently went out, requiring us to relight the coal and wood. We made diapers from the tails of worn-out men's shirts, folding them several times, with loops and ties sewn on. We changed them whenever they were wet, which sometimes amounted to two dozen times a day. To mitigate the load, we would suspend Violet over a chamber pot at regular intervals in the hope that a diaper washing could be spared.

Violet's clothing was extensive even in those early weeks, and while we were not affluent, we were unwilling to fall short of our charge. Being seamstresses, we sewed it all—the binder to strengthen her back, as well as the soft woolen vest with long sleeves and the large diaper, covered with another flannel triangle. We sewed the long flannel backwrap with shoulder straps through which her arms passed. We sewed the monthly that fell below Violet's feet and was pinned with a head flannel at the top. We sewed the nightdress with a veil, which we also stitched. We sewed the shorter clothes when she grew older, the dresses and petticoats that allowed her neck, arms, and lower legs to be bare, as convention dictated.

We answered the child's whims in many ways, beginning in those early months. While Anna still lived with us, Violet had no schedule. Anna fed, held, and cuddled her as she pleased, and we tended to all their concerns. When Anna departed, we continued to answer Violet's needs, following a prescribed schedule for feeding, sleeping, baths, and such. We also invested in a pram for trips to the park—a stunning blue one with a frill along the bonnet.

On Anna's departure, we fed Violet with a bottle. We sterilized the bottles and put dried milk in them, mixed with water. Fulfilling those responsibilities required additional time. When Violet was old enough, we added small amounts of cereal. She also sucked on ham bones and gummed crackers. We fed her well, so it was not uncommon for others to tell us that she was healthy. "As fat as a pig," they said. She was sleeping a fair portion of the night by then.

The work did not stop after her infancy. Violet was an attractive girl, dark, with tidy ringlets and the deep set, forlorn eyes of her mother. When we enrolled her at a school in town that required her to wear a gray frock and white gloves, we purchased the clothing as requested, rather than sew it, and dutifully paid the attendance fee. She was immaculate in dress and comported herself better than most, and we were exceedingly conscious of the importance of her presentation in avoiding further ridicule. We cooked her healthy meals, accompanied her to school each day, and raised her with the utmost attention to her manners, ensuring that her behavior was exemplary. She was a model student and abided by the prevailing social mores.

With respect to her origins, the question remained out of our earshot (though no doubt it was echoed in the town), and we rarely spoke of it, nor did Violet ask. We covered our ears to its reverberations. Yet we were candid with Violet from the start. "Hold your head high," we told her, and she knew implicitly to what we referred. When that insufferable child Beatrice barred Violet from entering her sister's sixth birthday party because she would pollute it, we did not cause a stir. We understood that she had been invited to the celebration, despite what the impetuous younger sister proclaimed. Nevertheless, we did not react to such cruelty. We simply took Violet's hand and turned. "She knows not what she says," we told her. "She is ignorant," we said. "You are stronger than her. Ignore," we advised. To other instances of prejudice, rare as they were, we responded with equal equanimity and strength. When Mrs. Delaney suggested that Violet corrupted other children by proximity, we told her that she knew not what she said and excused ourselves from her tea. "Rise above them," we said.

As far as the impact on our own good standing in the town, it was negligible. There is freedom in being a spinster, a freedom that allowed us to eschew unnecessary niceties when our Violet's good character was in any way defiled. We modeled this attitude for her while always treating her like the person she was.

Life with our little girl was in short wondrous for six years until the arrival of a letter, quick to read though long to comprehend. The request from Anna was an unforeseen rock thrown through our window, shattering our tranquil home, leaving us with shards that cut deep. Anna and her husband were reuniting the family, she wrote, a family that would soon consist of four. We became indignant. "How could she?" we asked ourselves. Could Anna not see that, far from reuniting a family, she was forever severing us from a child who had come to be our own? We had plans for our girl. She was to become a young lady, successfully raised by us, her two spinster aunts. She had earned a place in our town, in her school, at the table where every night we dined as a family, our unconventional-but-loving family of three. Now this self-proclaimed mother was declaring that she would give the child her husband's name as if that new name were an invaluable gift. But we had been the ones to bestow on her something far more meaningful and profound—pride and dignity not in whence she came but in who she was. This new name would be but a thin, impoverished veil, a guise, beneath which our Violet would now be forced to live.

More letters came. One from Aunt Priscilla and one from Cousin Jack, the father, who had never contacted us directly, having used his mother as a conduit for all these years. We tried to keep her. We did. But our pleas fell on deaf ears. And in the end, with no recourse at all, we accepted our fate. Violet's place was with her mother. She had to go. We might no longer feed her the stewed plums she so relished nor ride our bikes beside her to school. We might no longer mend her clothing or turn down her sheet; no longer darn her socks or cook her rice; no longer be able to tell her to hold her head high and to dismiss from her mind anything that undermined her noble spirit. But we also would not permit our lives before to be defined by these lasts that no longer were. We would focus instead on the firsts—on the first tiny front tooth pushing determinedly through a tender pink gum, the first teetering step across the kitchen floor, the first memories that would fuel and sustain us and that no one could take from us and that we would always share with her.

We waited to share the news with our little girl until the day before her mother arrived, unvarnished as we always did. We explained that her mother, the woman who gave birth to her, was coming to take her to live in London with her. She responded that she did not want her mother. She wanted to remain in Rickmansworth with us, her aunties. We told her she had to go. She asked us why and we said because children belonged with their mothers. She asked if so, then why had her mother not come to fetch her before. We said because her mother's house had not been big enough, because she was too poor, but now her mother had a home and a husband, and could support her. She told us she did not care how big her mother's home was, she wanted to remain with us.

In the end, we somehow got her to understand. We whispered our everlasting love as she squeezed us with her tiny arms, and we squeezed back firmly with our large ones. "We will always be here, and one day we will be together again," we said. "Promise?" she asked. "Of course," we said, knowing our lives had irreversibly changed but reminding ourselves that our memories would forever remain. We told her, too, to promise that she would be strong when her mother came. She said she would. We told her that she was brave and that she could withstand this, just as she did all else, and we reminded ourselves of the same. A love like ours did not abate, we explained, for its source was embedded too deeply within us. We could never sever her from us, nor us from her. She was a part of who we had become. Our little Violet who grew not from our womb but from our hearts.

CHAPTER 3

WESTON, MASSACHUSETTS — 2012

Children who suffer from child traumatic stress are those who have been exposed to one or more traumas over the course of their lives and develop reactions that persist and affect their daily lives after the events have ended. Traumatic reactions can include a variety of responses, such as intense and ongoing emotional upset, depressive symptoms or anxiety, behavioral changes, difficulties with self-regulation, problems relating to others or forming attachments, regression or loss of previously acquired skills, attention and academic difficulties, nightmares, difficulty sleeping and eating, and physical symptoms, such as aches and pains.[19]

On discovering through online census research that my grandmother Violet, aged six, joined Anna in London's East End slums, I know for certain that Violet's tale of the happy Rickmansworth childhood that she always shared with my mother and that my mother so cherishes seems to be, while not exactly a lie, a deception of sorts. I am in my mid-forties by this point, with a husband and three children whom we have been trying our best to raise. I often make parenting mistakes. I give my children what I deem to be answers when they would be better served learning the answers themselves. I too often try to make their challenges my own, to spare them from hurt, and to carry their pain. I sometimes protect them too much and in so doing, don't promote resilience as I could. At other times, I don't listen to them enough. I am apt to criticize myself for the parenting decisions I do or don't make, but I also know that parenting can be difficult and that, at the same time, it provides me reason to get up, to make my bed, to lay a meal, to come home. To see in my children their joy or their kindness or that pride that comes with accomplishment—that is a serotonin greater than I have otherwise known.

My children, of course, are not without their childhood challenges, even if smaller and more surmountable than those of so many children in the world. Nor am I without mine. All three of my children are entering or in their adolescent phase. My daughter is sixteen, a runner who is flat chested and trying to fit in among the fully developed girls. A boy likes her but she only likes him when he does not like her, and he only likes her when she does not like him. I hate to see her upset. When she comes to the dinner table not eating, I try to help her. I tell her just to go out with him even if she does not like him right now. She tells me that my advice is terrible and completely wrong. My son meanwhile is wearing rib protection and in pain as I told him to keep playing lacrosse despite what turned out to be broken ribs. Even if your ribs are broken, I advised him, there is nothing anyone can do, so play. He tells me both the doctor and his coach say I made a big mistake. His rib will never be the same. My other son has recently changed schools and feels excluded from the popular group. He does not believe he is smart, kind, and attractive. I tell him that he is, but he still cannot let go of the time I sat down on his bed and told him that he needed to make healthy choices with his food. He tells me I basically called him fat and that he'll never recover from it. I say I am sorry, that was not my intention at all. I'm here for you, I say. He turns away.

I know I often get parenting wrong. The seminal parenting moment came for me long ago during the hospital's parent education session for new mothers after I delivered my firstborn. I was sitting uncomfortably on a plastic chair in my blue paper robe with vaginal stitches from an emergency episiotomy to my anus while a deceptively equanimous lactation nurse explained to all us mothers how to hold an infant so the baby's mouth could latch onto the entire areola, how not to force, how to let the attachment happen naturally. There was no mention of the fact that my nipples would soon crust and bleed, of how painful the process would be. Nothing about how it might not work out. But then the nurse informed us that we might not succeed in getting our babies to attach and that this failure would mark the start of all that we got wrong as parents, of the questions we would not be able to answer, of the solutions we would not find. When she finished, the successful parenting lore I'd been fed suddenly seemed exposed as an expedient and well-propagated lie. Rather than be relieved, I was angry. Out of nowhere, I had just been informed that it was, in fact, not a given that my child would attach to my breast or that I would be a successful parent. Admittedly, I knew I was somewhat complicit. Pink and glowing and expectant and naïve, I had blithely accepted the messaging given to me—how simple breathing during labor could mitigate the pain, how during contractions we needed only to pause until the air seemed to "want" to come into the body, and how, once the contractions became more intense, we needed only to breathe lightly and shallowly with long exhales of *whos* and *puhs* like some sort of happily laboring Oompa Loompa on a hospital delivery bed. Even after the birth, with my sweet baby daughter cradled to my breast ("The most beautiful baby the nurse had ever seen. Did you hear that Lucian? Do you think it's really true?"), I too was content to erase from my mind the vomiting from the pain, the hemorrhaging, the doctors rushing in, the husband sent out, the passing belief that I might die and the wish that the fucking morphine would never stop.

I am under no false illusions about parenting now. I have long since dispelled that myth of perfect parenting. I sometimes tell my children that I parent like a machine gun, shooting bullets in the hope that one carries a small shard of something sage. I know the metaphor is not ideal but it's the only one that seems to resonate with them, having been reared by their father on Super Soakers and airsoft guns and introduced to that video game Halo way too young. It's not that I don't try. When I talk to them, I use recommended parenting catchphrases like "smart choices" and "positive sense of self." I am quick to sandwich criticism with healthy slices of praise. I remind myself that happiness, sadness, anger, and fear are what they are supposed to feel. I have even skimmed the book

The Blessings of a Skinned Knee. But all that knowledge does not mean I don't often lie awake at night, worrying about what I can say to make their latest disappointment less painful or persever-ating over my latest and greatest parenting mistake, which often stems from providing too much, from being too involved.

The irony is my relationship with my mother is in many ways the reverse. Perhaps my lack of responsiveness to my mother is steeped in the fact that my plate is already full, that while my children are hitting adolescence, my mother seems to be hitting a latent adolescence of her own. Despite her age, she has seemingly developed a complete lack of self-control. She cannot accept no. She falls into depressive episodes without reprieve. She spins on her stationary cycle until her heart rate becomes so rapid that the instructor tells her she has to *Please, God have mercy, stop!* No one can set limits for her, least of all my siblings and me. And even if I do know how to help her, I resist. I do not want to find solutions to her problems. I do not want to choose my words carefully with her. I am not responsive, attuned, and sensitive. I want to be a parent to my children, not her.

At forty-three, despite my age, I do not yet understand how unmoored she is and why she is that way. I have not yet read about the importance of attachment in the early years and how attachment to a caregiver serves as the foundation from which a young child learns and develops a sense of self. I have not yet learned that the regulation of emotion, thoughts, and behavior— what is known as self-regulation—develops out of co-regulation between a caregiver and a child in the early years when the care-giver models, guides, and instructs the child toward the develop-ment of these critical foundational skills. I do not yet know my mother never learned to self-regulate or develop a secure sense of self through early childhood attachment. I do not understand how much she struggles to bounce back from disappointment or how her past trauma impacts her emotions and behaviors or that I have to understand my own emotions, behaviors, and triggers in order to build a good relationship with her. I have not reflected on my own childhood and come to the realization that despite the lack of attachment and security in her own childhood and in her mother's as well, that she somehow found a way to provide that to us. I am not empathic toward her. I instead believe at that stage of my life that the growing number of discoveries about my mother and my grandmother's past that I throw at her like pasta to a wall might provide something for her to grasp in what I've decided is a vortex of her unmet wants from which I'm trying my hell-bent best to escape.

My online census discovery of Violet's move to London's East End after Rickmansworth is one such discovery, and after a few seconds of consideration, I decide to provide it to her.

"I have something to tell you," I begin during my weekly morning phone call with her. "You know your mother's early childhood in England?"

"Don't use 'you know.' You have a better command of the English language than that. Yes, I am aware of it. Go on." My mother's tone is clipped, suggesting that she is in ill temper once again.

"Well, you won't believe it. I was researching the other day, and, well, I learned that your mother also lived in London's East End. After Rickmansworth, before Germany. Isn't that interesting?"

"Sorry?" my mother says.

"Your mother's early childhood in England also included living in the East End in London, before the war," I repeat. "With her mother. She did not go straight to Germany after all."

"Are you sure?" my mother asks in her clipped English accent.

"Yes," I say, albeit aware that an uneducated German grandmother who lived in the slums is not an ancestry my English mother would want to embrace. I continue nevertheless, stubbornly maintaining that the added knowledge of Violet's origins will outweigh all else. "And, well, you know, it was in the East End."

"'You know?' Don't use that term. I've told you that. You're better educated than that."

"The East End means she likely lived in the slums with little education," I persist, becoming less certain of my decision to share.

"She always spoke well. She was fully bilingual. How do you know that she was poor and not well-educated?" my mother asks. Education is a sensitive topic for her. Although my mother's teacher recommended she attend the Sorbonne, her father, George, denied her the opportunity to apply, sending her to secretarial school instead. Her father's sexism was one of the reasons she insisted that her daughters had access to the same educational opportunities as her sons.

"It's in the census," I reply, recognizing her mother's poor roots actually might not be a fact she would like to acknowledge.

"The slums are not in the census."

"Your mother is. The whole family."

"That cannot be. She never told me that."

"Yes. The area with Jack the Ripper. The slums," I add in as sympathetic a tone as I can muster, realizing with some guilt that even forgetting her mother's East End poverty, the revelation is further evidence that her mother never truly confided in her at all and that they never enjoyed a trusting, reciprocal relationship, even when she was old enough to be confided in as an adult.

"Are you certain?" my mother asks.

"Yeah," I say.

"Well, I don't know why she didn't tell me that. And don't say 'yeah.'"

"Perhaps she preferred it that way?" I weakly suggest.

"Perhaps. But it's funny that she never once mentioned it. She never shared so much with me but then I never asked. We weren't close. She could be so good. But she had a temper. She could turn on a dime."

"I know," I say as I wait uncertainly in the silence at the end of the line.

"Well, I suppose there's nothing I can do," my mother says at last, recovering. "Another one of her secrets. Anyway, she only talked about those spinster aunts who sent her to that high-end private school. She loved Rickmansworth and both of them so much. She really did. They were her mothers. They loved her unconditionally."

"I'm sure you're right."

"Yes," my mother says, resigned. "I'm sure she did. At least that's what she said, and really that's all I have. Feel free to do with that what you will. And don't say 'yeah.' You sound so American. You're better educated than that."

I hang up the phone. I try to imagine what her mother, Violet, and her German immigrant mother, Anna, before her endured. I begin to write about Anna based on a small black-and-white picture that Neville shared with her and that my father sent to me. The picture is cropped just below Anna's breast and she wears a house servant's livery. Anna's hard, oval face suggests resilience despite hardship, years despite its age. Her eyes are dark, tired, and stare into the camera as if to say, *I can withstand this too.* I tell myself that, as a mother, I know how this feels. I know the importance of resilience and of fostering resilience in our own children, even if I don't always do it well. I know we need to let them feel sadness, anger, and indignation, and develop the capacity to recover on their own, to learn to self-regulate. I also know how challenging, but how important, promoting these capacities is.

And then I think about how Anna's and Violet's hardships were so much greater than mine. Parenting from birth is difficult enough, never mind having to begin or abandon parenthood when your child is six. Perhaps I did suggest my twelve-year-old son was fat. Perhaps I am responsible for a deformation in my other son's rib. Perhaps encouraging my recalcitrant sixteen-year-old daughter to date when she had fallen out of like was a bad course for her. But I have had the privilege of being able to make those parenting mistakes. My children have never been deprived of a parent, nor have I been deprived of my children. We have not had to suffer the long-term effects of mother-child separation on mental health that can persist long into adulthood.[20] I have been able to be present for my children as they work through their anger with me. We so often talk about the lucky circumstances of our birth. There also exists the lucky circumstance of our parenting. Violet and my mother were deprived of predictable, consistent, and supportive environments and relationships in their youth that research says can help you learn to cope[21] and the repercussions of which would manifest in later life in myriad ways for them both.

ANNA

BETHNAL GREEN, LONDON, 1910

Anna was traveling by train to Rickmansworth to meet her daughter. It had been six long years since she had moved to Bethnal Green where the German immigrants lived, where she had no room for a child. Until she met and married Louis.

The path here had been long. That first time she had entered his shop, one of many merchants in an overcrowded pier, she could not anticipate how accepting he would be, how tolerant, how kind, how after he had learned she was pregnant with another child—his first—he would insist that she bring her other child, her daughter by another man, home.

Anna had not been lucky with men. Since arriving to London, she had been attending the local German church. She had no longer anticipated marriage, at her age. She was realistic about life. She had secured a job on a factory floor and slept on a single cot in a dilapidated tenement building. She led a solitary life. She knew she was not pretty but she also knew that she was not without notice from men. She had large breasts, sloping shoulders, and a long forehead. Well-kept women, it seemed, looked past her from their church pews, without concern that she would draw attention from their men. She was in no way that delicate dessert—that small *Spritzgeback*, that *Vanillekepferi*, or that abstemious serving of *streusel* that some men believed to be their entitlement after they had eaten their main course. But in some men, there did exist a desire for her. She knew that too. There was something in her a little stolid, a little blunt, a little strong that appealed and that some sought to devour out of view only to return to their displayed dessert, having affirmed to themselves that they were large and firm. Perhaps she represented to these men the clandestine embodiment of their raw lust. Their secret affirmation, their God-given right. She did not know, but men like those were drawn to her. Jack, the father of her child, was one. Others were too. She had foresworn them all. And then Louis had entered her life, or more precisely, she had entered his.

That first day when she came upon his shop, he had not noticed her. When she opened his door, he had not looked up. He had paid no heed to her as he sliced her meat, cleanly and efficiently, or as he slid her cut, wrapped and tied, across the counter and rung her up. But despite the dexterity with which he cut, Anna could see that he did not have the manner of a butcher. She had seen it in the delicate way he handled the meat, in his gentle touch. In him was something different, something that appealed to her. When she had dropped her counted coins into his outstretched hand and he had brushed his long delicate fingers into hers without thought of the exchange, a frisson of recognition had passed between them. He had held her face in his gaze for a few seconds too long, not in a covetous way but in a way that suggested that he, too, had stood alone, and she had known at that moment that between them lay a thread of possibility. Between them, she had become aware of something else, too, something shared—a vulnerability, cloaked in battered skin, like a supple sole in a worn shoe—and she had had to suppress her desire to pull his elegant hand to her breast, to share her past, and to invite him to share his. To tell him that she understood.

"Are you new here?" he had asked as she put her coins in her purse.

She had startled. "No, I live nearby and work not far. On Sundays I take walks and go to the German church. Do you?"

He had let slip a small smile, responding that he was a Jew, which of course she had known, as it was a Jewish butcher shop, but in her fluster had forgotten.

"That's fine," she had said, and wondered what she meant by that. Fine for what? Still flustered, she had thanked him and left.

From thereon, she had begun to visit his shop once a week. Though well-accustomed to what was required to make meat taste good, she had never before enjoyed trips to butchers' shops as much as she then did. The stench, the sight of the carcasses hanging upside down outside the door, the men with their caps loitering outside—a butcher's shop for Anna had always been difficult to enter, like traipsing across a bloodied battlefield. But she now had found herself looking forward to her trips. Breathing deeply and focused ahead, she would briskly stride into his shop, where the floor was always clean, the countertop freshly scrubbed. She would admire his industriousness and ask him questions to which he would give short replies. When she had asked if his wife had liked the meat he served, "No wife," he had replied, looking straight into her eyes.

They had courted briefly. Louis was tall. Anna liked that about him. He rarely spoke. His face was thin. She would later learn that he had loved her from the start, despite that which preceded them and the inevitability of that which would proceed. She loved him too. She loved him for his steadfastness, for his silent acceptance, for his unwavering belief that a supportive nod was sufficient, for how he slept with his hand on her arm as a reminder that they were still both there, in the squalid, dark night. She found in Louis a stability she had lacked and despite the dinginess of where they lived, a comforting familiarity in all that surrounded them: the little grocery stores that smelled of pickled herring, garlic sausage, and onion bread; the casual laborers, hawkers, furniture-makers, general dealers, shoemakers, and costermongers; and the sound of German and Yiddish in the streets. It reminded her of home. Louis never spoke of what he had done in Germany or why he had left, and so Anna never spoke of her past either. While she had known from that first day they met that he had not stood behind a blood-stained counter in his previous life, she still did not know what he had done. He had been an accountant, perhaps, or some-one who held a pen. But now he was a butcher, and that was that. Why speak of their respective pasts, he would say with his barely discernible skip of his brow if she began to explore it with him. What for, he would suggest in his silent return to his task. She knew that he no doubt had arrived among the thousands of persecuted German Jews who had fled their homeland a few years back, but that was as far as she had learned. "The past is the past," he would respond when she asked.

So it was not until they married that Anna shared the existence of Violet with him, even though thoughts of her daughter were never far from her. She often imagined the color of her daughter's hair, the shape of her face, the size of her feet. She wondered how tall she was, whether she was talkative or quiet, obedient or unruly. She had so little to draw from, only that fleeting memory of her infant, suckling at her breast. She had filed every detail of her daughter from those first two weeks like contours on a map of a homeland that she had been forced to leave. And now here she was, going back to her.

Getting here had not been easy. When Anna had discovered she was pregnant with Louis's child, the news had been a surprise to them both, despite Anna's hard-learned knowledge that she could get pregnant with a touch. She had skipped her cycle for three months. Being forty, she attributed it to age. But then her already large breasts had begun to swell and so over dinner, she had told him. Louis was silent at first, which she misread as hesitation. "Are you sure?" he had asked. Not able to tell by his face if he was happy or not, she had defensively replied, "I know when I am pregnant." Hurt, she had abruptly risen from the table, escaping to their room.

Louis had followed her, visibly confused. "But I was about to raise my glass? Why are you so upset?" he had asked. So it was then that she had told him about her past. She explained that she had a bastard child in Rickmansworth whom she had not seen since birth. She had left her daughter there, she revealed through escaped tears. For six years, she had thought of her daughter every day, every moment, every breath, and yet she had done nothing for her, her child, her girl. She had simply let her be with those two old aunts, kept her a secret from everyone, even him. What kind of a mother was she? Why would any child, any man, want her to be a mother again?

Louis had held her then, stroked her sloping shoulders with one large hand while he swept away her tears with the other. "You will be a mother like no one else to them both," he had assured her. "You must go and get her. We can be a family of four then."

So now, here she was, on a train to a daughter whom she had not seen in six years.

Getting agreement from the two spinster aunts had not been simple. With Louis's help, Anna had written to them. She had told them, in the best English she could write, that she had married Louis Katzenstein and that they lived in the Waterlow Estate in Bethnal Green. She had thought the term Estate lent a certain prestige. The spinster aunts at first had not agreed to her request. Their refusal had surprised Anna. Anna had thought that they would have recognized that Anna, as her mother, must have hoped that one day she could bring her daughter home and that they would be relieved in some way to no longer care for their ward, despite the recompense they received. But judging by the letter Anna got back, her letter had been a shock. Short and uncooperative, the aunts had flatly refused. Undeterred, Anna had followed with a letter to enlist Priscilla's support and obtain, through her, Jack's consent as well. Anna had spoken neither to Priscilla nor Jack since her daughter's birth, but she imagined Priscilla's release from the financial obligation of supporting a bastard child would be welcome news, which apparently it was, as only a short time after sending the letter, a letter from Priscilla had arrived with the time and date of the arranged pick up. Enclosed also was one adult return train ticket, a single trip for one youth, and money for a cab to and from the station to the aunts' home.

Now, with growing anxiety, Anna stepped off the train into the bright May day in Rickmansworth, the sky an azure blue, the small town more picturesque than she recalled. Climbing into a nearby cab, she tried to push out of her mind the polluted streets, the unbearable stench, and the single shabby couch of her home, the place she was taking her daughter back to. It was all too beautiful by comparison here.

"But we will be a family of four," she repeated to herself in the cab. Then looking down at her large pregnant stomach, rumpled black dress, and swollen calves beneath black stockings, she whispered, "What have I done?"

"Sorry luv?" the cabbie asked.

"Nothing," Anna said, unfolding a small piece of paper in her purse and handing the cabbie the address.

Having told the cabbie to wait, Anna walked up the short front path of blue slate to the aunts' home. With a deep breath, she knocked. The aunts opened the door in colorful dresses and laced leather shoes and greeted her brusquely without remark on her pregnancy or inviting her inside. Violet was not with them.

Well then, I'll make this quick, Anna thought, assuring herself the sting would be less for it. She plucked up her strength. "I am here for Violet," she announced into a front parlor that had a beautiful oriental rug, painted walls, and two framed watercolors.

"Yes," May said.

"We know," Edith Mary confirmed.

Anna felt thwarted. Frustrated that they were making this harder than it already was. "Well, may I see her?" Anna asked.

"Oh yes. Of course," Edith Mary replied as if the thought had just struck. "Violet, dear," she called, the two sisters exchanging a knowing glance and turning their backs to the door in which Anna stood.

It was then that Violet emerged, face in hands, scampering across the floor like a field mouse seeking shelter beneath their skirts. With the bodies of the two sisters still turned, Anna could not see her daughter at all.

"Violet?" Anna asked, trying not to sound as desperate as she felt.

Violet did not respond.

"May I see her?" Anna asked.

The women turned, bringing with them Violet, who remained burrowed in their skirts. "Violet, say hello to your mother," May said, but still Violet did not turn.

"Violet?" Anna followed, as gently as she could, feeling awkward and out of place, as if she did not belong here at all.

"Violet, remember what we said," Edith Mary continued, and swiftly, Violet turned, wearing to Anna's horror an expression of unmistakable disdain on a face that Anna did not recognize at all.

Startled, Anna tried to compose herself. "I'm here to take you home," she said.

"But I *am* home," her daughter said.

The aunts then turned Violet back toward them as they lowered to one knee and took her in their extended arms, so that to Anna they looked like one. "Remember what we said."

Violet drew a big breath and again turned to face her mother from her ironed dress and carefully combed ringlets. The aunts then handed her a bag and, nodding toward Anna, indicated with their heads that Violet move forward toward Anna. "You know we love you," they said. "You can never forget. Now go," they told Violet.

"Alright," Violet said, and looking straight ahead, not so much as casting a glance at Anna, walked out the door.

Anna did all she could not to cry. "Thank you," she said, and hurriedly followed her daughter to the idling cab before one of them changed their mind.

In the cab, Anna tried to talk to her. She asked Violet a whole range of questions, from how she was feeling to what her favorite food was. But Violet did not reply. For the duration of the train ride, try as Anna did, Violet would not speak. So Anna, in the end, let their silence be, reminding herself that she could wait. Patience had become, if nothing else, a well-practiced trait for her. Six long years it had been. She could wait a little more.

After they had disembarked from the train and arrived at the street on which they would now together live, Anna said, "We're here!" as cheerfully as she could. Her daughter said nothing, her lips fixed into a frown. They walked up the narrow flight of stairs that separated the pairs of apartments on each floor. Still, Violet did not react. Anna knocked and Louis opened the door of the flat. Violet looked up at him and then eyed the bare walls, the adjoining room with one small bed, and the strangers in the other room of the flat they shared, and asked, "But where shall I sleep?" the first words she had uttered since leaving Rickmansworth.

"With us," Anna excitedly replied, although her voice came out as weaker and less confident than she would have liked.

Violet looked at her mother, seemingly considering what she said. And then she turned to Louis.

Louis straightened. "Excuse me," he said. "I've been rude. I don't think we've formally met. I'm Louis. Pleased to meet you. And you are Violet?" he asked.

"Yes, Violet," she confirmed, eyeing him up and down. "You are tall," she remarked.

"Yes, I am. And so are you," he said.

"Yes," she said. "You are the husband."

"Yes," he replied.

"So then what shall I call you? Will Louis do?" Violet asked, her accent and choice of words so decidedly middle-class.

"Louis will be fine. Now let me settle you in," he replied as he extended his hand, and Violet assuredly took it. And Violet Katzenstein she became—the eldest child in a family that would soon be four with a younger brother named George.

CHAPTER 4

SIMSBURY, CONNECTICUT — 1973

Behavioral tests showed that mothers which experienced separation were more depressive and anxious than control ones, also they had a lower litter size. Rats pups of the second generation whose mothers experienced maternal separation also revealed behavior changes akin to depression and anxiety. Thus, maternal separation causes depressive and anxious-like states on mother rats which experienced separation and has an impact on their litter size. Also, consequences of maternal separation seem to last throughout generations.[24]

I am six years old. It is summer and we live in a big house on a ledge that has flecks of mica that I think are gold. After breakfast, we go outside and my mother locks the screen door until lunch. My eldest brother has a thin red bike that he rides with no hands around the garage. He challenges me to do the same. I do not like my purple bike with its sparkling banana seat and two streamers coming out of the handlebars. I got the bike for my birthday. It is for girls. When I told my father I did not like it, he threatened to take it back. Ashamed, I said thank you, but I refuse to ride it still, choosing instead to play in the wood near the place where the chicken coop used to be until the fox took the chickens one too many times.

When my elder siblings play softball, I try to join them, but they tell me I'm a pain and to go and play with my little brothers instead, but my youngest brother is only three and he doesn't even know how to play. I have learned not to go near my sister when she pitches because the softball will hit me in the nose. It's just what happens, my sister says. She can't control it. My sister is President of the Kids' Club. My older brothers are Vice President and Secretary. My eldest sister is not in the club because she prefers to read. I am too young to be allowed club membership. My younger brothers are too.

At lunch, my mother unlocks the screen door and feeds my siblings peanut butter and jelly sandwiches and me cream cheese and jam because I hate peanuts. When we have to go to the bathroom, my mother unlocks the screen door but otherwise we have to stay outside while my mother cleans. She likes to move furniture, too, not a lot but so it all looks just right. In the afternoons, she gardens in clogs and walks around the driveway for exercise after she's gone for a jog. She lets us come with her. Today, for some reason, I am the only child who's decided to go with her. Our nanny, Dorothy, who hugs us all the time, is in charge of everyone else. As we walk, my mother holds my hand and I trail two steps behind, running every couple of steps to keep up. We do not talk, as I can't think of any questions to ask, but at the end of the walk, I think of one. I ask my mother her favorite age. "How old are you?" she asks. "Six," I proudly respond. "Well, six is my favorite age," she says. I realize she has told me her favorite aged child to raise, not her favorite age to be. She goes back inside our house to enjoy her afternoon cup of Earl Grey Tea and put her feet up for a few minutes to read. At 5:00, she unlocks the door and she gives us all a bath. My youngest brothers and I share one, my elder brothers share another, and my two sisters each get their own. By 5:30, we are in pajamas. My brother, who is two years older than me, refuses to sit beside me because he says my sneezes smell. We eat and get to watch one hour of public television. At 7:15, I go to bed and await my father to kiss me goodnight. I am the only child with her own room as everyone else has a sibling of the same sex who is close in age, which makes them a pair. A witch on a broom hangs from my ceiling on a thread. I watch it spin, believing it is calling the other witches to gather on the railing outside my window. I wait for my father to come and tell me not to be afraid of the witches outside or the monsters in my closet and beneath my bed. I know that my mother will not come. My father will kiss me goodnight for her. She will be too tired from all the cooking and the cleaning and the gardening and looking after us. Sometimes she gets sick from the exhaustion of it all and she becomes too thin. When I have children of my own, sometimes the same will happen to me. But tucked up in my bed, with my father having told me that there is no reason to be afraid, I know that tomorrow I will wake and eat and go outside and that if I need to go to the bathroom, my mother will open the door for me and that if I am sad, Dorothy will give me a hug, and that on the weekend, my father will take us for a tractor ride which will be so much fun. I sleep well knowing all this, unlike my mother who often does not sleep well at all.

ANNA

BETHNAL GREEN, LONDON, 1910 - 1915

Violet's acceptance of her new life took longer than Anna had hoped. That first year, there were so many times when Violet would have an outburst over the most innocuous of things—a lost sock, too many nuts on her cake. Violet's little face would flush and she would scream or run from her mother as if in need of an escape. At such times, Louis would shrug, knowing better than to get involved. "Let her be," he would say when Violet was particularly uncontrolled, and in time, Violet would return, composed as if nothing had transpired between them, the past forgotten again. "Give her time," Louis would say. For as composed as Violet often was, both Anna and Louis could see that Violet's forbearance was a thin armor to the struggle within her.

So Anna waited, always reminding herself that her daughter no doubt missed her home in Rickmansworth, her pampered life, the attention and sense of belonging she once got. She reminded herself that her daughter's attitude was to be expected and that in fact, given her change in circumstances, she was surprisingly restrained. Violet never commented on that single worn couch, or the stench in the narrow stairwell that connected all six flats, or the brazen woman above who entertained loud men in her flat at all hours of the night. Yes, she did carry in her a persistent and silent refutation evident in almost all that she did, in the unexpected check of her small head in response to what Anna had thought was a benign remark or in the stiff way she carried herself through the dirty streets to her overcrowded school. Admittedly, Anna sometimes found her daughter's aloofness difficult to bear, but she accepted what she saw for what she decided it had to be: a means for her daughter to cope. She tried not to feel hurt. She kept no record of the wrongs. Maternal love, she knew, was a love so different from all else, so vast and infinite, with no start and no end. It was a love that since her daughter's birth she had carried in every cell of her body, and having Violet home, in the flesh, was a visible rematerialization of what she had so long held, eternal in space. Divine in the true sense, patient and kind, protected and trusted, hoped and persevered. Forgiving. Just like they said.

But it did not help that the aunts still wrote. They wrote about how much they missed Violet and how quiet their house now was. After receiving those letters, Violet would cry in her room. Anna knew better than to join her daughter or to send Violet's letters back. Of course, Anna sometimes feared the aunts might ask that Violet be returned or, worse yet, if they learned how impoverished their life was and how difficult Violet was finding it to adapt, that they might demand that Violet be returned to them. More than once, Anna saw well-heeled British dressed in what they smugly thought befitting for visits to the poor, "slumming it," as the practice was known. Clutching Violet close, Anna readied herself should the two aunts reveal themselves in an attempt to steal her daughter away. *This too shall pass,* she told herself, just as Louis said.

Two years into Violet's habitation with them, her daughter's anger and insecurity had indeed subsided. Her outbreaks were less frequent. George was two and Violet relished being a big sister to him, her affection a constant reminder to Anna of all the love within her, even if she often concealed it to them. The letters from the aunts had ceased and Violet now called her mother Ma-Ma, as her toddler brother George did. The form of address admittedly may have started as a mistake, for although Anna had long ago asked Violet to call her *Mutter* as most German children did, Violet never had used that term, omitting in those early years any form of maternal address at all. But then one morning, after Anna had very gently rebuked her eight-year-old daughter for snapping at her little brother to stop all his noise, the word Anna had slipped from Violet's lips. Anna had tried her best to conceal her hurt, but her flinch was unmistakable even to Violet, the bruise to her heart no doubt evident in the quick contraction of her chest. In apparent recognition of the pain her mother had tried to conceal, Violet had abashedly corrected herself with "Ma-Ma" and from thereon, Ma-Ma she was. In her daughter's address, Anna found a seed of compassion for her that she had so long waited to take root. Love for her Ma-Ma, Anna was now able to assure herself, would soon come.

"She is adjusting," Anna told Louis one late evening after Violet had affectionately kissed her goodnight after a particularly trying day. She and Louis were laying in the dark in their small coil-spring bed, and Anna was thinking about her children, as she so often did.

"Yes," Louis said.

"Yes," Anna affirmed, as much to him as to herself. "She is."

Louis gently squeezed her arm. "That is good," he said. "She will be fine."

"You think so?" she asked.

"Yes," he said, "you have to believe that. Now sleep."

"Okay," she said.

And for a time, Anna did. Violet by that point was usually kind to her brother and to Louis as well. She loved them both, it was clear, but she could still be difficult with her mother, even unkind. In many ways, Violet still existed apart, with her clipped British accent decidedly middle-class, distinct from the cockney spoken by the other children and by her recognizably German mother, whose English was often difficult to understand. But it was 1912 and there was so much that Violet had a right to rail against. To her credit, her daughter usually kept her grievances to herself—in her tightly tied imaginary safe-keeping box, out of reach of anyone, most of all herself. The list of things with which her daughter had to contend was long: the lewd old man on the corner who heckled prepubescent girls; the angry xenophobic woman below who banged the floor between them and yelled "Sour Kraut" when she walked by; the foul smells and pervasive dampness that emanated from the river Thames; the garbage in the streets; the flooded alleys and the splashing from above by neighbors who were too lazy and too inconsiderate to dump their muck into proper holes. And then there were the constant headaches, which sometimes made her daughter sick and on occasion caused her to throw up, an illness that no doubt emanated from all of this.

Anna hated that her daughter had to endure so much, but she also understood that there was no solution, no antidote to the poverty, and so had come to accept and even appreciate her daughter's chosen method to cope. Her daughter's forbearance, the way she existed slightly apart from her family and her peers, was to be expected, even necessary to some extent. Whether that forbearance stemmed from willful ignorance or stubborn detachment, Anna did not know, but she decided that did not matter. Better her daughter learned young and was prepared. More hardship would come; it always did.

By 1913, that hardship had indeed come. Admittedly, life was much better in some ways. In the evenings, Anna noticed, Violet now hugged and kissed her goodnight, in addition to Louis and George. She now talked to her mother and asked her questions as well. Once, Violet even brought home a cut flower for Anna, telling her she was the best cook in the world. All this despite the struggles outside, despite the anti-German sentiment and the anti-Semitism, despite the growing xenophobia and the loudening chorus of Brits telling the Germans to go back to where they came from.

"Things are getting worse," Anna told Louis after yet another difficult day. "I am frightened for us and for the children as well."

"We will be okay."

"But what of Violet? What of George? Maybe we should not be here. Maybe I have made things worse."

Her husband kissed her on the head, drew her close. "We will be okay," he assured her.

Anna tried to listen to her husband, to permit him to allay her concerns. Louis refused to be deterred by what was encroaching on them. He often reminded Anna how lucky they were. They were now the only residents in their flat; they were one family with one roof, just as he had promised it would be. Once more, their building, which a philanthropist had built, was much nicer than many in the neighborhood that were kept together with mortar and street dirt. "We have it good," he said. As a full-fledged German Jew, Louis was subject to the rising tide of anti-Semitism and German dislike much more than the rest of them and yet, even now he found room for gratitude and positivity. She resolved herself to do the same. He had believed that one day they would become a family of four and now, just as he said, they were. He had believed that Violet would one day accept her and now, just as he said, she more or less did. She had to trust in him still.

But by 1914, the chorus of name-calling was more audible not only toward Anna but to her children as well, and as much as Louis reassured her, Anna was finding it increasingly difficult to keep her fear of what lay before them in check. She often could not sleep, wondering how she could protect Violet and George from all that lay outside. Sometimes Anna even gave in to thinking that Violet might have been better off in Rickmansworth. Had Violet stayed there she would not be Katzenstein, a German Jew by name, and therefore not subject to all that was becoming so hard to endure. There would be no threats and demands against her, that she go home to a country that had never been hers. Had she made a mistake? Anna began to again ask herself. *No, it will be okay*, she countered to herself. Trust, hope, kindness, and perseverance, that's what they said in church. Surely its presence, not just in her home but in all the other homes, magnified love's benevolent and redemptive force. Surely, love would win out and good would prevail, she tried to convince herself. But given what she saw, such reassurances were becoming more difficult to maintain, and Anna could not contain her fear. Would all that she and Louis had built splinter once again?

Then, some four years into her daughter's habitation with them, Anna had an idea. A solution, she told herself. The idea came at night, as ideas so often did, and in the morning, the idea did not go away. It did not seem to Anna foolish or inane, as night-hatched ideas had a tendency to be.

They were eating breakfast at their little wooden table when Anna presented her solution to Louis. Violet had not yet awoken, and George was sitting in Anna's lap, fiddling with the collar on her black dress.

"Some Germans are changing their names. Did you know that?" Anna asked through a beam of dusty light that lit up the room.

"Sorry?" Louis asked, and he shifted his chair so he could better see across the small dining table from him.

"A few have changed their names," she repeated. "I've been noticing the announcements in newspaper ads. Not many, but a few. I don't think it complicated. You know the Millers. They were the Muellers before. So I've been wondering. Maybe we should change Violet to Cross?"

"I don't understand," Louis said. His tone was steady. His voice did not inflect. Given the sensitivity of the proposition, she was relieved by that.

"It might protect her. And George," Anna added, combing her boy's hair with her hand. "Maybe he could have the same, born on British soil? It may protect him too?" Anna looked carefully at Louis as she spoke.

"Protect against what?" he asked, as if he did not know.

"All the German hate." She searched Louis' face for a wince, a furrowed brow. He showed nothing. So she continued.

"I'm not talking about us. I am Katzenstein, like you. But the children. It's just a name. I was only thinking. I have looked into the cost. We have saved. I just need to go to a Justice of the Peace. Get a few forms signed."

Anna was aware of the sensitivity of what she proposed. Violet had the Katzenstein name. Informally, anyway. They had given

Katzenstein to the Census only four years before and now Anna was asking if she could give it back. She was asking for Cross and the same for his son, the name of a man whom Louis believed had bedded her without consent, even if it was not exactly so.

"Louis?" she asked, wondering if she detected a small wrinkle of concern above one eye. Had she asked too much? "Actually, maybe it is a bad idea. You need not do that. It's fine." She started to get up.

"Sit down," he said. "That is fine. Good idea. Now eat."

"Okay," Anna said, and put her hand atop his, gently squeezing it.

As she finished her breakfast, with her son in her lap, Anna thought of how much she loved her husband, how lucky she was. "Thank you," she said, and kissed Louis on his head as he so often did to her.

The process was not difficult. It was easy to see what to do, given the Germans who had already posted their name changes in *The London Gazette*. Seeing a market, naturalization agencies had begun listing in German-language papers. To learn more, Anna visited one agency and then another, getting the information she needed without paying a cent. At a nearby Justice of the Peace, she picked up forms from an impatient clerk to be signed by her children's father, or the fathers in this case. Anna already had a copy of Violet's birth registration on which Anna had mentioned just that hint of Cross through the middle initial of C. She wrote to Priscilla, "Ma'am Cross," Violet's grandmother by blood. She kept the letter brief, asking her if she would kindly locate Jack to ask his permission to change Violet's name to Cross, and enclosing a copy of the form. Anna did not mention that Violet was actually Katzenstein. Anna was hopeful. Ma'am had never liked the Germans. She might agree to a British grandchild, even if she was reluctant to recognize Violet in her line. One less German at least. Anna only needed Jack's signature, nothing else, no money, nothing from any of them. Ma'am had a tough exterior but she always helped in the end. She was efficient too. She would get Jack's signature or forge it if she must. Jack was in Canada, as far as Anna knew, but Ma'am would find a way. She always did.

Two weeks later Anna received an unexpected letter from the two spinster aunts who apparently had learned of her request to change Violet's name to Cross. They asked that should Anna return to Germany, to leave Violet with them. "Those Germans will turn her ringlets to braids. Anna. Please grant us this request, for the sake of the girl." Anna ignored the letter and waited for Ma'am's response.

By June of 1914, Anna had her two completed forms, one for her son and one for her daughter, too, their fathers' signature on each. Both children were becoming Cross. She then scheduled an appointment at the Justice of the Peace. Louis said he could not join because he had a shop to keep; Anna suspected his absence was more complicated than that. With only one son, Louis would be the end of the Katzenstein line and Anna did not fault Louis for what he must have felt.

Anna arrived in the afternoon at the Justice of the Peace with her son and stubbornly English daughter with her. It was going to be another difficult day. When she told the clerk she was there to make a declaration of a name change before the justice of the peace, the clerk checked her in by handing her a number.

"Do you have the forms and the registration of birth?" the clerk asked.

"I have them," Anna declared. "Right here," she said, pointing to the contents of the black leather bag that hung from her shoulder.

"Name, registration of birth, what I said. Now wait." The woman looked past Anna, but Anna refused to feel dismissed by her. "Next," the woman said.

So they waited. Violet took little George from her mother and Anna reminded herself that she did not regret bringing her daughter home.

After twenty minutes, the clerk waved Anna back to a room in which sat a man with a mole on his lip behind a very large, raised desk. Anna felt very small in front of it.

"Are you the justice of the peace?" Anna asked.

"Yes," he said.

"I am here to change my children's names to Cross," she declared.

"I am aware," he said. "You don't have a solicitor."

"No."

Anna was nervous, and she could tell he knew. She handed him her documentation and she stood motionless as he reviewed it. He occasionally glanced up, scanned her face, and peered at the small boy holding her leg and at the ten-year-old girl standing at attention in her black shoes. When he was done, he asked that Anna bring the two children closer so he could see them.

"Hello," Violet proclaimed. "I am Violet," she announced, stepping closer to him.

"Violet who?" the man asked, less stern, and Anna wondered if she saw the beginnings of a smile in the upturned corners of his lips.

Violet looked at her mother, and Anna nodded. "Violet Cross," she said with even more force.

The corners of his lips raised even higher, and he gave a quick nod before turning his attention to the little boy, who had climbed back into his mother's arms, clutching at his mother's breast.

"And you," he said with a small laugh; he was enjoying this, Anna thought.

"George Cross," Violet interjected from the other side of the desk. "I am his sister. He is only four." The man smiled again and Anna was glad that she had brought her daughter here, to this place with her.

"Well, well," he continued. "Different fathers I see? Why are they not here?"

Anna bristled, her demeanor changed, more defensive than before. "One is in Canada as you can see, and the other has a shop to tend. But they agree that the children should be Cross."

"And your name?" he asked curtly of Anna, his demeanor changed as well.

"Anna Katzenstein, formerly Bracker," she said. He did like not Germans, Anna thought, before adding, "Both children are mine."

The man cocked his head toward Violet, as if to note something that he had observed. He no doubt had seen the *filius populi*
by Violet's name on the registration. *So she's a bastard*, he was
probably thinking as he looked at Anna and back to Violet again.
Anna did her best to remain composed, not to flinch. She could
handle men's looks. Violet, too, stood firm, seemingly impervi-
ous to what Anna now decided was a patronizing evaluation of
her. Then Violet blushed and the man opened his mouth as if he
might speak but, on further consideration, lowered his shoulders
and spoke.

"Fine," he said. "Cross, both of them. It will make no difference."

"Excuse me?" Anna asked. No difference about what?

"Is this your address?" he asked, ignoring Anna's question.

"Yes."

"Fine," he said, and looked again at Violet. Violet looked away,
and Anna saw in her daughter not stubborn detachment, or even
willful ignorance, but something else entirely, a desperate will to
persist.

Addressing Violet, the man continued, "I advise your mother
to take out an ad in *The London Gazette*. It is not much." He scribbled something on both forms. Violet still did not engage with
him. Anna worried Violet might run.

"Then it is all right?" Anna interjected, reaching for her daughter's hand. Violet did not take it.

"You're dismissed," he said, dropping his gaze from Violet and
fixing it back on his desk. He pushed the documentation across
his desk.

Anna stepped toward him with George held in the crook of her
arm and took the forms, placing it awkwardly in her bag before
grabbing Violet by the hand. She then quickly left, as she so often
did, afraid the man might change his mind.

They did not speak on the long walk home but just as they were
entering the flat, Violet asked, "Is it done? Am I Violet Cross?"

"Yes," Anna replied, uncertain how her daughter would take
the news.

To Anna's surprise, Violet squealed in delight and hugged
her brother walking beside them. "We are both Cross, George,

finally!" she exclaimed and Anna was both saddened and relieved. *How unpredictable my daughter is and how hard to understand*, she thought.

They then walked up the stairs to their flat, a mother and her two children who carried different names. Before she opened the door, Anna reminded herself that she had done well, an immigrant who knew so little of this country but who had at least done this.

"Meet Violet and George Cross," Violet triumphantly announced to her stepfather after opening the door.

"Well, well, well," Louis said to his stepdaughter, with what Anna could have sworn was a wink. A wink—so uncharacteristic of him. He turned to Anna. "Well done," he said to her, and she could not read if Louis was pleased or resigned.

Later that evening, Louis brought out two beers and raised his glass to his wife, and Anna raised her glass to him. "Thank you," she said.

"We are family, no matter what," he affirmed.

"Yes," she said as she tried not to think about what the judge had said, that it would make no difference at all.

The days proceeded. Anna published the announcement of the name changes in the newspaper, and Violet announced to her class that she had a new name. Every evening, Violet practiced writing it. Violet Helene Cross. "It looks good doesn't it, Ma-Ma?" her daughter asked.

"Yes, yes, it does," said Anna.

Anna wrote the aunts, too, informing them of the changes. Ma'am, she wrote, had agreed, as had her son Jack.

The situation grew worse. On August 4, Great Britain declared war on Germany and *The London Gazette* was filled with announcements of Germans changing their names, just as Anna had previously done. Anna was glad she had had the foresight to change their names before the war broke out, but even a changed name, she now feared, would do little to protect her children from the surrounding hate. Every day the papers carried news of Brits taking up makeshift arms to attack what they deemed enemy establishments in their midst, and Anna was petrified by what she read. There was the attack on the Polish tobacconist and confectioner in North Finchley that involved some two thousand angry Londoners, among them reservists from a nearby barracks. There was the crowd of a thousand who attacked and set alight the shop of a German in Keighley, near Wakefield, and the two thousand who gathered outside the house of a Quaker, throwing stones at his windows because he had shown charity to destitute aliens sent by the Society of Friends.

Then came news that enemy aliens would have to register with the police and were forbidden from using names they had assumed since the outbreak of the war. Because she had changed their names before the declaration of war, Anna assumed her children's names safe, but she worried nonetheless about them and about her husband as well.

"I changed their names before August of 1914. Are they safe? Will we have to register them too?" Anna asked Louis after reading the news of the registration.

In the dark she could feel his gaze resting resignedly on her cheek. "I'm afraid so," he whispered. "Yes," he repeated more loudly, to make sure he was understood.

So register they did, two Katzensteins and two Crosses. To Anna, the registration signified the beginning of the end. Their lives were so restricted now, their freedoms gone. As alien enemies, they had to obey local curfews and refrain from entering prohibited areas. They were not allowed to own cars or motorcycles. They were not allowed to own cameras or military maps. They could not be members of German clubs. They could not read German newspapers. The people had turned against them as well. Storefronts declared "No Germans need apply," and businesses began to discharge their German workers, for fear of being implicated with spying.

The fear was splintering around them. Even Violet was now visibly insecure, the daughter whom Anna had once thought so strong. Her mask of disdain and indifference was completely gone, her vulnerability exposed in its most raw form. When Violet came home from school, she now climbed straight into her mother's arms and hugged her brother too. Anna felt so guilty for having ever wanted her daughter's armor stripped. The aunts wrote again, imploring Anna to let Violet remain with them. Anna did not reply.

In May of 1915 came the news that the *Lusitania* had sunk. A German U-boat struck the liner down, and within eighteen minutes of being hit by a single torpedo, over a thousand passengers and crew lost their lives. In the days that followed, even deeper hatred set in. The Germans were going to pay. The newspapers published images of mass graves in Ireland, where many of the bodies from the *Lusitania* had washed ashore. Rioting began, and the shops, businesses, and homes of anyone believed to be German came under threat. Louis barricaded his shop. The very next day a brick knocked in the front window of a pork butcher's shop and a crowd wrecked the place, smashing everything suggestive of Germany. Then the government announced full-scale internment for all men of German descent between the ages of seventeen and fifty-five. Within a few days of the announcement, Louis reported to the local police and was detained for a night in a prison cell.

Anna and the children visited Louis in jail. Anna brought him a book. Violet hugged him, told him that she loved him, that he was the best father a girl could have, and cried unabated. Only four years before, Anna would have welcomed such a vulnerable display of love. Not so anymore. Violet's hard shell had completely dissolved, like sugar in rain.

CHAPTER 5

FAIRLEE, VERMONT — 2017

Toxic thoughts can lead us to react more harshly to challenging behavior . . . toxic thoughts can leak into our facial expression without our verbal awareness. And because abused youth have had to read non-verbal cues to stay safe, these toxic thoughts can wind up harming our relationships if we don't catch and correct them.[23]

I t is 2017. My mother's younger brother, Neville, has had three strokes. He has lost his ability to speak. I cannot ask him about my maternal history although I have in my possession a great deal of his research. He has long been interested in his mother Violet's story. Well, at least the historical context of it. He has never seemed to be much concerned with communicating underlying emotional narrative. He has preferred, for the most part, to be accurate and succinct. When he wrote, he used acronyms for long names, such as GEC for his father George Edward Cusworth. When answering his phone at work, he simply said, "Cusworth." No "Hello," no "How are you," just "Cusworth" with an expressionless tone that always made my siblings and me laugh as it was such a contrast to his in-person warmth, to the way he responds to my mother and to us. It is as if he can regulate his emotion with a switch depending on the context.

My uncle was trained to discern fact. He studied law at Christ Church, Oxford, and advanced to the top position at a legal publishing firm. Throughout his professional life and before he retired and had a stroke, my mother was quick to boast of all Neville had achieved and what he had attained. She liked to tell people that Neville was a member of London's Garrick Club, for men of the arts, especially theatre, with an enormous library and large leather chairs, in an expensive part of town. Charles Dickens, H. G. Wells, and Kingsley Amis were all members of the Garrick, she often pointed out. Neville let her boast of his achievements not, I suspect, because he liked to be aggrandized but because he saw that she took great pride in him. As a consequence, he did not correct her when she made these lofty comparisons. He did not, for example, interject with the fact that, while he loved the arts, he was not an artist himself and claimed nothing akin to that. He let her speak on his behalf. He let her speak of Oxford and his professional life, as if in tacit acknowledgement that she never was given the opportunity to pursue such interests herself. Despite the fact that she gave birth to seven children, in some ways he fulfilled the role of her first-born, having been cared for and protected by her in those abusive foster homes when he was only eighteen months, even if when she cared for him, she was barely three years old herself.

When I am fifty and after he has had his strokes, I cannot learn what he thinks about our legacy of maternal trauma. I cannot discern if he believes, like my mother, that history repeats itself and that there are wider implications to it. When anti-immigration sentiment sweeps the world and young children are being separated from their parents, I cannot ask him whether what my mother calls our return to fascism and persecution also is affecting him. My mother feels she is witness to what led to Hitler's rise. She is addicted to current events and to her phone alerts. Violations of human rights trigger her physically and mentally. She fears what is happening in the world will do to the next generation of children what was done to her. By the time I become interested enough in Neville's work and in him, I do not ask him if he agrees. He cannot speak. His writing hand is clawed. His eyes are still lively, suggesting he has more to share, but I do not know what. He smiles all the time with those he loves, but I cannot get to what lies inside him, though I'm not sure I ever could.

Neville is different from my mother. Based on his past writing, even his interest in the family history has always seemed to me a predominantly intellectual pursuit. His writing is informative and succinct, even somewhat removed. In all his work, there is only one reference to himself in a scene in which he runs into his mother's arms. Aside from that one memory, he himself does not feature in his writing at all. He quotes historians and lists facts. Personal subtext seems almost a narcissistic indulgence to him. I can only guess why. Perhaps he views it a mistake to presume that our life has relevance to anyone but us. Or perhaps he thinks life too short to get lost in the emotional complexity of our youth.

But Neville carries secrets too. He was the one to discover the letter from his grandfather, Jack Cross, revealing Violet's illegitimacy. He found the letter in Violet's chest of drawers after her death of colon cancer in a little damp cottage in Sussex. When I am fifty, my mother still frequently mentions that letter to me. "Why did she never share it with us? Illegitimate, can you believe that? All those years. Amazing, don't you think?" When he could still speak, my mother asked Neville for his perspective, but he preferred not to speculate. If their mother had not shared it with them, she must have had her reasons, he apparently said. Neville also was the one to learn from an old Cross aunt who lived in a nursing home in the west of England that their maternal grandmother, Anna, gave birth to another child in Germany when she was very young. Again he shared the information with his sister whom he thought, I assume, probably put too much focus on it. "Why did he not find out more?" she asked me. "Why did he not pursue it? It would be so interesting to know, don't you think? I want to know." But Neville apparently saw no reason to press. The old aunt is blind, and pressing, he explained to us both before his strokes, would be too upsetting for her. Better to let the secret die with her and stick to the accessible facts.

I do not know what my uncle thought of my research into his mother's life. Sometimes, I think he may have believed that I did not understand that some rocks were better left unturned and that focusing on the tragedy of one's youth, or indeed of the youth of one's parents or grandparents, was not the best course.

That evening with me when I was twenty-two and his half-cousin Angus refused to speak of Uncle George's falling out with Violet, Uncle Neville was the one to turn the discussion to the innocuous Prime Minister John Major instead. Angus seemed to resent being asked about the family, and Neville had apparently decided not to delve too deeply into what Violet herself did not disclose, into what clearly made others uncomfortable, into the details of what we could not know. Perhaps Neville believed that we must transcend our past, and he did not want his sister setting me onto Violet's life like a hound on a scent. He was willing to share some facts with his sister, my mother, Barbara, and if she wanted to share them with us, her children, so be it, he would not.

At fifty, I assume that informing Neville's approach to his sister was the reality that she already had absorbed too much, that in her adult years she needed to hold fast to the few happy remnants she could sew together from those early years, just like their mother did. When Neville heard from Angus that in fact his mother and her stepbrother lived in London's slums after Rickmansworth, he apparently did not share it with her. I assume he did not share it because he believed why take from Barbara the one story his mother had entrusted to her. Barbara treasured that story as if an heirloom. Indeed, to her own children, Barbara had willed it again. Why make fiction out of what she held as a stabilizing truth? He was protecting his sister, just as she long ago protected him when they were young, a protection she herself never had. It was I who revealed Violet's residence in East London to her after finding her address in his notes.

I will never know, but sometimes I think that perhaps Neville thought that history should not be an entertainment to which we claim some outsized hereditary right and that we should not feel entitled to make it our own, inventing where we like. I would like to believe, however, that he would support me trying to lend a voice to those who preceded us. As a man of the law who also enjoyed a club for the arts, I suspect he was well aware of the fine line between fiction and fact and that to understand our mothers' past and its effect, that line could be crossed. In his writing, he himself may have preferred to stick to fact, believing it important not to view history through too emotional a lens. But I do not think he would fault me for what I wrote. When I visit him after his strokes, he does not appear to judge me. He engages with me if not through his speech, through his eyes. I can see the emotion that dances in his eyes and I feel it in his hands that linger on my shoulders as he holds me at arms length and embraces me in his gaze. He seems to know the importance of getting to what is felt even if he does not speak of it himself. He is neither distracted nor emotionally distant to me.

At fifty, I know I can learn more from him. When I think of my Uncle Neville and how attached my mother is to him, I am reminded of what I have learned from that organization where I work that specializes in trauma-informed care. The organization's literature addresses the importance of being aware of our own emotions and how we communicate our emotions to those we care for. We need to show them that we understand and that we do not judge by how we respond. If we get triggered and our emotions run away, we need to stop and breathe. We need to reframe the way we think about why someone has responded in a particular way by taking the time to understand the source of the behavior. We then can choose not to dislike, judge, or dismissively look away. We can engage, be attentive, and be more empathic. We can fix our face if we are communicating negative emotion or disdain.[24] When I visit my uncle, I think about the fact that my uncle is handling his stroke fine, much better than my mother is handling it. I wonder why my uncle has not been triggered in later life as my mother has. Studies I have read suggest that early trauma for male rats is not as harmful as it is for female rats.[25] I wonder how much of his emotional well-being is attributable to genetics and how much to how and to whom he attached in early childhood.

VIOLET

HAMBURG. GERMANY, 1932

Dear Diary,

My father's dead. My real one. Not Louis, but the one I never met. The one I thought was rich but apparently was not. The one who sent me back that letter I have sworn to you I will always keep, the letter that came in response to the one I last year wrote and that asked that we at last meet. (He said no, you'll recall.) So aged only 28, I've lost yet another parent, proxy or not. It's getting decidedly hard to keep track!

Anyway, and here's the big news, real grandmother Priscilla apparently told Ma-Ma that real father Jack killed himself! Suicide by arsenic poisoning with Paris Green apparently. Paris Green sounds cruelly romantic, doesn't it? But not to worry, wife Lena apparently said real father Jack's death had nothing to do with the letter I wrote to him asking to meet. Thank you, wife of real father. That makes me feel so much better. You're so kind. Anyway, wife Lena told real grandmother Priscilla who told Ma-Ma who told me in case I was sitting around waiting for the invitation to visit him.

Not that I really, actually care very much. Well, I do care a bit as now I definitely never will meet him but I'm not sure I would have liked him. I had gone to all the trouble of writing, badgering Ma-Ma to get his address that, I must say, was within my rights as his biological offspring, and he writes back that letter so full of excuses. Too kind Ma-Ma politely attributed his refusal to "The Depression" which she says is much worse in Canada than here in Germany but I would not let him off the hook as easily as that. I told her I thought he was weak and she said something like he was the black sheep of the family and always went his own way and it wasn't quite as simple as I thought. She, of course, was just being the way she always is, trying to make the best of a situation. He probably forced himself upon her, but she never said that either. She in fact never shared anything of my origins with me for so long. I told you about that time when it all came out after I pressed her when she said something about me not actually having Jewish blood because my actual father was not Jewish at all. Something anti-Semitic had happened, I can't remember what, and that comment slipped out. Hitler by the way has only become more popular since then. He and the Nazis just won with more than a third of the popular vote. A terrible man. Mark my words. I worry about Louis with him around.

But anyway, in retrospect, maybe I should not have written him, but I was just so tired of not knowing so much. Ma-Ma never mentioned him, and the aunties, though always upfront with me, never were forthcoming with details about him. They were wonderful. Don't get me wrong. And Louis was a decent replacement. He respected me from the start. That's why him being taken away was probably the most terrible morning of them all, awaking to find him and thousands of others escorted by soldiers with drawn bayonets and the crowds spitting at them, throwing insults and rotten food, jeering, calling them baby killers and huns. Ma-Ma thought I did not know what was happening, but I did. You could not help hearing or looking out the window at all those men being marched down the street. I actually completely broke down when he was sent to Knockaloe Camp. I love Louis, always did, and that was overwhelming to me. In fact, a lot of things have been. Going to Bethnal Green. Not that I blame Ma-Ma anymore. I have learned not to hold it against her. But I did hate going back to Germany too. I did not speak a word of German then, as I've shared with you before, and the Germans were not at all kindly to me. The teachers slapped my knuckles with a ruler every time I uttered an English word. Of course, the British were never much better, forcing us back to Germany, sending Louis to that awful camp. Neither country is much good, if you ask me. But I try not to get too worked up about things like that. Not anymore at least. I exist apart from it, just like my aunties taught. The only difference is when I was very young, I was much more strident. I believed I could change things. Now, I'm more resigned, more apt to accept, probably like my real father who committed suicide. I did, by the way, get my hands on the *British Medical Journal* when I found out he offed himself and I looked up the word suicide. It said something like "the genetic seed of suicidal thought takes root when one believes one is no longer able to endure suffering in the present or pain in the future."[26] And actually, the theory makes sense to me. I mean think about it. Said father went his own way for so long until one day, he realized it was all for naught. I get it. Life can be a lot to bear, and the only way to go on is not to think about it all too much, to avoid focusing on the past or what will happen hence, and certainly not to talk about any of it or think that you can change its course. I mean, you can't blame Jack for wanting to get out. Hate to admit it but I'd probably do the same.

Well, I'd better be quiet before I say something I'll regret. Sorry for ending on such a morbid note! Here's his letter anyway. Transcribed by moi.

Believe me yours,
Violet

p.s. I like the way he signs.

Dear Vie,

I received your letter yesterday and was pleased to hear from you and to hear that you have recovered from your illness and are enjoying life again. Well, the reason I had not written to you before was I expected to get my pension through the first of last month but it did not come through so I chased after it and then had to have a medical examination sent in, as I have not heard anything more I think probably that I will get it in the beginning of next month. If so, we will let you know right away and if you are still in the mind to come out, I will send for you but I must tell you things are very bad out here at present and I have only been working two days per all the summer and now I am off until sent for as the motor car trade is flat and in fact everything is bad. Lena got laid off her last job and did nothing all the summer but now she is working at the Eastman Kodak so of course that helps a little, the wife has been laid up with rheumatism and is still hobbling round so talking it all through I have had a rotten summer but I think things will soon start picking up again at least I hope so. You asked me if I was a wandering Jew in my younger days. Well I certainly was pretty wild and took a long time to settle down. Lena is about the same she is like a blue bottle fly all over the place in a few minutes and as restless as a hawk. Yesterday was Armistice Day. It's kept very solemn here. Do they hold it in Germany (also my birthday)? I expect they are still pretty sore on us yet. Well Vie I haven't any more to tell you but when we meet I guess we will have a lot to talk about so must conclude with best of wishes,

Believe me yours,
E J Cross

CHAPTER 6

LONDON, ENGLAND — 1991

Epigenetics adds a new and more comprehensive psychobiological dimension to the explanation of transgenerational transmission of trauma. Specifically, epigenetics may explain why latent transmission becomes manifest under stress.[27]

A t twenty-three, I am aware that my mother has a tendency to spend, even if I do not yet know the future financial repercussions or the source of her behavior, even if I have not yet read that childhood trauma casts a long and wide-ranging shadow, even if I have not studied the literature showing that childhood trauma carries with it a greater risk for mental illness and can affect functioning, including financial.[28] When I am twenty-three years old, the extent of my knowledge around financial functioning is limited to having borne witness to what I perceive as my mother's draw to expensive things, her ability to intuitively pick out the most expensive piece of clothing on the rack. This ability is in fact a point of pride for her, but I have never appreciated her love of valuable things. Actually, I try to live in opposition to her in that respect. I wear hand-me-downs from friends and take equal pride in being unkempt. I know that this dichotomy with her is in many ways false, as I have attended private schools, never been in want of a thing, and am now living in London's most desirable section of the West End. But when my father receives an inheritance from his mother, I am nonetheless disapproving of my mother's decision to contract the construction of a big new

Vermont house on a hill that commands better views than the small home below in which my parents currently live. However, my main concern with their decision is not their financial health but instead the fate of my beloved Vermont home.

"What will happen to the pond by our old house and the rock in the middle of it?" I ask when my mother calls me to speak of her new construction that also includes a tennis court and a new pond to replace the one we had. The rock in that pond has always been my favorite spot. As a teenager, I often lay in view of the rock on the pond's dock, in the shadow of Glebe Mountain, my feet dangling in the water with the mud rinsing out from between my toes. Now my mother is talking about replacing it, taking away the fixture of my teen years!

"It's important to me," I protest, aware of how spoilt I sound.

"Well, the new tennis court and new pond will be better. The house will be, too, you will see. This old one is far too small."

My mother goes on to explain that the new house has three bedrooms upstairs, a master bedroom downstairs, off of which my mother is planning a blue slate porch that will be installed in the spring, and on which she and my father plan to sit at night with drinks to watch the sun set. The kitchen has been designed with Mexican tile and an AGA imported from England; AGAs are apparently the most logical choice in Vermont because of the heat they consistently emit. My mother does not know why no one else imports them. She is also planning to put an outdoor shower out back, in which anyone can stand naked with a view of the wood. In the spring, the front of the house will have a big garden with a stone wall and a sloping meadow through which the grandchildren will be able to run. My mother especially loves the master bath. It has a bidet—"only Europeans use bidets"—and the library will be paneled and lined with shelves for books so my mother can read to her heart's content. Beside the garage she is going to put a flagpole, from which she'll fly the Union Jack and beneath it the American flag. The American flag has to go beneath—not that she wants an American flag, but my father has insisted on it. He wants the house, too. It reminds him of the house of his youth.

"Do you really need all that?" I ask her on the phone from their kitchen table in London. I know I am judging her, but I nevertheless persist. "We're all basically out of the house. It sounds too big, too much. I love the old house. I love that rock," I repeat, though if I were honest, I would have to admit that I do not quite love the rock as much as I did in my early teenage years. It all got a little more burdensome the day my mother christened the rock her own. "Barbara's rock," she called it and from then on, whenever I lay on the dock, I could not help but visualize my mother, making her way toward me with her wide-brimmed hat and her waxed legs breaking the tall rough weeds. She would walk across that ground beneath Glebe Mountain, its summer hair bending to her step, the ground crushed under her bright red clogs, and announce, "Elizabeth, I'm here. Time to swim to my rock!" My silence pierced.

"I really do love that rock," I repeat, whining a bit.

"Well, it's time to move on. Forget the rock," my mother says, somewhat heartlessly, I think.

"But Dad's business hasn't taken off yet," I continue. "Is it really the right time?"

"Hush. You're out of the house now. This is my home. It's none of your business. It's done."

"But he said he may have to be selling the London flat. Can you really afford all this?"

"It's fine. Anyway, I'm not selling the flat. I don't care what your father says. No one can tell me what to do. And anyway, if I sold the flat, where would you live?"

"But you already have a house that we love, and none of us are home much, and Dad hasn't got his business going, and not everyone is out of school. Why build that house? Why not put that money toward keeping this flat? This does not seem viable to me."

"Don't get involved, Elizabeth. It's none of your business. It's done. I never had a proper home growing up. You don't know what that's like. I have nothing from then. I don't want to talk about the new house with you."

"But, Mom—"

"It's my life. I'm not going to discuss it any more." She pauses. "How's the research going anyway? Find out anything else?"

"Not really."

"I'll be coming over again in six months. I need to get to London again. See Neville. We can talk more then."

I hang up the phone. There is nothing more to say. I do not anticipate that in two years' time my father will become acutely ill, my parent's financial strain will become insurmountable, my mother's bouts of acute depression will begin, and her friends will seem to her few. I do not know that later, long after that house has been built and I have children of my own, I will wonder if this expenditure was the point at which the course of her adult life began to redirect and whether, given the trauma and the maternal history that preceded her, there always was an inevitability to it. I have not yet considered why she and her brother responded so differently to what befell them. Epigenetics will one day help me understand. Through it, I will come to see that genetically identical twins can look entirely different in both color and size due to the alteration of the expression of their genes, that behaviors and appearances can be passed through generations and appear in one offspring and not the other. Environmental triggers can turn them on[29] and not just environment but childhood abuse can induce what is called epigenetic variation as well.[30] Non Maternal Care (NMC) in early childhood, like the care my mother provided Neville or that which Violet received from those two aunts, can serve as a protective factor,[31] but childhood trauma and lack of attachment can still result in long-term effects that persist.[32] At twenty-three, I have not read such findings. In fact, they do not even exist and even if they did, I suspect I would not have cared. Instead, I continue to collect and sometimes write about my mother's past. I do not consider how my grandmother's struggle may have impacted my mother and even me to some extent. I do not think about my tendency to emotionally distance myself from her or to distract myself. I do not think about how the anxiety our mothers carry and how they cope may be expressed in us. All I know is that when I get anxious about my future, I do things like think about that rock that my mother is about to take away. I do not realize that my mother has no such fixture from her past on which she can consistently rely and that the fixtures of my grand-mother's childhood also were taken away young.

VIOLET

HAMBURG, GERMANY, 1935

Violet had never thought she would get married to a Brit named George, but then she also never imagined that Adolf Hitler would seize power. Violet had long ago learned that there was no point in projecting. Would that have made any difference at all? Hard times could not be prepared for, and anyway, what for?

Now living in Hamburg, Violet was marrying in four months' time in Hull, her fiancé George's hometown. England was as good as anywhere, though if pressed, she would concede to reservations about holidaying in Yorkshire after the nuptials. Too cold and too damp, by the sounds of it, and she was not at all sure she liked George's mother very much. Having listened to George recite the letters his mother wrote, she—with her girlfriends' agreement—had decided that the mother seemed a closed-minded Yorkshire matron who demanded far too much of her son (though Violet was trying to reserve judgment until she met the mother in the flesh, of which, by the sounds of it, there was quite a lot!). She would have preferred to be married in Hamburg in front of her stepfather Louis and her own (admittedly not very svelte) Ma-Ma, who was somewhat embarrassingly pleased that her daughter was at last marrying ("And to a clever Englishman too!"), but in actu-ality the land on which Violet stood when she said "I do" held no sentimental value for her. In fact, with the exception of that small patch in Rickmansworth, Violet held no real affiliation with—no bond to—England, but neither did she identify herself as German, despite having lived in the country for the past (could you believe it?) twenty years! Who could have guessed she'd be in one place for so long? Not that anyone would know exactly where she was from when first looking at her or, for that matter, listening to her. Germans only detected a slight British accent when she spoke their native tongue, and the English, once they got to know her, labeled her German, not because they heard a German accent but because of the nationality of her mother and, on further consideration, her dress. Not that she liked the German language very much. Too guttural. Too harsh. When she had emigrated to Germany with her mother and brother, George, back in 1915, she had been unable to utter a word of the language and had learned it by force. Still, she preferred not to think about that time, or about her youth beyond the age of six (children at that age were jam, sweet and best when preserved, she had once said to a friend, and the friend had laughed and laughed; Violet had not considered the observation a joke but was happy to have amused her friend nonetheless).

People could call Violet trite. She did not mind. Trite was a privilege unable to be grasped by those who had not experienced what she had endured, which she chose not to discuss. She never mentioned details about growing up in London or Germany to her fiancé, her colleagues, or even herself now. (In any case, "growing up" was hardly the accurate term, as by the time she moved to London from Rickmansworth, she considered herself already "grown up.") Rickmansworth, she had decided, was the only mentionable bit, and even that was veiled. All else was fluff, or lint, or whatever English or German word one wanted to use to suggest the detritus of her youth past six. She had decided once and for all to jettison it all for her own good health.

Not speaking of her past had its challenges, but Violet found ways to overcome. When she met someone, for example, the other person often inquired into her past in some form. Where one was from was frequently the initial overture to a conversation, but Violet had become adept at evading such questions. Ambiguity ("England and later Germany") and deflection ("And what about you?") usually sufficed as an effective pivot point. Deflection and ambiguity allowed her to avoid discussion of a past that had passed and which she had absolutely no need to relive.

Yes, Violet did her best to focus on what was good in life. In Hamburg in the 1930s, she could. She lived in a comfortable and very well-appointed flat with Ingrid, a friend who had brown, chestnut hair that each morning seemed to accumulate every last bit of the static electricity in the flat. She and her flatmate frequently joked that if only they could figure out a way to harness the static in Ingrid's hair, they would not only be able to heat the kettle but also be very rich! Ingrid also was dating a British man and they often laughed about the eccentricities of The British Male. The British Male seemed to them to be the only race for which mention of a bottom was considered both a clever punch-line and a flirtatious remark. Talk of atrocious weather, she and Ingrid agreed, was also a conversational mainstay for The British Male. Drink was their universal God-given right.

Such light talk of The British Male was just one of many things that brought a smile to Violet's lips. Clothing was another. Violet loved clothes and she was entitled to all sorts of discounts on couture clothing she wore (wholesale price!) as a buyer for the Franz Fahning Department Store, a job she very much enjoyed. She had friendly colleagues at work with whom she ate what was more often than not a delicious lunch, and on the weekends she got to sit for hours with one or two friends at noisy cafes, chatting away and sipping hot *Kaffee* in beautiful demitasse cups. She dressed very well, too, positioning her hats at a perfectly calibrated angle atop her head as was the style of the day, and she wore well-tailored, silk-lined women's suits that tapered tightly at the knees, exposing her attractively slim calves (her favorite color was black, even if she did not consider it an authentic color). Her friends told her that she had dark, impenetrable, brooding looks, and she had not decided if that was a compliment or not, but she had decided to take it as such. She felt energized by somber hues.

When George pursued her, following a chance meeting at a restaurant bar one evening, Violet was in no way looking to become a wife, but neither did she dissuade him as pursuit by The British Male was a bit of a lark. On first meeting, she liked him enough not to resist. He had a large head and a wide girth, but he also had a clever British mind (as her mother liked to note) and in that British Male tradition, he liked to brandish it about, which was appealing in its way. He had a deep, hearty laugh and thin red hair that, to everyone's surprise, was already going white, despite his relatively young age—but when paired with his quick smile, it did lend him an infectious charm. Admittedly, she was not necessarily attracted to him at first, but he was so dogged in his pursuit of her that she found a way to be attracted to him. They dined out frequently, and she embraced the indulgences that came with being chased—the small gifts, the delectable foods, the held doors, the strong arm at her side as she strolled down the wide Hamburg sidewalks. When he proposed to her, she accepted; at thirty years old, she felt she might as well, and anyway, she had grown rather fond of him by that point. Yes, he had an eye for the ladies, but what British Male did not?

Once they were engaged, Violet felt no need to imagine what life with George would bring. The prospect of marriage for her was in no way the realization of some long-held dream, nor would her impending marriage be her little girl's fairy tale realization of char girl turned princess after meeting her British Male frog prince. No, Violet never had been one to project, and so she did not get carried away with furnishing an imaginary married house, one with burgundy-red upholstered chairs or small wooden rocking horses for children that she did not yet have. She was not so foolish as that. Indeed, she went so far as to suggest pragmatically to George that, after they were married, she should remain in her job so that they could go on happily as they were. Her friends at first wondered if her suggestion was a rebellious act, a refusal to embrace marriage for what it was, but she explained that her suggestion was not a refutation; rather, marriage to her was just another segment on the track she took through life and at the moment, she was enjoying the current segment of her ride quite a bit. When she shared her view with George, he laughed just as her friends did. She may have detected a slight edge of dismissiveness toward her in his laugh, but she dutifully ignored it. At that point, she had not yet learned to discern the subtle variations of his laugh. When George learned that his account firm Ernst and Young was transferring to Düsseldorf in the spring, she likewise told her friends that she did not mind a stitch, despite how much she clearly enjoyed Hamburg. They voiced their admiration of how relaxed she was about everything and how quick she was to accept. She paid little heed to their praise, but she appreciated their support. Change in her past never had led to good, but she chose not to dwell on that. What was enjoyable to her remained the exploration with her friends of life's more innocuous twists and turns. To sit and chat and discuss, that was a privilege she embraced. The freedom to repose in the quotidian, what fun! Call the discussion boring, call her boring, call it all boring—Violet did not care!

And yet, Violet was not ignorant, despite what her appearance might suggest. She was aware of the larger context in which her decisions were being made and her life being laid. She could hear the rumors in the café, the whispers, the asides. She was not ill-informed. She was not naïve, even if some might think she chose to appear that way. She merely opted not to engage in that which she could not control. She had never liked Hitler or his National Socialist party, and she recognized that she was fortunate to have a job when unemployment was high. She put little stock in Hitler's promises to provide more jobs. As Chancellor, Hitler had certainly not made the economic situation worse; she could credit him that if absolutely forced. His election in 1933 and his amendment of the constitution, consolidating his power, had in no way not concerned her, but she saw no way that a single or soon-to-be-married woman such as herself could do anything about his rise at all. And yes, his banning of all political parties and his self-declaration as *Führer* did, deep down, frighten her quite a bit. Sometimes, when the morning alarm sounded, and she and Ingrid picked up their brushes to corral their hair into their tight buns, she had to silently remind herself that everything would turn out alright. And most times, she did succeed, even if she knew all too well that nothing good came from prejudice and hate, even if she had once lived amidst that contagion and seen her stepfather interned, even if her Aryan friends at work frighteningly claimed their lives were growing better under him. Despite that knowledge, she saw no point in becoming an activist or dedicating her

time to canvassing support for Hitler's removal. She had taken no
vow to join the table of young people talking in the corner of some
cavernous café about what could be done. She did not delude herself with the belief that a thirty-year-old department store buyer
could do anything to stop Hitler's inexorable march. It was not
that she lacked the courage to stand up, but, honestly, what was
the point? The future path of what would become history, she had
long ago realized, was outside her control.

And yet. Had one asked her, as she sat wrestling with her hair
at the vanity, Violet would unabashedly have answered yes, she
believed that each person was entitled to his or her beliefs and
no, she did not want anyone telling her that she had to accept
their opinion as truth. Hitler's stance on Jews was beyond offen-
sive to her, and she was not afraid to declare that point of view
if asked, but she saw no benefit to bringing up the topic or discussing it at length. She refused to Heil Hitler (she had to withhold her inclination to spit at the mere mention of his name),
but she was not so stupid as to gather among those little conspir-
ing groups of angry men and bluestocking women who endlessly
discussed what would or would not be. Such activities could benefit no one, nor make any difference at all. She might not be the
most informed, but she had at least learned these essential truths.
She thought about her half-brother George, who had the name
of Cross but was half Jew, and about her mother, Anna, who
was married to her stepfather, a Jew, the biggest concern for her
of all. But better to let sleeping dogs lie, she actively reminded
herself.

So despite Hitler's rise, Violet carried on. In Hamburg, she
continued to work and dine with her betrothed and chat with
her friends and eat and drink and enjoy the pleasures of life.
Sometimes, she would go out with her half-brother George, meeting him at a window table of the art-deco Café Heinz or, when he
would agree, beneath the ornate Art Nouveau tile mosaics in Café
Paris. Her half brother did not particularly like the Café Paris, due
to its proximity to the Rathaus, but Violet loved it, the way she felt
entering it, like walking into a celestial tunnel of white, its almost
effervescent light refracted by a glass entrance with windows that

doubled as doors. It was like passing into heaven itself, absent St. Peter and his gate.

While her brother never felt comfortable there, Violet relished everything about the place: the glistening bases of the stools; the long narrow bar that curved at both ends like a split ship; the polished tile walls embellished with large, swirling fingerprints; the Jugendstil décor; and, of course, the café's famous *trompe l'oeil*. Most of all, Violet appreciated sitting outside at one of the circular tables, arriving fifteen minutes prior to the appointed time, outside the shadow of the Senate and the Bürgerschaft and the green copper roof of the neo-Renaissance Rathaus, home to stately rooms and tapestries and coffered ceilings and glittering chandeliers, and the festivals on Rathausmarkt. To her, the beauty of Rathausmarkt outweighed almost everything else. Sitting there, she was able to watch her half brother walk toward her down the Rathausstrasse between the grand stone fronts, albeit beneath those ugly limp Swastika flags, and remind herself of how good life in Hamburg was and tell herself that everything would be okay.

As she sat, she would invariably detect in George's quick gait, in the way he locked his gaze on her, a growing furtiveness, but she chose not to focus on that. Hamburg was filled with Gentiles of undisclosed Jewish descent—half Jews, like him. But like her, many of them chose to trust that nothing too bad could come to pass, at least not in Hamburg, which had a greater number of Jews than anywhere else. Each of them—Jew, half Jew, or Aryan, all of whom were in her strangely blended family—were in fact aliens of some sort, no one better or more pure than the next, and surely, in a court of law (if it ever came to that), no one could deny the impurity in all of them. All people, she assured herself, contained multiple identities, donning them like hats—sometimes feathered, sometimes not, just like her. Purebred German did not exist, and surely most Germans, at their core, understood that. Violet's mother's family, for example, so seemingly German, hailed from Schleswig-Holstein, and so even Anna was actually Danish beneath her German cloak. All of Germany—even if not mixed with Polish or Romanian or some other "lesser" deemed race—were in some form mutts. In the end, surely reason would prevail and the country would recognize that truth; surely the insanity of the whole absurd classification system would be put to rest. *Never mind the thought of German purity*, she would repeat to herself as her half-brother George approached her with those furtive looks. *Bah. Forget that.* And she would order herself another *Kaffee* and do her best to savor its simple, yet delicious, bitterness.

The problem, of course, was that her brother could not forget, and during her coffees with him, he was becoming more trying than she would have liked. Although he rarely verbalized his worry, he constantly put it on display for all to see, especially Violet. She could see it in the speed with which he sometimes spoke, as if at any moment his right to voice his thoughts might be revoked. Sometimes, when they walked around, she swore that he was looking about as if planning an escape. If he arrived first at the café, which she did her best to avoid, he always sought out a table in a corner or in the shade, as if he did not want to be detected.

She knew he was fearful. She knew he worried about the fate of his father—her stepfather—and she did, too. He had been through so much at that camp. But one had to prevent one's worries from eating holes into one's life like a nest of hatching moths. One had to dispense of them, as best one could. One could not allow oneself to be anxious. It did no good. She sometimes wondered if she had been remiss when she and her brother were young in not verbally sharing that lesson with him. Throughout her life, she had done her best to model strength and the dismissal of destructive thoughts by not indulging them. Not that she had been successful all the time. Now he could no longer contain his fears, despite her efforts to try to assuage them by example and, if necessary, by redirection as well. When they strolled alongside the Hamburg harbor, for example, and he stared at the vast German S.S. *Imperator* and, searchingly, at the other remaining ships, she tried to divert him. "Don't those pastries in the window look sumptuous? Look at that queue, have you ever seen such crowds? Should we stop? Have a bite?" Usually he would ignore her remarks, which riled her a bit, but on she would press. "Please let's go," she would say, and he invariably would ignore her or sometimes, of late, even try to put her down, like the time he had told her, after she attempted to redirect his gaze to the window display of a fashionable clothing shop, that the shop had once belonged to a Jew and that by drawing attention to the shop she was being callous toward the owner's plight. *Why bother even trying?* she had asked herself, salving the hurt from his small prick. She had merely been attempting to distract him for his own good. Could he not recognize that? She took a similar approach with respect to referencing his father, her stepfather, Louis. She had recently seen him, she would note. He seemed well, didn't he? George never replied. She wanted then to remind him that Louis had survived British internment at Knockaloe Camp during the First World War, that he had done his bit as a German when the British turned against them and that surely, the Germans would not, in the end, turn their backs on him. When Violet spoke to her mother, Anna took the same approach with her. The family was well, she said. Louis had his job. Everything was fine. They did not speak of Hitler. Willful ignorance is not such a bad thing, her mother once told her when she was young and they had just moved to Germany. She had not known what her mother meant at the time but she appreciated it now.

Her brother had a different approach. Despite her modeling, George did not conform. He retreated toward anonymity instead. He stopped meeting her, for example, at the Paris Café or anywhere near Rathausmarkt. Following the National Citizens Law, when they met at another less beautiful, more anonymous café, her concern for her stepfather Louis had admittedly grown, but there was nothing any of them could do and nowhere anyway he could go, so she did not talk of it. Britain had evicted Louis years before. In Germany he had to remain. She had to trust Louis would be alright because if she thought too much about it, she would feel sick. George, too, would be fine, and she went so far as to tell him.

"You're a Cross. We may go through hardships, but we get on," she told him.

"You don't understand," her brother mumbled back before abruptly rising to go to the loo. When he returned, she wanted to tell him not to mumble, to be proud, to go on as he was, but she did not. By that point, too much time had passed and any assurance seemed both futile and too late.

Then, following the Law for the Protection of German Blood and Honor that outlawed marriages between Jews and non-Jews, George—who at twenty-six was in love with a non-Jew—became almost unhinged. He was short not only with Violet but with everyone else. Hamburg, the country, the world, even the noisy bird in the tree (couldn't it be quiet?)—everything was against him. When he bought his *Kaffee*, he swore while miscounting his change. They had made the light too dim to see, why were there so many small coins, the café was too cold to count, why did the *Kaffee* cost so much, did all waiters have to be so rude? Violet pretended she did not see or hear and she found herself having to check her anger now. *You need to persevere*, she wanted to say. And anyway, Jew or not, one had to live proudly, head held high. And, lest he forget again, he was a Cross.

"I'm concerned that you're not happy," she told George one day.

"Happy? Happy?" he asked with contempt. And, ignoring her, he turned away, more interested in a piece of litter on the ground (that he did not pick up) than in what she had to say.

Of course, the truth was that at this point, Violet also was starting to feel afraid, but she saw no reason in discussing that with him. She was not stupid, though in his dismissiveness George made her feel as if she were. Hitler was a bigot, a racist, an awful narcissistic despot so awful that every insult came off as looking better by comparison. Heil him she never would. She never raised her arm to Hitler. She had no false presumptions about the rationale behind the implementation of the Nuremberg Laws. She could see that these laws were in no way mutually beneficial for Aryans and German Jews. Encouragingly of late, the acts of violence may have subsided somewhat, as the newspapers often pointed out, but speaking ill of Jewish people was still commonplace as she noted among her colleagues at Franz Fahning who often made disparaging, anti-Semitic remarks. Still, Violet was just one person, and George was just one person, too, also with the name of Cross, and what could they do? As his elder sister, she could model for him, try to convince him not by what she said but by how she acted. She could show him her strength of belief that the moderating influences would in time win out and that the Nazis would fall from power as more sensible minds prevailed. The doors of power had revolved before, and they would revolve again. Admittedly, even in liberal Hamburg, such a perspective was sometimes hard to maintain, she would grant her brother that. Sometimes she, too, felt anxious about their future, about their past repeating, and about being caught in another awful war. He had to try to believe that good would prevail, believe in her, in them, in Germany doing what was right in the end.

And then one day, George broke. Out of nowhere. George, who was never so bold as to voice his opinion in public, arrived at their coffee emboldened and angered. He told his sister that it was time to get out, that she was a fool, that they were fortunate, that they could go to England, and that for so many emigration was hard, but not for him or for her. They had an obligation to get out, he maintained. They could not only voice but also show their disgust with Germany, their complete rejection of her, with their feet. They were "Christian," he said, putting finger quotes around the word with a brazen and sarcastic nod and huff. They could leave with their assets intact. "You're even marrying a Brit, for God's sake!" he exclaimed. He was relentless. Things were worse. Irreversible, he said. There was no going back. She had to stop pretending. He was harsh.

"Stop," she replied at last. "Have faith. Shhhh."

"Faith," he said with audible derision. "Faith." With a spiteful sigh, he shook his leg, in the way he often had, ever since he was a young boy, when he was frustrated and used his body to vent, not that he thought she ever paid much attention to him.

"Relax," Violet said, but he persisted, until she could not endure it anymore. "Isn't this *Kaffee* delicious? Just try to enjoy it, please, George. It's good," she begged.

"Good? Good, you say?"

"But it's taken so much for us to get here," she implored, more insistent. "Please, sip, sit back. Louis is okay. You are okay. We all are. Look at the way the woman over there laughs so hard, throwing her head back and kicking her toe out, almost hitting her companion in the shin. Life is good. Please, George."

He asked, "Are you such a fool? Face the music!"

"I am listening to the music," she returned, almost desperate. "Beethoven, I think." She was being obstinate. But his behavior required it. She would continue to refute their circumstances by example. It was the only way. She persevered.

"No," he replied. "If you must talk in metaphors, recognize the music for what it is. It's the Horst-Wessel-Lied. You hear it as well as I do!"

"Please stop!" she demanded, angry, and he asked if she had seen the pamphlets. He was speaking too loudly. It was really frightening her now. Did he want another cup? Could he come to her wedding? Could he? At the wedding, they would be serving roast beef and potatoes and Yorkshire pudding. "Very English. You have to come."

He stood up then, looked at her, opened his mouth as if to say something, but then did not. He reached into his pocket, dumped all his change onto the table, and left. She was insulted. Furious. But she composed herself, paid the bill, and left.

Four days later, when she stopped by his flat, he was not there. The landlord had not seen him. She tried contacting his girlfriend. No response. She could not track him down.

She was breathing hard. She adjusted her hat, wrestled her hair into its tight bun, took a moment and another moment, admired some shoes in the display window of a shop owned by a Jew, which had not changed ownership under Aryanization yet (*So there, George!*).

At last she resolved to ask Ma-Ma about him, girding herself for the response. "He has left," her mother said. "He tried to convince us of the same. But we will see where the cards fall. It will be okay." Violet returned home and let herself scream and cry. Damn him. Even their mother said it would be okay. She brushed her hair hard and threw her hairbrush across the room. She lay in bed, comatose. Did not move.

The next day, she got up and resumed her life. She spent the next two months working hard, dining with her betrothed, the remaining George in her life. She again talked about the inconsequential with her friends. She got married in Hull and, as she anticipated, did not take to her new mother-in-law, who was provincial and closed-minded, as Violet had suspected she would be. Her half-brother George did not attend her wedding, despite it being in Hull.

After that, she moved to Düsseldorf with her new husband and became pregnant with a child. When people later asked why she and her brother rarely spoke, she simply told them that they had had a falling out. One day she would answer the same to her child, Barbara Christine, if she ever asked. What else was there to say? Digging into one's past had never served her well. Better to leave it. Better not to pass on the burden to someone else.

CHAPTER 7

LONDON, ENGLAND — 1991

The most important principle of attachment theory is the need of a child to develop a relationship with at least one primary caregiver for healthy emotional and social development to occur.[33]

S till shy of twenty-four, I do not yet know how it feels to have a child. I am in love for the first time. I come home in the morning from my boyfriend's flat to change before work. I unlock the front door, walk up the four flights of stairs to the white painted door, take out my second key, and am stopped by a chain. My parents are visiting and the previous night I had called to tell my mother I would not be coming home. I have told her to please ask my father not to chain the door but he does, forcing me to squeeze my face into the gap between the door and frame before yelling: "Could someone please let me in?" My father shuffles to the door and opens it without remark and returns to the kitchen to make my mother's tea. His silent omission of a greeting is how he tells me that he does not approve of me sleeping at my boyfriend's place.

My mother often tells me that my father and I have a special bond. During his treatment for testicular cancer before my mother becomes pregnant with me, the doctor informed him that he would be sterile. My father was therefore convinced when I was in utero that I would not survive or at best emerge deformed.

On seeing at my birth that I was healthy and intact, he said how lucky he and my mother were and bought a large bottle of champagne for our nanny, Dorothy, to celebrate with them. When my older brother later learned of this story, he joked with me that my father never should have bought the champagne. Hadn't his fears been affirmed? Had I looked in the mirror of late? After my father passes away, that same brother will tell me that he always thought my father had a special place for me. I will have not thought of the bond with my father that way, even if I always have known that when I am with my father, I am my best me. When I was very young, my father and I had an unspoken code. When I held his hand, I squeezed it three times to say "I love you" and he squeezed four times back to add a "too" to his "I love you." When I was sick, he knowingly took me in the car for a drive because I would feel better getting out from the house. I am close to my father, but I also know that he and my mother provide different things. She provides structure, routine, and consistency, and he provides what I can only describe as calming joy. They both provide love, though in different ways.

I think my siblings believe I view my father with rose-colored lenses. My Uncle Neville says my mother views her father this same way. Despite what she maintains, George was not perfect, he tells me one day. When I share that I had learned that my grandfather had an eye for the ladies, he does not respond. When I press, Uncle Neville provides no details except to say my mother adored her father despite everything. When I mention that same suggestion to my mother, she says she does not know. He was charming, very bright, she says. When I am older, my mother will share a letter from her father that Neville photocopied for her. It is dated 1937, from her father to her grandmother once they have moved to Düsseldorf, Germany, before the outbreak of World War II. He is clearly besotted with his newborn.

When I have children of my own, I will think about what my grandfather calls in his letter the topsy-turvy world into which his daughter is born. I will think about how in that moment after the first birth, the rest of the world falls away. I will think about George beholding his girl who at this point he calls Christine and how for him, she is the center of his world and how he sees in her a reflection of himself. I will think about how we all are prone to think that a firstborn baby is the smartest or the most beautiful in the world and the most darling as well. Because to have a child is so miraculous, this body of life that appears into thin air, pure and full of promise. An embodiment of hope. It is how I will feel about my own daughter at her birth, and my husband will as well.

But when I am just shy of twenty-four and my father insists on placing the chain on our door, I do not yet know how a baby will change me, how hard it will be to ever let go. When I move into my boyfriend's flat because my parents are selling their flat, my father will not tell me he would rather I did not. My mother will tell me she does not mind what I do. She will tell me I am an adult and can make good decisions on my own. In the future, I may seek reassurance from her but I will seek to model myself after him. I will not blame him at all for their financial situation. Unlike my mother, I will cast no blame on him.

But when I have children of my own, I also will begin to know how a mother feels when the last of her children have gone to college and her treasured home is being sold and she believes she does not have enough money for old age. When my own children have left home, I, too, will realize how it feels to have been the parent who set the rules and what it takes to let go, having been so attached to them. And I will recognize how important she knew it was to support the father-child bond, especially as you struggle yourself.

GEORGE

DÜSSELDORF, GERMANY, 1937

Dearest Mum, Dearest Dad,
I am sorry you have not received a letter from me for such a long time.
It is not that I have been too new-fangled with being a father in fact
I have scarcely realized it fully as yet. I have been weighted down
with worry and anxiety for the last five weeks. [Barbara] Christine

is five weeks old today. They are both still in the hospital and likely to remain there for some weeks yet. Christine will probably be there until the beginning of August and even then we shall probably have to get a trained nurse for her. Violet is, however, the chief worry. Her temperature once went up to over 104 so you can imagine how I feel. She has had terrific pains in her body and leg and one seems so powerless to help her. The professor says it is a very rare case and at one time they were all really anxious. She seems to be considerably better now although she is not yet free of pain. Her temperature is back to normal. Her internal organs were examined again today. They were unable to do it before on account of the fever. Apparently the cause of the trouble in the abdomen is lots of blood or phlebitis just the same as in her leg. They actually applied leeches today, just the same as doctors did centuries ago. I was horrified. I do pray that she will continue to improve. The terrific expense involved is worrying enough but we shall get over that in time. The kind firm has advanced me a substantial loan. If only my family is restored to their good health.

You can imagine that I have spent every available minute in the hospital. When in Düsseldorf, I am there running, noon and night. Lunches do not seem necessary at such times. When away from Düsseldorf, I could rarely concentrate on work. So I trust you will understand and forgive me for appearing to neglect your letter. I assure you that I love you and think about you just as much as I have always done.

Christine is progressing very satisfactorily. I have not had the pleasure of touching her yet but the doctors and nurses all seem to be very pleased with her progress. Today, she weighed 43 German pounds or about 5 English pounds, not much for a five weeks' old baby. She is just the smartest thing on earth. Even all the nurses say so. She is the darling of them all. I do wish you could see her. She has the biggest of beautiful big blue eyes with fair hair and a real Cusworth face. The nurses all say she is the image of her father. I wonder if I looked like that as a child. I do wish you were not so far away. . . . Everything seems topsy-turvy at the moment but I firmly believe that everything will come out all right. Trust in our God is the only reliable thing in this world.

I am sorry to burden you with my troubles but I do think you will want to know what's going on here.

Now darlings, please look after yourselves and cheer up.

With all our love. Ever your most devoted son,

George.

CHAPTER 8

OLD SAYBROOK, CONNECTICUT — 2018

Survivors' immediate reactions in the aftermath of trauma are quite complicated and are affected by their own experiences, the accessibility of natural supports and healers, their coping and life skills and those of immediate family, and the responses of the larger community in which they live.[34]

It is Easter and I am without my children again. I am sitting on a pew in church with my eighty-two-year-old mother between my oldest sister and me. I am close to fifty-two years old. I am working on my capacity to self-regulate and to be more emotionally aware. I have downloaded free apps onto my gold-cased iPhone 8 Plus and practice yoga in hot rooms. I take deep, mindful breaths at work when a colleague becomes irrational. I remind myself what I can control and what I cannot. I identify my emotions and try to regulate them. I do not dismiss anger, understanding that it is a primary emotion, like sadness, happiness, and fear, and try to do the same with my children who are now close to adults. I know it is not the emotion but what we do with that emotion that matters. I try to smile when I can and avoid facial expressions of disdain. I have stopped killing insects except for ticks, brown-spotted moths, and caterpillars. I strive to find joy in the present. Sometimes I do spew a litany of 'fuck-a-duck's when I drive. Sometimes, I tell my youngest if he refers yet again publicly to that time in fifth grade when he claims I called him fat, that I will make something up in return like he has got to increase my supply of crystal meth. My children still tell me that hugging me is like hugging a metal post, but they also watch my eyes closely for when, at the mere mention of something sentimental, tears well up in them. But often, when I am with my mother, I continue to completely emotionally shut down, just as I often have.

I also am well aware of how imperfect we all are, and how far from a model parent I have been. Given that research shows that early childhood and adolescence are the most formative period to help children make the transition from co-regulation toward self-regulation—from a dependent to an independent and self-reliant adult—my window with my own children has arguably shut. Even if I try to prop that window open with the pervading cultural argument that adolescence in modern culture is delayed, I acknowledge that my parenting sell-by date has largely expired and my children are who they are. My youngest may still fall under the you-can-die-in-war-and-have-a-cig-but-not-order-a drink-at-a-bar classification, but even he is at college and no longer lives at home. He can be recalcitrant in his quiet way, but he is kind with an infinite capacity for empathy and love. My middle son is dogged, persistent, and stubborn at times, but fiercely loyal, protective, and compassionate. My eldest is determined, devoted, reflective, and always grateful for what she has. I still offer all three of them advice and they still occasionally ask but I also recognize at their age, my parenting decisions bear little influence on who they are—if indeed they ever did—and we all have still done okay. We were attached and supported when we were young. We learned to self-regulate; in fact, most of the time they manage their emotions and behaviors much better than I. They, for the most part, understand others' emotions and express how they feel. Sleeplessness from worry, occasional passive-aggressiveness, and lack of patience may remain a part of who I am and occasionally surface in them, but none of us has to struggle to manage the effects of a difficult past.

And yet even with my newly acquired knowledge of the importance of early childhood and the secure childhood that my father and mother provided me despite her past, I continue to struggle with being what I have come to call a "good enough child" to her. This Easter, she is wearing a new pair of designer suede boots that she can in no way afford. Sitting beside me, she has started to uncontrollably shake. The trigger for her emotional, physiological, and, I suspect, cognitive dysregulation (although it is church and so she is not voicing her thoughts) may have been the flowers at the altar that my brother bought in my father's memory, her suppressed anger that I have not been to visit her in a while, or the memory that she first met my father in a church and now he is dead and she is broke, lonely, and abandoned. Perhaps her trigger is all of these. I do not know.

My siblings remain much better at helping our mother move from a state of dysregulation to one of self-regulation, a skill that I now understand she did not learn in early childhood through no fault of her own. Because I work in psychology, I can talk a blue streak about issues like these. But when my mother starts to shake, it is my eldest sister who puts her arm around her as I sit idly watching my mother's shaking subside. When my mother looks to me, the shaking resumes. After some time, I will myself to respond like my sister would do and I reach out to hold her hand. Her shaking again abates until I let go and it starts again, and I think, *Well, I had better try to do something else*, so I do what the caregiver training organization where I work promotes when working with very young children. I stop and ask her to take slow, deep breaths. I look at her. Together, we breathe. Then I give an affectionate touch. When I leave, I hug her and kiss her on each cheek, tell her I love her, and slip in the importance of breathing to her before scrambling away. Mine is a cameo performance at best.

I know that I am far from an exemplary caregiver for my mother. This admission is not falsely cast or falsely modest. I still do not fully know why I am this way. I sometimes err toward dodging responsibility by explaining away behaviors like mine as being etched into my DNA. But if so, why am I the least responsive of my siblings who carry similar genetic material to me? I often tell my psychologist friend Beth at that nonprofit employer that provides caregiving support for trauma-impacted youth that she needs to write a guide not just for caregivers of children but for caregivers of trauma-impacted parents, cold fish like me. Intellectually, I can understand the genesis of my mother's challenges and how they manifest. I know, too, that it is important for me to see past my mother's mask of trauma to her core self; that her behaviors are her trauma talking, not her; and that I have shortcomings and triggers that affect how I respond.[35] I know I need to accept that her brain as an adult in her senior years can never fully repair, grow, or change. I know that I must try to better model emotional competence with her and to think about my tone and the facial expression I wear when I'm with her (resting bitch face is not helpful). I need to try to stop and breathe before I react to her justifications of what I perceive as unnecessary expenditures, and to be aware that I have a tendency to detach and judge. I need to remind myself of the quote by the comedian Russell Brand that depression stems from worry about the past and anxiety from worry for the future, and that unlike her I have nothing in my past to worry about, even if I worry about the future a lot. I can do better, I know.

When I am home, I read an article about avoidance coping and its manifestations of procrastination, passive-aggressiveness, and rumination, all behaviors that I exhibit with my mother. I reread the recommended tips:

1. *Understand what [avoidance coping] is and why it doesn't work.*

2. *Recognize when you're doing it.*

3. *Use stress relief techniques.*

4. *Practice emotional coping techniques, such as journaling and meditation.*

5. *Identify active coping options. . . . Is there a way you can reframe your thoughts?*

6. *Practice communication skills.*

7. *Take small steps . . . then take a larger step next time.*

8. *Find help.*[36]

I remind myself that to have helped my own young children do all those important things, like teach them to move from a state of co-regulation to one of self-regulation and to guide them toward appropriate behaviors in response to the emotions they felt, I must have used some of these practices, unconsciously at least. I know my husband helped me on this front, but I was not a complete failure. I moved my children a little bit along the continuum, didn't I?

After Easter, I go to visit my mother again ("When are you coming down? I barely see you anymore"). But despite what I know about the importance of being present for my mother, when I see her, I proceed to tell her the start of my son's college game and my visit with my sister in the hospital mean I can only stay for ten minutes. When I arrive, she nevertheless thanks me for the Starbucks latte and granola-topped yogurt that I have bought, even if she is vaguely aware that I went to Starbucks to buy my own latte first. She then lets flow a stream of unbridled thought. She is clearly lonely with my father dead, but I have little patience as she tells me that she will eat the yogurt tomorrow for lunch because she has no money and her refrigerator is bare and that her doctor has told her she is becoming too thin but she does not have enough money to eat. All I can think as she unloads her financial stress on me is that she is telling me this information despite the money we regularly send her, despite her social security, despite the fact that my siblings own her condominium on the water and her car. I point to the hundreds of dollars of plants that she has bought that are still in pots outside her garage door and she tells me she bought those on her Walmart account so they do not really cost anything at all. I refrain from commenting further, but I become avoidant, telling her that I am running late. I quickly kiss her goodbye and leave, hands-free on the phone with my sister as I drive north on I-95, venting. I don't know how we are going to afford moving her to a senior community, I tell my sister, but if she moves into my home with me, no one will be able to bear living with me. My sister knowingly agrees. I am undone once again.

I return home and recommit to practicing mindfulness. I read an article that says that mindfulness can help with self-regulation by allowing for the delay of gratification and the management of emotions. I read that by thinking about a situation in an adaptive way rather than in a way that increases negative emotions, and by becoming aware of transient feelings and monitoring my body to get clues about how I feel, I can better self-regulate.[37] *Okay, I can do this*, I tell myself. *Ohm. Namaste.*

I return to my mother. This time for the night, resolved to try harder, to be a better daughter, to help my mother more. When I arrive, she is sitting at her kitchen island, scrolling through alerts on her phone, as I myself often do. I acknowledge that we are not as different as I think. I take the time to look at her when I arrive, to observe, to be attuned, to respond. I notice that she is still beautiful, that woman noticed when she walks into a room—head held high, shoulders back, her aquiline nose and her tall, poised frame that together confer on her an air of regality reinforced by her clipped British voice and a countenance both formidable and strong. It announces to all that look at her that yes, she has endured. She sits erect, her no longer fair hair a silver-gray, thick, cut short in the back and in the front swept away from still crystal-clear blue eyes. She wears a white, high-necked sweater with no makeup. Her skin is freshly moisturized, neither pinched nor drawn, and with inexplicably few lines, unaware she has entered old age. Her legs are crossed, an elegant patent leather shoe kicking out from beneath the kitchen's marble-topped ledge. When she gets up to greet me, she slightly wobbles when she walks as the limb beneath her arthritic knee has gone askew, but unlike most her age, she has not lost even an inch of her height, still five foot, seven and a half inches. I breathe. I acknowledge that she looks well.

"Thank you," she says. "Glad you're here. I have so much to talk to you about."

I stay for the night. She talks to me from her kitchen island as I work from her dining room table, getting up to help her whenever she asks. She reads me phone alerts about the policies of President Trump, voicing her disgust and informing me she's not sure how much longer she can go on with him in charge. She talks of the world's return to fascism and the persecution of refugees. She speaks of how appalling it is that immigrant children are being separated from their parents, how lasting that damage will be for them. When I enter the kitchen, she shows me a book about the Regency period in England, one of three that she is currently reading that sits on the kitchen island of unpaid bills and birthday cards. Twenty-one grandchildren, seven children with their spouses mean she spends far too much on cards, she remarks, before turning back to her book and the lack of sexual mores of the Regency period. So different than the Victorian period, she continues, before telling me that she prefers the Regency period as she herself has always refused to be constrained by Puritan ideals.

"I am a European at heart," she says. "Do you know I showed up naked in your father's room when I was only twenty-two? He was so shocked. So American, so Puritan. I loosened him up a lot. I did."

Mindful of what I say, I refrain from remarking on the newly repaired carpet that sits wrapped in packaging at the door, the new doggie bed, and the other new purchases by the door—all of which I could not help but notice when I arrived. She reads me quotes from Oscar Wilde in her book. Then her phone beeps with an alert about Trump and she starts reading it aloud.

"Mom, I don't think you should read so much about Trump," I begin tentatively, trying to be aware of my tone and my expression as I speak.

"What do you mean?" she asks. "I am not going to sit here with my head in the sand. I'm not going to ignore what's going on in the world. What good comes of that?"

"I don't think it's healthy," I gently respond. "You read about those children being separated from their parents at the border and you think about your past and then all you had to endure. It's destabilizing for you," I suggest.

"Perhaps," she says. "You could be right," she adds. "But I don't care."

Over dinner and breakfast, we talk more about her past. She tells me how hard it is to have been left so little after my father passed away. I tell her I understand. I tell her that given her past, how hard it all must be, how she must struggle still. And then she surprises me.

"I'm fundamentally insecure," she declares. "That's why it's so hard to have nothing of my own now. I never had a home. That's why I was so angry at your father when he died. He left me without anything."

I listen. "But Mom, he also gave you so much else. You lived so well for many years. He loved you unconditionally. He gave you the home you never had. We all were so lucky with him."

She nods. "We were," she says. "I was."

I continue. "But I know childhood was terrible for you, Mom, and that you and your Mom had a difficult time."

"We did. I never had a relationship with her. I loved her and I know she loved me, but we just could not make it work. We were the victims of circumstances outside our control."

"I know," I say. I do not know what else to say. As I leave, she tells me how helpful our conversation has been.

"Do your siblings know all this?" she asks.

"Yes," I say.

"I'm not sure they do. Please tell them," she says.

VIOLET

WASSENAAR, HOLLAND, 1940

"Hull Family in Dutch Road Smash; Car Down 15-Foot Bank: Mother and Daughter Injured" —*The Hull Daily Mail*, April 2, 1940."[38]

Violet had not heard the window shatter, her family shriek. She remembered only the sight of the charabanc, the swerve of the wheel, the glimpse of the parapet. She heard not even a murmur when the car plunged, and later she recalled only silence, when life was suspended and God decided which way He would let fate fall as they crashed down the embankment.

She awoke to find a nurse bent over the bed, fate having saved her this time.

"Chris—" Violet stammered.

"Your daughter will be fine," the nurse said.

Encouraged, Violet felt the world begin to slowly spin. She noticed the light in the room and the sky outside and she pressed forward, on her slow train of life, rocking ever so steadily, side to side—another segment of track before her laid. When her daughter engined her way into her room with a bandage wrapped around her little head, Violet felt stronger still. Her daughter, with her beautiful thick, blond hair, cut at the chin, and her piercing blue eyes, Violet loved her so. She spoiled her. She knew. She let her sit on her bed, low to the ground, framed and sheathed. She allowed her to twist the lamp bent over the pillow like an outstretched neck, and she encouraged her to play as she deftly avoided the cords on a floor that was checker-tiled, black-and-white like a board. Violet loved that no matter the circumstances, Barbara Christine played. She was proud that somehow despite all that had transpired in her early years she had fostered that in her. Her daughter enjoyed the moment. Violet hoped that propensity in her would remain.

Once her daughter healed, Violet was moved to a convent hospital in Wassenaar, Holland, just outside The Hague, to be closer to the family home. She did not like being away from her three-year-old daughter and one-year-old son, but she remained so glad that her daughter had healed. Each evening they would arrive, Neville, George, and Barbara Christine wearing her shiny red shoes. On arriving, Barbara Christine would run toward her mother and with her fat little fingers, she would caress her mother's motionless arm injured in the accident. Placid Neville would be dropped into her lap like an offering from George until Neville's restlessness required him to get down.

When the children came, she and George did not talk of Hitler. Not at first. When they had lived in Germany only eight months before, they had not either, choosing not to talk of such things. Each morning in Düsseldorf, they had arisen and Violet had sat with her husband for a breakfast of juice and a pastry. On sunny days, she would look down at her sweet children in their beautiful pram, with the lace trim around the hood, and simply admire the splendor that existed around them. "Please let's not now," she would say to George when, on rare occasions, he began to touch on what the future could bring, and he, in respect of her, would acquiesce to her implicit wish, even as the threat of their time ending became more palpable to them both. Had someone pressed even when they lived in Düsseldorf, Violet could have conceded that with each passing day, Hitler was finding his way into their hallowed home, like some sort of toxic smoke slipping beneath their front door and from which one day they would have to flee. She was not in denial of that fact, despite what appearances might suggest, as by the late 1930s, no one could deny the inevitability of Hitler's rise. But she chose not to speak of it. George was less inclined to hold his tongue, even if he did so with her. On a business trip to England, George had gone so far as to warn his British colleagues what awaited Europe and the world. For his outburst in front of Parliament, he had been thrown in jail for the night. He had not told Violet of his plans to protest but had he sought her counsel, Violet likely could have warned him of the sheer futility of protest. But he did not. In fact, without a word exchanged, in 1939 she had named their second-born child Neville in hope of peace, despite them both knowing it was a futile wish. And less than one year later, when they left for vacation in England from Düsseldorf, they had known they would not return though neither had said such. As they rushed out the door that morning, Violet admittedly had lingered, reluctant to close the door, but when George had gently reminded her it was time now to move on, she had accompanied him without protest.

And yet, despite her seeming acquiescence on some matters, no one could describe Violet as acquiescent on matters of the family well-being. She still carried in her an obstinate streak on which George knew better than to remark. He let her have her way when that streak showed or when she veered into impatient ill temper, which on occasion she did. For example, after they had left Germany and were living with his parents in Hull, England, she had been the one to insist on joining George with the family in Rotterdam when Price Waterhouse decided to relocate him to work as an accountant there, despite the risks. "Too dangerous," he at first had protested. "You can't leave England with the children to join me in Holland." But Violet had not relented, grew furious with his insistence that she remain, and so he had relented. Violet knew her occasional flash of defiance in her otherwise seemingly compliant countenance could be perceived as a flaw, like a small birthmark stamped on what some might call an otherwise beautiful face. But she also knew that the very otherness of that birthmark could be what differentiated that face and was the indelible mark of her toil and pain, that it was inseparable from who she was. A man could choose to live with his wife for his entire life and never once mention that birthmark so as not to label it in a way that would upset her based on how she herself had come to terms with it. George chose that. And so on they went, avoiding talk of such things, and proceeding as best they could, the preservation of the family always their first priority.

In Holland, at first, Violet and George saw no need to discuss what was becoming more obvious outside. But when Violet awoke at 4 A.M. on May 10, 1940 to the sound of aircraft and antiaircraft guns, she knew that they could avoid Hitler no more. The family's safety was undeniably threatened. With Violet still partially paralyzed and convalescing with the nuns and the children living separately with George, their departure would be fraught with risk. But when the parachutes started raining down, littering the ground, and George came to her, telling her that the Germans were closing in, she accepted what he said as truth. She let him explain. She was not so foolish as to refute what he proposed. He detailed to her that the Germans were attacking nearby airfields to weaken Dutch defenses; that Ypenburg was falling; that the airfield at Ockenburg was going down; and that the partially constructed airfield at Valkenburg was blanketed in German paratroopers now. Despite the onslaught, the Dutch had so far held out though not for long, he said. The Dutch may have bombed their own besieged airfields to protect themselves and the German ships may have so far been destroyed, but eventually, George explained, Hitler would win. We will need to find a way out, he told her, and she accepted what he said without resistance.

The next day, when the Germans had occupied Valkenburg, some bridges, and the buildings of Katwijk along the Old Rhine River, George returned and told Violet that tomorrow they would leave. The Germans had so far failed in invading The Hague but that would come, he warned, and again, she agreed. Despite the Dutch successes, the holdout would be short-lived, he said. They would not be safe. Violet was not delusional. She had lived under Hitler in Germany. She had seen Neville Chamberlain resign and Winston Churchill take over the British government in his stead. Air raids had risen to some nine or ten a day where they lived in Holland. Appeasement was no longer an option. War had come.

They left on the afternoon of May 12. George came to pick Violet up, the nuns carrying her half-paralyzed body into the front seat. George had organized passage on a ship and had some of their things loaded on board ahead of time. Her children were strapped into the back seat of the car, and a stretcher was folded into the trunk. The children slept as George drove, the car waving through checkpoints along his carefully plotted route as the air strikes rained down. They took shelter in roadside ditches to avoid exploding bombs dropped from German warplanes. It was a har-rowing trip on roads overcrowded with fleeing Dutch.

When they arrived at Ymuiden, the quays were teeming with people desperate to flee, to be transported across the Channel to a safer place. George somehow found a place to park, awoke the children, and told Barbara Christine to remain quiet in the car with her mother and brother while he went to find help. Barbara did exactly as she was asked. Violet also maintained her calm, despite the discomfort she felt, paying no heed to the lights in the sky and the deafening sounds that engulfed them, and awaited George's instructions from the inside of the car. Outside were many people, pleading, circling, as Violet and her two children sat in their sealed, protected space.

Their journey had been meticulously planned out, as things always were with George. He had never missed a day of school or work in his life. Despite the bombs and the attacks and the crowded roads, he had managed to arrive at the appointed dock at the appointed time and located two people to carry Violet onto the ship with her children at her side. As he had requested, they did not utter a peep. The six of them forged their way through the crowds. Violet tried not to listen to the pleas: "How much do you need?" "We don't take much space." "We must." "We are Jews." "We will not survive." She tried not to look at the bandaged wrists from those who had foreseen the futility of remaining in this life with Hitler. Lying prone, she was relieved to not have to see their faces as she was transported to the quay. She focused instead on her children and kept them in sight as she was loaded onto the ship.

Their Dutch steamer was called the *Van Rensselaer*, and Violet was laid among the others, pressed tight, the smell of the evening's dinner of broth soups and canned meats hovering between them, her children close. She loved her children so much, perhaps never so much as then. They were so well-behaved at that moment, and she was so proud. She vowed that one day, when they got through all this, she would put her daughter back on a pile of pillows to try on shoes, as she had in Italy when George had sent the two of them abroad to enjoy life and rest. She had spoiled her daughter, laughed when her daughter had thrown every pillow on the floor so the red one would be on top. The Italians had fawned over her little girl, her *bellezza*, her *capelli biondi*, who loved red so much. She did not regret that trip. She vowed to always cherish it.

They embarked that night. For many years after, Violet would try without success to forget what followed: the force of the German mine, hurling people in every direction and crashing them down, like pebbles crushed in waves. When they hit the mine, their Dutch steamer, with one hundred and fifty refugees on board, had not yet left the harbor; the south pier was still in view. They sunk fast. Violet would always recall the jolt, the suspended stillness, the fear, the children breathing in stutters, the sinking, and the realization that the steamer had landed on a sandbar, the passengers pushing their way out with Violet herself unable to leave. Years later, she would dream of that night. The passengers in her dreams were bats, screeching, one wing tied, their flight uncontrolled in a cave.

In those years ahead, she would remind herself that George decided to stay with her that night, giving each child to a stranger to put on a lifeboat and vowing to remain by his wife's side.

"Go with them," she pleaded.

"I'm with you," he said. "They'll be fine. They'll be safe. And we will figure this out."

Eventually, George did find a steward to help lift his wife out, and together they, too, escaped. A few did not—the captain, for one—and Violet suspected again that only by the grace of God had she survived, though later admittedly she would sometimes wonder why and wish she had not.

That night, however, Violet felt fortunate. They once again lost the few possessions they had left when the boat sunk, but when George, the steward, and Violet reached the shore, they found Barbara Christine wandering not far from where they landed. Violet was able to concentrate on the good fortune of that. While Neville was nowhere in sight, she was able to maintain the faith that he would be found too. When she asked her daughter if she had seen Neville, Barbara Christine had said no. "But he's some-where," she had added, and Violet was comforted by the spirit of her three-year-old girl.

Even as they pushed their way to their car, Violet was able to remain calm. With the steward's help, George placed his wife in the back seat and laid their little girl to sleep, her head in Violet's lap. George thanked the steward, kissed his wife, and set out to find their boy, and Violet turned her attention again to her little girl, cupping her daughter's head with her good hand, actively reassuring herself that her son would be found. She was in physi-cal pain almost everywhere at that point, with the exception of her paralyzed left arm. The pain of the injuries from the car accident had again, for some reason, taken a newfound hold. The right side of her body felt as if it were being stabbed with small knives. But, at that moment, with Barbara in her lap and her perspicacious remark that Neville was "somewhere," Violet decided to embrace the pain, using it as a palpable reminder that she was alive and present in this world with her girl. She did not permit herself to be overpowered by it.

As Violet and Barbara sat in the back of the car, George searched. Over the following hours, he brought them little gifts: bread and a blanket, small pieces of news. The car was, for Violet, a refuge of sorts and she felt safe in it. When she learned that the Dutch royal family had escaped on the British destroyer HMS *Codrington*, she stubbornly maintained her conviction that George would find Neville and that he would secure them passage as well. She had no reason not to trust him. He would deliver, just as he always had. It was fine. They would be alright, she said to herself.

In time, as promised, George did deliver her little boy. He had found Neville in a Dutch Army barracks, singing for the soldiers. He returned, and Barbara Christine sat up, and George placed Neville in his wife's lap, and Violet kissed him all over his tiny, sweet, chubby face, rejoicing in him. She was a mother to two children still.

"How did you get so filthy, my sweet little boy?" she asked. "You look like a street urchin."

"I'm dirty too," her daughter said, and showed her mother a spot on her dress.

"Yes," her mother agreed, though her daughter had actually fared quite well. "And where are your sweaters, my children?" she went on, realizing for the first time that they both had lost them.

It was at that moment that Violet could no longer contain her worry. For while Violet acknowledged that a spot and some dirt were nothing, the thought that her children had lost sweaters and she had not known was unnerving. For the first time that night, she began to feel that their little protected sphere that she had striven so hard to create had opened a tiny bit and the awful world was beginning to creep in, never again to be kept out. It was a terrible thought and she felt herself shake. To offset her worry and calm her nerves, she tried to think how she, relegated to the car, could locate new clothing for them or, failing that, two jackets at least, as her husband worked outside to secure spots on another ship. The passage across the Channel would be damp and cold, she reminded herself, even though it was May. Outside the crowds pressed and the skies whirred, and Violet did her best to block the noises out and focus on her children. How could she help them? *We are fortunate*, she reminded herself. "We will make it," she said aloud.

In a short time, George returned. So briefly had he been away that Violet wondered if he had even left or if he had just gone around the back to relieve himself. He opened the door, and the children exclaimed, and he told them he had something to share with their mother, so could they be still, please? Violet noted the crack in his voice, so unlike him, and she again subdued the disquiet threatening to overtake her. Her control loosened still. The car door was open, the outside noise loud.

"I have secured passage on another ship," he told Violet hesitantly.

"Wonderful," Violet managed to respond.

"Yes," he said, pausing for a breath. He looked at the children. "But the captain tells me he can't fit a stretcher onto it."

"Sorry?" she asked, not knowing what she was saying or whether, amidst the noise, she had accurately heard what her husband said. This was George. He figured situations out. He did.

"I've been working to find another," he continued. "I haven't found one yet. But meantime I've asked the captain to please allow you on the ship. He so far has refused. The ship leaves soon. The authorities have told me I must take our spots."

These authorities, who were they? Violet did not ask. "How soon?" she asked.

"In an hour," he said, adding, "I can send the children and remain with you." She noticed he was looking away.

"The authorities—" she began.

"Yes, the authorities," he said.

Violet tried to block out the air raids outside, the sounds nearly deafening, but she could not. "It will be fine," she told George, not believing the assurance herself.

"I'll stay," he said without conviction. They both knew there would not be another ship.

"We're leaving?" Barbara Christine asked.

"Yes, dear, yes," Violet said, and looking into her daughter's transparent blue eyes, she said, "They cannot remain. Go with them."

The door remained open. Outside, people were scrambling. The whirring in the sky seemed to have reached a climax by that point.

"Alright," he said, and kissed her on the head. Was there relief in his voice? She could not tell.

Nearby, an ambulance was waiting. George told her to stay put and walked over to it. A nun came back with him. It was Sister Meike, the young nun from the convent where Violet had lived for the last few weeks. Violet began to wonder at the coincidence, then stopped herself.

"Hello, Mrs. Violet," Sister Meike said.

"Hello," Violet said.

The nun pulled the stretcher out of the back of the car and unfolded it. Together, she and George helped Violet onto it.

"I hope I'm not too heavy for it," Violet said, knowing she was not. She tried to laugh.

"Never," the nun said. She was pretty. Violet thought that someone like her would make a good wife for George, compliant and sweet, if only she weren't a nun.

Sister Meike opened the doors.

"Kiss your mother goodbye," George said.

Violet was not going to cry. She was not going to give Hitler that.

"Why?" Barbara Christine asked. "Why are we saying goodbye?"

"Because I'm not going with you now. I'll come later," she said, glancing at George.

"You will?" Barbara asked.

"Yes, of course."

Barbara leaned down to her mother, and Violet hugged her with one arm. George picked up Neville and tipped him toward her like a teapot. Violet tried to smile but could not. Then her husband kissed her on the head. Barbara Christine asked why her father was wiping his eyes, and he told her it was because good-byes always made him sad but not to pay attention to him.

"Get the children jackets," Violet told her husband. "They've lost theirs somewhere."

"Where will I get them?" her husband asked.

"Just ask," she said. Husbands could be so useless. They did not know how to ask for help. Mothers and wives did. "Do that at least," she said.

"Of course," he said.

She was loaded onto the ambulance with Sister Meike at her side. George told the children to wave, and she waved back with her one good arm. *I'll hold onto this memory*, she told herself, *my children waving at my husband's behest*, as he shut the ambulance doors. *Damn him. Damn war.*

CHAPTER 9

LONDONDERRY, VERMONT — 1994

*Chronic exposure to a mother's depression is proposed to contribute
to a maladaptive pathway in which children's empathic responses
arouse anxiety, sadness, guilt, and self-blame cognitions and prompt
'costly' altruistic behaviors (e.g., role reversal in which the child cares
for the parent) that lead to internalizing problems.*[39]

I am twenty-seven. While I know my father is ill, I am not prepared for what awaits me when I arrive. I fly into Boston, drive
up to Vermont, and walk into my mother's hot kitchen, with
its blue AGA stove that never turns off, transforming the kitchen
into the family sauna in which we all sit. I enter its now fragile
silence, broken only by a whistling kettle and the interminable
airing of NPR, the din of our youth. As I enter the house, I immediately begin to sweat.

"Hello, Elizabeth," my mother says from her stainless steel
sink, niceties dispensed with, impatience edging her voice. "Your
father is panting all the time, can't even make it up the stairs."

I walk toward my mother, who is dressed in sweatpants tied
tightly at the waist and shining new red Ferragamo shoes. "Hello,
Mom," I say. "How are you?" I give my mother my cheek for her
perfunctory pink-lipstick kiss.

"I don't know why you always do that. You always give me a
cheek. I'm your mother. It's been miserable here."

"How is he?" I ask, ignoring her remark.

"He's not well," my mother whispers loudly.

I loudly exhale.

My father enters, his stride labored and slow. One week home from open-heart surgery, he looks worse than I feared. He is pale with black circles around his eyes, but his greeting to me, as with any of his children, is reliably upbeat.

"Elizabeth, hello!" he exclaims with an energy that belies the visible struggle with which he moves and the pallor of his face. When he greets us, he always uses our Christian names first, as if announcing us to a large audience. (The greeting for my eldest brother includes his middle name, which is also my father's.)

"So great to see you. How was the flight?" he continues. "You look so well. Let me take your bag." He extends a weak arm to the backpack I have slung on my shoulder. Unlike my mother, I travel light. Unlike my mother, I buy few clothes. Unlike my mother, I own no self-care products and keep my possessions few. But looking at her with her bobbed hair and pointed face, I cannot deny that we are also alike in many ways.

"I've got it," I say as my father kisses me on the forehead and pats me on the back.

"Leave it, Stephen," my mother says.

"How are you, Dad?" I ask.

"I'm fine. I'm great!"

"No, you're not," my mother counters.

"I'm great," he repeats, dismissing her remark. "Great. And I've lost so much weight—positively svelte!" He pats his stomach.

Sponging the glistening steel sink, my mother rolls her eyes. "Don't listen to him. Your father's not well."

He waves the air with his hand, swatting the comment away.

The phone starts to ring. My mother glances at the kitchen desk on which the phone sits and then at my father. He pays no attention to her or the phone.

"Should I get it?" I ask. My mother again glances at him.

"No, no," my father says.

"They're always calling," my mother says. "They never stop."

No message is left, and my father slowly shuffles to the kitchen table, pulls out a Smallbone chair that my mother purchased and shipped from England along with the AGA, and he lowers himself into it.

"Sit, Barbara," my father says, sliding the French coffee press and china cup toward the seat beside him. "Fresh coffee, Elizabeth? I can heat up the milk."

"I've got it," my mother says, walking toward the stove. "Stay, Stephen. You have that coffee, Elizabeth. I'll get my own."

"Fine," I say, allowing my mother to look after me as she always has done.

I relax into my chair. Despite the evident tension, I am relieved to be home in their familiar pull. A month before my father's surgery, my mother had called me at my apartment in Hong Kong to tell me that my father's aortic valve would be replaced with a pig's and that I needed to come home. In the build up to the surgery, my father had never let on that he expected any other outcome than great. When I had asked my father about the surgery, he had told me not to worry, that after the surgery he would make a pig of himself at meals, that it would be easier to bring home the bacon then, that he'd soon be living high on the hog. The pig jokes had continued whenever I called. He had told me he had started wearing the tie that we gave him that had pink little pigs. It will be fine, he had assured me. No big deal. My mother, meanwhile, had said caring for our father was getting her down, that things were difficult at home. She was frequently ill with nondescript ailments. I did not know why. I had told her that I would come home after the surgery to help. Fine, she had said. But you need to come home. It is your turn. Your siblings have been doing their fair share. It is time for you to step up. I had not expected the recovery to go any way but well.

"Sit down, Barbara," my father says. "Elizabeth's here. The coffee can wait."

"I can see she's here. I'm not blind. I'm heating the milk for her. It will otherwise be cold," my mother replies, their marital dynamics unchanged: my mother the put-upon realist and my father the unfailing optimist.

"I can heat my own milk," I offer.

"Sit down with your father," my mother interjects. "He's seeing double. You need to take him to the optometrist in Springfield."

"Seeing double? From the surgery? What's that about?" I ask, worried.

"I'm fine," my father says.

"The appointment is at 11:00. You need to take him," my mother says.

"That's in an hour," I observe, glancing up at the kitchen clock.

"Yes, it is," my mother says, as if I were stating the obvious. "You can put your things away and go."

"Barbara," my father says. "Give her a moment."

"Just leave it," my mother replies.

I say okay, pour heated milk from my mother's pan in my cup, and carry it upstairs. My mother reminds me to bring the cup back down to the dishwasher when I am done. It is very boring to be always picking up everyone's empty, dirty cups, she says.

I quickly shower and help my frail father to the car. He is using a cane and clutches me with his free arm.

As we drive down the driveway, he tells me how wonderful it is to have me home.

"But you're seeing double?" I ask.

"Yes, a little," he replies. "I'm sure it will be alright. I'll sort it out."

By the end of the dirt road, he has fallen asleep, hunched in his seat, his breath labored. I wonder if he will die. I think back again to the time I was ill at home for days and he came to my room and enthusiastically said, "How about we take a little drive, change the scenery for you?" For twenty minutes, he drove me around the small Vermont town—past the gas station, with the attendant who once told my father that even in the summer he did not take off his long underwear, as life was easier that way. We drove along the winding river that in the fall and spring threw fresh bursts of cold wet air onto the road. Afterward, I felt so grateful for my father, for his enthusiasm, for his measured silences, for his humor, and for the fact that he always showed up when my mother had too much going on in her life.

When we arrive at the office, I wake my father and he smiles. "Elizabeth!" he exclaims. We slowly walk into the satellite hospital building, and once we've been ushered through the waiting area into the patient room, I inform the optometrist nervously that the onset of double vision surely must be related to the surgery that has taken place only one week before.

"We can't be sure," the doctor replies. "We need to consider all the possible causes."

I bristle at his equivocation from my small, straight-backed chair that has been relegated to the edge of the office, pressed flush against the wall. My father says nothing, and I try to respect his unspoken request that I be patient, but I am frustrated by the deference he gives to this doctor, a respect he believes everyone deserves. "Consider all the possible options?" I ask, challenging the doctor.

"Yes," the doctor affirms, and my father glances at me in a way that asks that I keep my mouth shut.

My father has verbally reprimanded me only twice in my life that I can recall: once when I was a young child, for treating his big stomach as a pillow with a slam of my head, and once in my ninth-grade parent-teacher conference, when I disrespected my teacher by not removing my hat and interrupting her twice. He told me on leaving the conference that he was never so embarrassed by me. "Very rude," he said. I felt as if I were hit in my gut, my transgression so grave that his usual silent omission of approval was deemed insufficient. I vowed not to disappoint him ever again like that.

The optometrist dims the lights and begins the evaluation, moving a large white arm with two oversized, owl-like mechanical eyes to mask my father's round, tired face. His body below looks small and vulnerable—slumped and powerless and exposed. He sits behind the contraption silently, speaking only when asked a question. The optometrist moves dials and changes beam colors and requests that my father look near and far. The exercises seem futile to me, his double vision unchanged. "The problem is the heart!" I want to yell, but out of respect for my father, I restrain myself.

After a few minutes, the optometrist moves the machine away from my father's face, exposing him in his entirety, tired and weak. The optometrist spins on his little black stool, flicks on the bright light, and slides across the few inches of his blue-carpeted floor to his nearby desk. I imagine the optometrist as a child who dreams of sliding stools and oversized machines and laser beams that will allow him to see the nerves behind a pupil, nerves no one else can see. The doctor looks so empowered by the technology as my father sits patiently waiting in the ash-gray leather chair. The doctor toggles and jiggles his mouse, typing words onto his screen. My father combs his slick, still-black hair with a cupped palm, as if reminding himself that it is there. I feel sick with worry for him.

"I suggest you go to Hanover and have more tests run on your eyes," the doctor says at last. "I can't see anything here, but I don't have all that I need in this office."

"As we said, he had open-heart surgery last week. Certainly it's related," I interject, furious, unable to restrain myself this time.

My father glances at me. "I'll be fine," he says curtly.

"I just can't say," the doctor says. "Call Hanover."

"But—" I begin.

My father interrupts me, slowly standing up. "Thank you, doctor. I appreciate your help." He reaches out and shakes the doctor's hand.

I do all I can to nod. *This doctor is an idiot*, I think. My father undoubtedly feels the same, though he is not so impolite or mean-spirited as to say it.

"I'll be fine," my father repeats to me as we leave the office. "I always am. Thank you for taking me." He kisses me on the forehead.

As we pull out of the office lot, Springfield feels dark and dreary. I drive alongside my father to the measured beat of the windshield wipers, which intermittently reveal a winding road. It is late afternoon and raining—a cold, early-December rain that should have been a snowy blanket for my mother's gardens that each fall she works so hard to put to bed.

"You see that house up there?" my father asks. "I see two of them." The house is brown and falling down, the windows sealed.

"It's not right. It has to be related to your surgery. The optometrist had no clue."

"He was doing his best," my father replies.

We drive in silence for much of the forty-minute trip home, along the ascending road through Chester. We pass the large brick inn, the narrow bookstore, the New Age crystal store with hanging wind chimes, and the closed deli. Springfield, with its abandoned factory and vacant shops, is at last behind us. I feel sick with worry for him and frustrated that he is not worried himself.

"How are you doing now?" I ask.

"I'm great," he says.

As we pass the Tater Hill Country Club, he says it is my mother I should be worried about. "You need to ask how she is."

"What?" I say, despite having clearly heard what he said. He is focusing on our mother again. So typical of him.

"No one can figure it out. She has no energy. She doesn't feel herself." He stares into the distance. "Dr. Lamb has no idea what it is. She needs to see someone else. Maybe they can figure out what's wrong with her. I'm fine."

"No, she's fine," I say, thinking about my sister's comment that when the doctor opened our father up during surgery, he found that his heart was enormous, the biggest one he ever saw.

"I don't think so," he says.

We drive up the dirt road, past the Coles' place and their Scottish Highland cows with the curling horns. As we turn into my parents' long driveway, I fight back the recurring thought that his loss of vision is the beginning of the end. If only I had a stronger belief in God like my dad, I might pray, but to pray now, if God did exist, would be dishonest. I decide that tonight I will pray without using God's name, so that if God does overhear, He might forgive me. I hope He will understand.

We reenter the house and immediately the phone starts to ring. I trail after my father through the mudroom into the kitchen. He checks the caller ID.

"Can I answer it?" I ask.

"Leave it. They're not nice people," he says. He uses the word "nice" all the time. So do I. It drives my mother crazy. Shows lack of imagination, and she doesn't understand why we can't find a better word. You're so American, she says.

"Could you go check on your mother?" my father asks, pulling the kitchen desk chair across the immaculate Mexican-tile floor as the phone continues to ring.

"Okay," I say. "You alright? Can I help you?"

"I'm fine," he says.

As I move into the library, I find my mother sitting in a gray tweed chair, reading a book under the light of a standing brass lamp. Her refusal to look up means she wants to finish her page. As children, we learned to wait.

"How did it go?" she asks at last.

She has had her hair washed and set, and her face is wrinkleless and smooth. If she is ill, she remains striking in her looks.

"They want him to see another specialist," I say.

She has changed into a pair of new, yellow-strapped shoes. Ferragamo again, I assume. I look away through the window toward Glebe Mountain behind us.

"Ridiculous," my mother responds. "He needs to call the cardiologist again. I told him it was a waste of time. Go talk to him. He's getting worse. Have you heard him panting? Go get him, will you? I want you to talk to him."

"Okay," I say, and as an afterthought, I ask how she is.

"Life is stressful. This is all too much. Just please go talk to your father," she says.

I obey, as I always do with my mother. I return to the kitchen. The phone starts to ring, and my father glances at the caller ID while thumbing through a pile of envelopes. This time the caller leaves a message. "We've been trying to reach you. Please call us back immediately. We need to talk to you about a debt you owe." The caller leaves a number, and my father pushes the stack of bills aside.

"Ridiculous. I'm going to go check on your mother. Would you come tell us about Hong Kong?"

He stands up, using the edge of the desk as support, and begins to shuffle his way to the library, his slippers leading him ahead. I follow, ensuring that he does not fall.

"Hello, beautiful," he says to my mother when he arrives. He bends with such strain to kiss her forehead that I wonder if he will be able to straighten. "How are you? Elizabeth is going to tell us about Hong Kong."

My mother says okay and puts down her book to look through the bay window above the red couch that has been reupholstered since I was last home. I take a moment to gather my thoughts before I begin. Outside beneath the crook of Glebe Mountain is the closely mown croquet lawn, the immaculate tennis court, and the pruned pear trees that have yet to bear fruit. I was married on that lawn, inside a tent. My parents organized the entire affair. My father called me in London after finding the Wild Turkey Window Smashers to perform as the guests arrived. He was so excited by their name. "Good Vermont trio with a great name," he said. "Smashing!" My mother at the time thought it all too much, a musical trio greeting the guests and a dancing band, but my father could not resist. "How can we say no to a name like that?" he asked. I arrived home in late September, a few days before the wedding, and assessed the centerpieces on the tables and asked to listen to the demo tape of the band. My parents patiently acceded to all my requests, and I consciously deafened myself to the hushed arguments about the costs that had begun to emerge. My father's business was failing, I knew that even then, but it was my wedding and I did not want to know the details of their financial situation or be privy to their financial stress. On the eve of the wedding, I went into my parents' room, as if I were a small child, telling my mother I could not sleep. On the third visit, she invited me into their bed, which I had not shared since I was eight. I fell asleep instantly between them. On the actual wedding day, the fuse for the space heaters blew and the stove went out and my father shuttled countless hot trays for the caterers from our neighbors, the Coles, who lent their kitchen to us for the event. During his toast my father wiped his brow, and a man danced with my mother before my father had a chance to ask her himself, and I renewed my vow to make my wedding the best day of my life, and it was perfect, just as my parents planned.

"How long do you think the markets will remain strong?" my father asks, propped in the ladder backed chair with long armrests that my mother placed in the library so that he could more easily get up and down. He winces as he adjusts the needlepoint pillow at his back.

"It's all so uncertain," I say.

"What do you think of Chris Patton? What will happen there?" my father continues, turning to his wife. "You were talking of him the other day, Barbara, weren't you? You had some interesting remarks."

My mother turns her gaze from Glebe Mountain toward my hair. I suspect she is thinking it has grown too long given the small size of my face.

"Everyone is trying to guess what will happen," I say, turning away from my mother's gaze.

"Do you get up early there?" she asks.

"4:30."

"I used to get up at 5:00 every morning to bathe all of you. For many years."

"She worked very hard," my father says.

"I know," I say.

The phone starts to ring, and I decide not to ask this time if I can pick it up. I instead begin to talk over the deafening sound, pretending that no one is calling. "I like Hong Kong," I say. "It's exciting there right now."

"How many shows do you produce a day?" my father asks, and I say two and, seeing how he waits, go on.

I then speak of a typical day in the newsroom in Chai Wan, of the training program I have initiated, of how it feels to be a *Gweilo*, and of how everyone congregates at the Time is Only Now Café. I speak of sitting in the Foreign Correspondents Club with its beautiful striped façade, and of the surging Hang Sang Index, and whether the free market can be at all free after the British hand-over to the Chinese. I speak of the viability of one country, two systems, and the way the island looks out onto the South China Sea, and of my runs with my husband in the wooded hillsides in the territory's country parks, and of the conservation implications of the territory's plans to build a new airport on Lantau, and of the high cost of real estate, and of universal suffrage, and of how people walk around in clothing with the price tags and brand names still attached. (My mother cannot believe that. Why do that? What brands do they wear?). I talk of life abroad, and my parents listen, and for a brief moment I decide that something has been restored, that their worries have been displaced by the details of my life, that my father actually will be alright, that I could have been in London in their flat again, my mother lying in the tub and concerned only about the eczema on her arm.

My mother asks if I ever see John Gray, the chairman of the Hong Kong Bank, reminding me that they had been friends in Germany when she was in her late teens, before she met my father. "I led quite a life then," she says. "I was very free. I never said yes to your father, you know."

"Yes, Mom," I reply. "You've told us that."

"I moved here without having said yes to your father. I didn't want to be tied down. Your father picked me up from the boat, and I was flirting with everyone. I was so carefree. I had lots of options."

"She did," says my father, readjusting his position on the chair.

"The ship's doctor made an advance on me," my mother adds. "It was inappropriate."

"Yes," I say, having heard reference to that advance and many others, many times.

"I'm really a European. I'm not a Puritan."

My father laughs self-consciously.

"Have you seen that picture of my mother on my desk, Elizabeth? Do you like where I put it?"

"Yes," I say, and peer over at it. "Your mother looks sad," I observe and regret what I say as soon as it comes out of my mouth. She turns her gaze back to the space above the couch. "She was pretty and stylish," I quickly add.

"She was," my mother replies, turning back toward me. "Very beautiful before the war. But then the war changed her. We never had a relationship after that. I was sent from place to place. I think she was often depressed. That's why this is all so hard. I never had any security and now it's being pulled away again." She looks at my father. He looks away, struggles to stand and supports himself by the arm of his chair.

"I've got some things to do," he says.

After my father has shuffled away, my mother asks me whether I can call the hospital to set up another appointment for him. "It doesn't seem right, does it?" she asks.

"What?" I ask.

"Any of this. Go talk to him," she says, and returns to her book.

When I arrive into the kitchen and ask how he is, he impatiently tells me he's fine. "We need to look after your mother. She just can't get better."

"I know," I say.

"They've run lots of tests. They can't figure it out. She's just not herself. No energy at all. She's the one who needs looking after. I'll be fine."

"Okay," I say, growing frustrated with talk of her.

"It's hard for her," he continues.

"Yes," I say, feeling conscripted into this now not-so-gentle pull and tug of who is looking after whom.

One week later, after I return to Hong Kong, my father has open-heart surgery again, replacing his infected pig's valve with a mechanical one. When he awakes from the surgery, his double vision is gone. The issue has been miraculously solved, he exclaims. When pigs fly will be the day he gets another animal valve in him, he tells me before my mother gets back on the phone.

"I forgot to ask while you were here. How's that book going?" she asks.

I don't know how to respond. Since moving to Hong Kong, I've done no work on it, the story she recorded in London collecting dust in a drawer.

"It's going fine," I say. "Making progress," I add, believing that's what she wants to hear.

"Good," she says.

"Great," my father adds, who's now hopped on the line.

I call my sister. She tells me that no one has diagnosed my mother's ongoing illnesses, no matter how obvious in retrospect they will seem. My mother isn't well but my father's health remains of greater concern to me.

GEORGE

YMUIDEN, HOLLAND, 1940

"Hull Man Was in Mined Ship Now in England—But Wife Left in Holland"

"The Cusworths of Hull are still dogged by danger. Last night, the "Mail" told of how Mrs Violet Cusworth, wife of Mr G.E. Cusworth, the Hull accountant, had been aboard a mined ship, which was just leaving Holland. It was reported that she had been saved. To-day the "Mail" was told that Mrs Cusworth is back in hospital in Holland. Mr Cusworth and the children are in England, after escaping from the same sea disaster. Now, after lying desperately ill for weeks with a fractured skull, Mrs Cusworth is thrust back into a grave condition by the combined horrors of bombing and terror at sea.

At Ramsgate

Mr Cusworth, torn between loyalties to his wife and children, wanted to stay with his wife, but the authorities persuaded him to take what remained of available transport and bring his children home. Mrs Cusworth, senr., of Heathcote Street, Hull, told a reporter to-day: "My son telephoned me last night from a Ramsgate hotel. All four of them were on the mined ship. His wife was on a stretcher and they had to take her back. My son wanted to wait a day, to see if she could come, too."

"Terrible Air Raids"

"You have your children to consider,' they said. So he came. All their possessions have gone down [with] the ship, except for a few things the people gave them. My son is just heartbroken. "He doesn't know what to do. His mind is still dazed by the horror. He hesitates to bring his kiddies up here because of the danger, and is considering going into Devonshire. "They have been in some terrible air raids. . . . Nine and 10 a day, he said. That is what upset his wife."[40]

George was standing on the deck of the ship, his children with him as he ushered passengers on board, his free palm pushing air. *Go right back*, he motioned as the approved passengers hurried past, silently obeying, their feet shuffling to the quarters below, having ascended the gangway. He had offered to stand here, to help load. Three stewards guarded the other end of the gangway, matching names to a list, a human gate that opened just wide enough for the approved, impassable for the rest. Watching, for George, was a penance of pride—so many having been turned away, his wife among them.

George reminded himself that this was not his fault. Because of him, forty-two *Van Rensselaer* survivors had secured passage on this ship. It had all happened so fast. Only a day prior, a soldier had directed George to the captain of the Dutch steamer Johan de Witt. On his way to the captain, he had come across the group of *Van Rensselaer* survivors. George had felt a certain responsibility toward them, having helped organize their failed passage. Some, too shaken by the sunken ship, had gone home, unwilling to risk another hit, but many had remained. To those, George had given his word that he would try to seek passage for them, while seeking the same for his family and his son whom he had not yet found. No promises, he had said, but he would try. He then had found the *Johan de Witt* captain, who on learning that Violet was in a stretcher, said her passage raised a question of numbers, so many in need of a spot. One person on a stretcher equated to three able bodies, he had said, and even George had not been able to argue against the math.

So now George stood, telling the boarded passengers to mind their step and to move toward the stern. As he spoke, he held his placid son in his arms, and his daughter stood restlessly beside him.

The night was wet and in the darkness, his children looked disheveled to George. Fortunately, before boarding the ship, he had found, discarded on the ground, two children's jackets that were far too large for his own children. They wore them now and George tried not to consider why they were abandoned. He focused instead on the fact that by some odd stroke of luck he had succeeded in granting his wife her departing wish. If only he could have told her. She would have been pleased with him.

"I'm tired," his daughter said.

"I know," said George, whose arms were growing tired too. Laying down his sleeping son on the deck, he told his daughter to watch over her little brother, which she did, her eyes fixed on him. She was his protector now.

George tried at first not to get distracted by thoughts of his wife. Since leaving her, he kept his attention focused on immediacies, such as sorting out the broken zipper of Neville's new jacket or wiping the mucus streaming from his daughter's nose. His children were the reason he had made the difficult decision to come, to be the parent in place of his wife.

"How much longer?" his daughter asked.

"As long as you can," George replied.

For the most part, George was succeeding in not letting uncontrolled emotion hijack clear thought. He was being rational, as he had most his life, rarely veering—at least not until of late. Albeit, they had been lucky hitting that sandbar after he had given his children to strangers, having decided to go down with the ship with his wife. After disembarking, he had found his daughter right away and then his son singing to five soldiers in blue-green uniforms with socks pulled up to their knees. Violet had been so grateful. She was good that way, quick to express her appreciation of him, though on occasion also quick to come undone. When he had given Neville to her, he had not been able to tell her that she would not be joining them. Instead, he had left, briefly, to collect himself, before sharing with her what he had done. Sometimes it was hard to be the rational one.

"Where is Mummy?" Christine asked, beneath the flashing sky. She was playing with the sky's refracted light on the toes of shoes that he did not recognize as hers, as if dancing with a fairy only she could see.

"She is not here," George said.

"Why?" she asked.

"Because she couldn't fit."

"Why?" she persisted, abandoning her dance.

"Because of the stretcher," he said.

"Why?" she continued.

"Because," he answered, deciding it too complicated to explain, the inflection in his voice revealing an impatience he was trying to contain.

Barbara Christine frowned and disengaged from her father, straying from his side, like a kite at the end of a string. Hair in a ribbon, she was drifting from him in her oversized red dress, given to her by someone George did not know. It was peeking out from beneath her coat with a little hint of lacy frills.

"Stay by my side," George said, fearful that his daughter would stray more.

"But I want Mummy," she demanded, awaking Neville whom George had then to pick up. "I want Mummy," she repeated.

"She's not here," he reprimanded.

"But I want Mummy," she insisted.

"Can you be quiet?" he asked as his daughter recoiled and cried. "Christine," he offered apologetically, using his pet name for her. She remained sullen and aloof, and so with his free arm, George reached out to her and slowly, coyly, his daughter came back to him.

George checked his watch. His wife was probably at the convent now. The gangway was up, and yet George stood, fixed on the deck. George could not make sense of why. He always had been a math man, found practical solutions in his personal and professional life. He had always found the answer, received top marks and never missed a day of school in his life. He had married the beautiful woman whom he had methodically pursued. She had produced two beautiful children in quick succession, just as he had planned.

And yet here, beneath the rupturing sky with him and his children so at risk, he seemed unable to do what everything around him told him he must: go below deck.

This was not the first time. Somewhere along the line, amidst Hitler's rise, George had become prone to disregarding fact, to permitting himself to be a casualty of hope. For even after going to England to warn Parliament about Hitler, even after taking that brief stand, he had returned to Germany with the misplaced hope that things might change. Even after having been forced to leave Germany and returning to England where it was safer, at least for a time, he had gone on to Rotterdam, knowing that Hitler would likely invade. Worse yet, he had let Violet and the children join him. Consistently, over the last three years, he had let sentiment pollute judgment, hope coerce logic. And he was doing it now, waiting for a wife to come whom he knew never would.

The captain appeared, out of nowhere it seemed. He was rushing, probably on his way to the bridge. He ran short fingers through thick, brown hair as he strode across the deck.

"What are you doing here? Take your children below deck," the captain barked. The captain's eyes were expressionless, his nose flattened, noisily sucking air. His breathing was loud and quick.

"I suppose we're leaving?" George ventured, ashamed of the crack in his voice.

But the captain did not indulge George with a response. He turned and strode away.

George, knowing his question had been rhetorical, decided to answer it for himself: "Yes," he whispered. "Yes," he repeated more loudly as he looked out at the sea one last time. The night was orange and black mostly, with streaks of yellow and pockets of blue. No stars. Even the moon had disappeared. The boat rocked and the water pinched so hard that the skin of the sea seemed to tear, spilling salt water on the flat wooden deck. George decided it was time to go. *I should have done it long ago*, he at last told himself.

He grabbed his daughter's hand. "It's the right thing to do," he declared aloud, and Barbara Christine asked him what was the right thing, what was he going on about.

"Nothing. Nothing at all," he replied. She was brazen, that girl. Outspoken. He liked that. It would serve her well if she grew up to be that way, if they survived this.

"We're going," he continued, drawing both his children closer to him. Together with them, he stepped over the wet, descending the stairwell, reminding himself that all questions had one right answer. The rest was semantics: six of one or half dozen of another. Stay or go. Yes or no. He had gone far by that knowledge. Until he had not.

He found a spot to lay his children down and the steamer embarked. Over the course of their journey, he knowingly indulged himself in thoughts of his wife and the life they had built. He gave himself that. It would do no harm, not now, at this point, after all was done. He thought about how lovely Violet had been and how he would never deny her that. As the children slept, he thought about how he had met her at the department store, clipboard clutched tight, her thick hair tamed in a bun, standing at the till, her accent so fine that he had thought she was German, a supple mouth that made the harsh German language sound soft. He had visited each day after first meeting her, in search, he had told her, of the perfect hat. They had begun dating, just as he had planned. He so enjoyed walking down the street with her, her arm hitched to his, passers-by turning to look at her long neck, her slim calves, her delicate self. Her body so beautifully arched, exquisite that first time he entered her. From behind. She had been so surprised. He smiled. It had been good. Yes, as a wife and then a mother, she was at her most beautiful. Violet, smoothing the cover of the bed, the sheet turned down like the mark of a page. Violet unbuckling her purse to buy Barbara Christine an ice cream cone or calling her "sweet pea in a pod" on pillows she had carefully propped. Violet handling rounded melons from the crate, her thumb pressing each tender tip, her nose inhaling slowly, her eyes lazily lowered, the sweetness running through her like a slow inhale; or concentrating on clothing beneath the iron, her upper lip pursed, her face folded in thought. What man could resist? What man would? Perhaps he could not be faulted for not wanting to give it all up, for proceeding despite all that portended around them. Excessive comfort stunted men.

George rested after that, for a short time. When he awoke, they had landed at Ramsgate. He collected his children, disembarked, and telephoned his mother from a Ramsgate hotel that had offered to house the refugees for the night.

CHAPTER 10

NEW YORK, NEW YORK — 1996

If children reach adolescence without achieving stable parental attachment, the professional task becomes one of damage limitation, aiming to give as safe as possible a transition to independence, and to halt intergenerational perpetuation of dysfunctional attachment.[41]

A t twelve, I wake in Cape Cod to find my mother sitting outside our seaside bungalow. She is ashen and unmoving as if frozen onto her chair. The air is still, even the nearby sea apparently silenced by what has befallen her. My father is the only moving player in this scene, tending to my mother, collecting his car keys, telling the rest of us children that something terrible has happened and that our mother is finding it difficult to cope. There has been an accident, he explains. My eldest brother has caught fire hiking in the mountains. A gas burner has exploded in his face. My father says he will be driving up to New Hampshire. My mother is repeating: "He may never see again. He may not survive. He is so badly burned. I may lose him." Before he leaves, my father tells us that it is a very difficult situation for our mother. Such things are hard for her. We must be good. He will be back soon. She does not have the strength to join him.

Twenty years later, my father continues to do what he must for my mother. I have moved back from Hong Kong, left my job as a television news producer, and am starting an Internet magazine with a younger brother, who also lives in New York. I am a mother of three months to a beautiful baby girl. I have set up a desk in my bedroom, and after the sitter, Yolanda, arrives, I squeeze in what time I can to edit, interview, and write before I nurse. My father has recovered from both his heart surgeries. He has a three-day consulting job in New York and is trying to find his way out of debt. Each week he drives down from Vermont. To save costs, he often stays with my husband and me. He remains a man of puns, superlatives, and few needs. When he stays, he does not remark on my chaos, on the Avent bottles lined with stains of milk left curdling in the sink, or the soiled laundry in the pin-striped cloth hamper by the door, or the nightly infant cries from his cluttered room. Content to be in the same room as my baby, he sleeps on the beige Jennifer's Convertible Couch. The couch is the most comfortable bed, he exclaims. The tiny bathroom with the changing table and all of our baby supplies is also absolutely perfect for him. When he returns from work at the end of the day and greets his newest granddaughter, he remarks on how bright she is or what a fascinating gurgle she has made or the extremely serious way in which she is evaluating him. She's clearly bright beyond her years.

I don't disagree. There is nothing in the world like my new baby to me and my father seems to recognize that, leaving me to exist in my sacred mother-child space, which in the evening I share with my husband and from which in the day I only partially step away to that other semi-professional space in which I will never again exist in quite the same way, forever mixing into it thoughts of my daughter and later my sons as well. Even when I age, young parents holding children of their own will evoke in me that same feeling of being pressed against my baby's soft, warm flesh, comforting and secure like the memory foam of that perfect mattress on which I have never actually slept but which I like to imagine I did. Crusted nipples forgotten. Stitches dissolved. No need for fucking morphine at all.

But when my mother joins my father in our New York apartment, I struggle to keep my footing in this space. I move my colicky daughter to my room so that my tired mother can sleep. I transfer baby supplies from the small bathroom so that when my daughter awakes, my mother can use the bathroom that she says does not have enough surface area for her toiletries. And when my sitter, Yolanda, arrives, my mother invariably walks in without so much as the perfunctory knock on the door of my bedroom where I work.

"Hello, Elizabeth!" she announces. "Will you have breakfast with me so we can chat about things, now that Yolanda is here?"

"Well, actually, I've just sort of settled in," I respond.

"Fine," she says, not concealing her hurt. "But remember, I'm only here for a few days. And one day, I'll be dead and gone."

Then she tells me I never have time for my "dear Ma-Ma" any more, and she does not understand why I can't spend time with her given that Yolanda is here. I respond that between mounds of laundry and unfinished work, I need time to work. Raising a baby is so much more demanding than I thought.

"You don't have to tell me," she replies, and abruptly departs.

My mother is right. There is nothing I can tell her about parenting that she does not already know. She learned everything she knows from our pediatrician and for the next twenty years, I will learn everything I know about parenting from her. When I ask, she will tell me when to introduce solid foods and how many hours a child should sleep, at what frequency, and at what stage of development. She will tell me when I see broken capillaries around my son's groin and unexplained hematomas on his legs that I must take him to the doctor, not to waste a moment more. She will tell me that I am right to be concerned about my toddler's speech and that I need to start speech-language intervention right away. She will tell me that boys are more difficult when they are young and girls when they are old and that no one will fight for my child like me. She will provide affirmation of my decisions when I seek affirmation and unwavering belief in me when I need support. She will remind me what children need most is routine, security, and love, and that she always provided us all three. She will know the importance of a mother not conflating her child's accomplishments with her own. "Who is really interested in hearing about other people's children?" she will frequently observe. (When I was given a manicure for my eighteenth birthday, my mother's manicurist was surprised to hear that she had a third daughter, let alone four boys. "Seven children," said her manicurist of more than twenty years in utter disbelief. "I never knew.") You must admit that I was a good mother, she often will tell me, using the past tense to remind me that her job is done. And I admit it. She was.

That doesn't mean that as a mother myself, I can accept her inability to respect the sanctity of my space. When we were children, we were not permitted to enter her adult world, to interrupt dinners with my father after we had been fed; to sit on her formal, silk-upholstered couches that seemed to always have been recently reupholstered; to interrupt her ceaseless reading; to eat her Godiva chocolates in her just-polished pewter tins; to knock on her and my father's bedroom door every Sunday afternoon when they disappeared for "adult" time. But now, she seems to me to feel entitled to enter mine at any time.

Perhaps I should not be surprised. Except for the boundaries she set for us, my mother never paid any heed to the ones that society set for adults. She transgressed them all the time. She was the first in our small town to wear a bikini at the club, host gay friends in the same bedroom as overnight guests, or ask a Caucasian head of school how the predominantly white parents of her affluent school responded to her black husband at school events. She did not mince words or conform to societal expectations if she did not see the point. When she wanted her guests to leave her dinner party, she told them the dinner was over by running a vacuum cleaner beneath their feet. One of my most salient memories of our trip to Europe as children was riding around Paris in the sweltering summer heat with my six siblings and two of our childhood friends in the back of a rented van with broken air conditioning. Having left the side door open while my father drove so she could get the air circulating in the back, she wore only a bra and very short shorts in the front passenger seat because it was "just so damn close." "You know the term close, don't you children? It is a British term. You don't use that term in the States but there's no better word to describe how this air feels. You all must agree," she said in her own defense, in her mortifyingly transparent bra through which we all could see her nipples poking out like two protruding head-lights and which together with her looks, seemed to be drawing the attention of every passing man. Despite screaming for her to put her shirt back on, she stubbornly refused. "You children aren't going to tell me what to do. The Europeans don't care. It's you Americans who get so worked up. I will do what I want." She told me the same when I was young and came home with a friend to find her vacuuming the house in what I swore was that same bra. "Don't be ridiculous. You're so modest. So American. So Puritan. No one can tell me what to do or think," she told me. *But Mom*, I wanted to say, *I'm only eight years old, can't you see how embarrassing this is for me? This is not what moms are supposed to do!*

At 1:00 P.M. she returns from Elizabeth Arden Salon. "Time to eat lunch," she says.

I tell her that I have eaten, that I am tired, that my baby is only three months and she has kept me up most the night, and that today is the day I intend to work.

"Well, you can just sit with me then while I eat," she says. Her legs are casually crossed, her head on my pillow, and her red shoes dangling over the edge of my bed. She looks as beautiful as she always does. "That picture of you two is nice but the glass could use a clean."

I ignore her criticism. "Yolanda leaves at 4:00. How about I join you over tea?"

"I have a hair appointment then. That doesn't work. I need to talk with you today."

"Can't you wait?"

"Not really."

"But I just can't talk now," I say.

"Fine," she says, hurt, then rises and shuts the door loudly behind her.

After she leaves, I feel guilty for how I interact with her. Two years have passed since my father had his open-heart surgery and admittedly, she is better than she was. Gainfully employed with his health restored, my father is not under the same financial stress and so neither is she. She does not seem as depressed. Her nondescript illnesses are fewer and further in between. That's not to stay, however, that she is any less demanding of me.

My father, meanwhile, remains reliably unchanged: as upbeat and as protective of my mother as he's always been. At 6:00, he returns home from work. He brings with him a bottle of white wine, gives my new daughter a kiss on the forehead, asks how I am, and offers my mother and me a drink. My baby is crying and my husband is devotedly tending to her, walking her incessantly around the room as I cook. My mother does not move. She is reading a 650-page book beneath a lamp with her Chardonnay. At dinner, when my mother says she has barely talked to me all day, my father tells me that my mother has come all the way down from Vermont and I need to take a bit more time with her. I say okay reluctantly.

But the truth is that despite knowing my mother will never do what other grandmothers do, that she will not leave me to work in the few free hours I have or step into the kitchen to fry the potatoes so I can settle my child down or be the grandmother who plays and laughs on the floor with her grandchildren, just as she never did with us, I will wish she would. I will wish that she carried in her more joy. At night, on rare occasions after a drink, she might shimmy across the floor to my father, her head tilted back, shoulders up with a bat of her eyelids to him, but those glimpses will remain infrequent and almost always rest in him. Life, I know, has never been easy for her. And increasingly, it will seem to me as I age that my mother in some way will feel she deserves recompense from us for all the child-rearing she did and for the childhood she never had. She often will remind us that she dedicated herself to parenting and to child-rearing, awake at 5:00 A.M. to bathe whomever the youngest was. She will tell us that she had to cook two dinners every night, one for us and one for my father. She will talk about how much cleaning she did, about how she advocated for us at different stages of our youth, about all the driving she did. By her account, raising children will often seem to me to have been for her a job for which she was never paid, while for my father, child-rearing and parenting will seem to have been and to remain a respite, a sacred place in which he held us in his outstretched arms like suspended exclamation points of delight after a long day of work. In my early parenting years that expectation of recompense for my mother will seem to be defined as time. When my parents later come under financial duress again, it will include financial support as well. When my children have grown, I may understand how she feels, but I will nonetheless struggle with caring for her as her adult child.

In the meantime, my father always will do for my mother whatever he feels he must. Until his death, he will protect her, support her, honor her, reward her, and expect the same of us. When she hangs up the phone on us in anger, he will call to ask that we apologize to her, the mother of his seven children who has succeeded in raising us despite the childhood she endured, the mother she was separated from.

Looking back after he has died, I will not know why he responded this way to her. Perhaps because his father died when he was five years old, he established a pattern of caring for the women he loved. I will not know for certain. Whatever difficulties he endured in his childhood, he never spoke of them. When my brother was burned or their finances were tight or she was in any way having trouble coping with her life, he did for her whatever was required. Perhaps he thought he owed my mother for giving him a family whom he adored and was his greatest pride. Perhaps he felt we children owed her as well. Once more, I will realize, when my own children have grown, that my husband is in many ways like him: emotionally aware, with a patient ear and sympathetic touch, and for whom family sits above all else. And it is only then that I will wonder, *If he is like my father, how much am I like her?* I will remind myself that I am more fortunate, that I was able to attach and through the responsiveness and attunement of those who cared for me, I have been able to begin to learn how to manage my own emotions and those of others, how to regulate in a way that my mother cannot, even if I still have ample room to improve. And for that, I will be grateful to my father, to Dorothy—the woman whom my mother hired to help care for the seven of us—and to my mother as well.

VIOLET

WASSENAAR, HOLLAND, 1940

The inside of a tin can. That's how the ambulance felt to Violet, prone in the back. She lay with her body tilted up in the cot, her vision restricted to a skyline defined by the frame of a small window, her five-foot, eight-inch body shivering. Was she near the Gordelweg River? She did not know. The damp air had permeated her skin, lodged itself within. The sounds around her were loud, fading but never quite dead. The slightest of noises echoed in her ears: a pebble bouncing up from the tar, resounding against the ambulance's steel; a loose door rattling; the springs of the cot squeaking like an unoiled hinge. Her ambulance bumped along the crumbled road, wheels jumping, and she was so uncomfortable in it. She hated being helpless, forced to lie in this *ziekenwagen* with its red cross emblazoned on the side while her children sought passage on an escaping ship. Had they got out on that second attempt? Had they been torpedoed? Were they alive?

The young nun Sister Meike sat beside the driver in the front seat. How George had found Sister Meike at the port was something Violet preferred not to think about. It had all been so chaotic outside. The harbor had been packed with people trying to flee and there, at the port, Sister Meike had appeared. How had she got there? Why had she not left? Violet tried in vain to push the questions out of her mind, but what else was there for her mind to do, trapped as it was? This journey back to the convent was so insufferably long. She just wanted to get back. To find someone, anyone, to ask her family's fate. She felt ill, her stomach twisted in knots, and the ambulance seemed to be taking so many alternate routes. Where was she? Where were they? Between Zwembad West and Horwathweg, perhaps? She had once admired Queen Wilhelmina. She had never thought she would abandon her people as rumor now had it. "All for one, Queen Wilhelmina," Violet announced with a wry laugh to the empty truck. She repeated the name, exaggerating the letter L twice. Perhaps the rumor was untrue. Perhaps, like her, the queen remained in this neutral country. Neutral? What had that status brought? Violet listened to the pellets of rain gunning the roof of her ambulance. A part of her wished the rain were real bullets, then the questions would stop, questions which all lead to one: Were her children alive? If she were dead, she would not have to worry about whether her children made it to safety or not. She tried to envision them. Was Barbara Christine holding the hand of her little brother as he toddled across the boat? Where was George? George. Deep breath.

She had no idea of the time. The ambulance had stopped, was idling. Had they arrived? She raised her one good hand and knocked on the partition between her and the driver's cab. The tinny sound echoed in her ambulance chamber. No response. She knocked again. She heard voices. She was unable to tell if they were speaking in German, Dutch, or English, or what exactly was being said, not because she did not speak the languages but because from the back of the ambulance, the sounds were unclear. A door opened, more words were exchanged, voices were raised and abruptly halted, and the ambulance turned and accelerated again. Violet thought she might get sick. She wanted it all to end. She wished she had gone down with that first ship with George. She imagined putting a gun to her mouth and firing it. A quick end. Her head would explode. Her brain obliterated once and for all. Perhaps she could take a gun from the driver. He must carry one. Everyone did now, didn't they?

Eventually, they made it back to the convent. Sister Meike opened the back doors and, with the help of the driver, carried Violet to her bed. Violet was shaking, her paralysis worse. "Any word on the *Johan De Witt*?" she demanded. Sister Meike did not know. Stupid girl.

The night somehow passed, Violet's questions unanswered and unabated, her mind reeling and unchecked, draining her of whatever in her remained. When dawn broke, the morning was eerily quiet, broken only by a single BBC voice on the radio that someone had switched on in the night. Violet listened to the radio in the silence, answering the announcer with an internal narrative of her own. Holland was apparently negotiating a surrender with Germany, the BBC announcer said. *Since when did neutral countries need to negotiate?* German parachute and airborne forces had secured key bridges at Rotterdam, Dordrecht, and Moerdijk, as well as in Belgium at Maastricht. *So much useless detail.* German parachutists, disguised as Dutch soldiers, farm boys, and Roman Catholic nuns had overrun Holland. *Hitler thought he was so clever.* The Dutch were apparently ready to give up. *Of course they were.* The Queen had made it to England. *So the rumor was true. But what of her children? What of them?*

"Any word?" Violet asked when Sister Meike came into her room to bring her toast.

"None," Sister Meike said.

Each time someone entered, Violet asked again. Each time, the answer was the same.

In the afternoon, Violet lay in bed counting the squares in her ceiling, and by late afternoon, the bombers came. Violet shook at each whirring sound and listened to the sirens and *ziekenwagen* dispatched in the bombs' wake. *This was Hitler. There was no end, despite the reports, no stop to this war, to the invasion, to this insufferable life.*

Violet looked out her door. She told herself that at least the casualties coming into the convent were fewer than she had anticipated but then wondered if the reason was that the rest of them were dead. She tried to trust that her children were not among those she saw, that they had gotten out. She kept her eyes fixed on that open doorway. She watched the people rush past, evaluating the size of each person in each gurney and wondering whether each was a child or not.

"Any word on whether my children's ship got out?" Violet asked again.

"None," Sister Meike said, hurrying away.

The BBC blared. "Surrender or feel the consequences," the Germans had reportedly said before they attacked with their planes. The attack had been short but devastating. Flat Holland wiped down. Violet later learned that the smoke was so thick from the land fight that those German bomber pilots claimed not to have seen the red Very lights clustered above the city, warning them that the raid was off, the Dutch prepared to surrender. The hundred Heinkel IIIs of Bomber Group 54 had reportedly flown in two columns and dropped ninety-seven tons of explosives onto Rotterdam. The old timbered houses caught fire like matchsticks, and the obsolete two-wheeled pumps of Rotterdam's citizens' fire brigade were not able to cope. First reports said that thirty thousand civilians had been killed. "Unmitigated barbarism," the reports said. Violet could have told them that.

After the bombing, Violet waited and watched. If her children had not escaped, she wished she would die before finding out. She wished a bomb would hit her room. Annihilate her. Eradicate all trace of herself. The longer she waited, the more palpable her fear that they had died became: a dead weight, her body taking on her rising fear like water on a sinking ship, all hope displaced. She felt herself losing hold of life's point. Holland was overrun, her children's fate unknown.

When Sister Meike walked into her room the next day, her pretty face drawn, her shoulders slumped, her demeanor aged, Violet knew what she was going to say before she spoke. She thought about asking the nun to leave or, at the very least, not to speak. She braced herself.

"We have received casualties from a mined ship," Sister Meike began.

"You're talking too quietly," Violet told her. "Speak up." The convent had become so noisy; it was impossible to hear oneself think.

"Casualties from a mined ship," Sister Meike repeated more softly and more slowly, as if Violet might not understand.

No need to go softer, Violet thought, *to go slower. The content won't change.*

"Casualties," Sister Meike repeated, making certain the word was heard.

"So?" Violet asked. *"Casualties" was such an ambiguous term.*

Sister Meike persevered, moving still closer to her bed, and whispered, "I don't know how to tell you this. They're all dead."

Violet did not respond.

"Dead," Sister Meike repeated gently. "A mined ship."

This isn't a game of clues, Violet thought, choosing obstinacy over loss.

"There were children," Sister Meike added, stroking Violet's head.

Violet jerked her head away. She did not want Sister Meike stroking her. "Of course there were children," she said. *Don't come to my room to state the obvious,* she thought.

"Two children," Sister Meike added. "A little boy and a little girl."

Violet would have vomited if she had eaten anything at all in the last two days. *On this nun. Serve her right.* "Go away," she said, but Sister Meike ignored her.

"Two children around your children's ages, we think."

Who was this "we"?

"We can't be sure," Sister Meike said.

"We can't be sure," Violet mocked. "And the name of the ship?" The most important information was either being withheld or remained unknown. "The name of the ship," she repeated. "The name of the ship."

"We don't know," Sister Meike replied.

"Well, then don't tell me this!" Violet was furious now. *Why come into her room with such vagueness, such uncertainty? What was the point?*

"But there were children," Sister Meike added, stroking Violet's head, stressing the verb in the past tense. *As if that mattered.*

"Have you seen these children? Do you know what they look like? Have you looked? And please stop stroking my head."

Sister Meike pulled her hand away. "I'm just telling you what I know."

"What was the name of the ship?"

"We don't know. As I said."

"We don't know the same of the ship, and we can't identify the children." Violet emphasized the "we."

"I just thought you'd want to know. I'm sorry. So sorry." Sister Meike's voice was trailing off.

Violet turned her head, did her best to control herself. "Please don't tell me any more as long as you know so little. You can go."

Sister Meike paused, then rose to walk away. Violet paid no heed. Instead she screamed, a scream so loud, so uncontrolled, so shrill and piercing that Sister Meike jumped. But the nun did not turn. She scurried, like a frightened mouse, out of the room. *Run,* Violet thought.

A few minutes later she returned with another nurse. Violet was not moving; her body was limp. She did not listen to what Sister Meike or the other nurse said. She did not look at them. They were bodies in the room, filling space, breathing her air. She wanted to evaporate into that air. She wanted to disappear, to be gone, not to have to exist, to die. Poof! They gave her medicine. Violet did not know what the medicine was. She did not care. She hoped it would make all this go away. She hoped she would never wake up.

The next morning, however, she did. Her eyes opened to Sister Meike again.

Violet asked her to hold a mirror to her face. Opening her eyes to look at her reflection took all the energy she had.

"I'm dying," she told Sister Meike. "My hair is turning gray."

Sister Meike told her it was not.

"Was the steamer the *Johann DeWitt*?" she asked. "I don't think they're dead," she said at last to the nun. "I dreamed last night that they were safe. I want to go to them."

"Yes," the nun replied dismissively.

"But they are safe," Violet insisted, making sure Sister Meike understood, suspecting the nun thought it was the drugs speaking, not the voice from her dream.

"Perhaps, by God's grace."

Violet did not respond. She would not begrudge Sister Meike for her faith. Everyone needed something they could hold, to persist, to survive.

The days passed, and Violet went in and out of medicated sleep. Rotterdam burned, the night sky pulsed, the heat from an inferno shimmered on display outside Violet's window late at night, like a canvas being painted with neon light. In the day, Violet tracked specks of ash floating outside—black snow, they called it—and listened to the radio. She heard that hundreds were dead, tens of thousands of houses destroyed, schools and churches razed. She did not, however, learn the name of the ship that had gone down, but she remembered the name of the second ship George and the children had taken, the *Johan De Witt*. Her hair had turned completely gray, but, without confirmation otherwise, she maintained the belief that her children were alive and did not surrender herself to death.

Weeks passed, and still Violet learned nothing. She maintained her vow to exist, passing through days that held no meaning other than the possibility that outside the realm in which she existed was the possibility of an alternative realm in which her children lived. She did not have the energy to imagine what her children did each day; believing they were alive was enough. Holland had been occupied and Violet did not do much more than wake, eat, and try to sleep at night. Her realm was her room, even if outside it was a park, a city, a country that had been overrun. In her world was a window, a bed, a chair, and a bureau, and the occasional intrusion of Sister Meike who liked to report what she saw through the window in the park outside.

When Violet got word through the Red Cross that her children were safe, Sister Meike came running into her room, embraced her, and said that it was the most wonderful thing. But without her children and under the harsh conditions of this occupation, Violet knew that something inside her was gone, eaten away, the ballast of her ship eroded so that it would never quite be righted again.

CHAPTER 11

OLD LYME, CONNECTICUT — 2007

Adverse childhood experiences dramatically increase the risk of attempting suicide.[42]

My mother's ailments are becoming markedly more pronounced. There is never a single one: she complains of feeling lethargic and not being herself; she has asthma, eczema, bronchitis, infections in her bladder, and a succession of illnesses that, she says, have brought her down. Despite her health, she forces herself to exercise each morning, for hours without rest.

I have three children in five years, nothing compared to my mother who gave birth to seven in eleven. I am forty years old. My youngest is just seven years old and my eldest is twelve. I am in the throes of parenting, my days filled with standing on the sides of playing fields, transporting children, cooking meals, and advocating for my children's interests in any way I can. Those age-old parenting adages have held true. The moments go slow, the years fast. You are only as happy as your unhappiest child.

Due to his health, my father meanwhile has not gotten out from under their debts. After he overcomes another form of cancer, this time pancreatic, they are forced to sell their Vermont home. They are paupers, my mother frequently remarks. She tells us that she does not want to be a burden to us, but our father has left her with no choice and she needs to rely on us. When I remark on what I deem unnecessary expenditures, she tells me that she is entitled to indulge herself once in a while, and that she has worked hard all her life raising us and deserves the little she buys. When I comment on her newest pair of shoes, she acknowledges with a certain pride that shoes are her greatest weakness, on account of her mother having spoiled her before the war, before her mother was interned. The prewar stories of my mother refusing to remove her shoes at night or demanding red ones at the store are among her favorites. A leopard doesn't change its spots, she reminds me in her defense. In contrast to her, we children have benefited from a happy childhood. "Remember that trip to Austria, all those trips to England, the one through Paris, and that trip out West?" she asks. She worked so hard for all of us, and we all have houses and take our own children on fancy vacations. But life for her is very difficult, she points out. She is a wandering Jew, even if she is not technically Jewish, though her step-grandfather as a matter of fact was.

As the debts mount, my mother begins to lose her voice. To me, her voice seems more misplaced than lost, as if she has simply forgotten how to speak. When she speaks, she forces sounds out of her mouth through labored breaths. She tells me that she hates the noise she makes, the effort she has to expend. When her head starts to shake, she says she does not want to go out in public because she looks and sounds so strange. Dr. Lamb prescribes Xanax to help her cope, but she quickly habituates to the increasing dosage he prescribes. With each increase, her voice briefly improves and her shaking temporarily subsides, before worsening again. My father rarely remarks on her voice or her physical state except to remind us that he is trying to sort out their finances and that our mother is doing her best.

When my brother and I confront our mother one night about her spending, she tells us she might just take too many pills and end it all that night, so no one will have to worry about her anymore, just as her mother tried in Germany when my mother told her that she would not commit to marrying my father. I call Dr. Lamb later that night, but Dr. Lamb says that because of patient confidentiality, he will respond only to our mother's wishes, not to those of her children, and hangs up.

My mother does not overdose. Dr. Lamb refers her to an Upper East Side psychiatrist, whom we children call Dr. Love because he increases her prescriptions so much that in the afternoons she can no longer walk a straight line. She takes her doses throughout the day, and her resulting lack of balance means she frequently falls. Bruises cascade down her limbs. Her doctor appointments increase. She tells us that the doctors think she has dysphonia, just like NPR's Diane Rehm and one of the Kennedys, though she can no longer remember which one. "Very rare condition," she explains. "Medication is the only option. I'm a very rare case. The doctors are all so intrigued. They just can't figure me out."

She is constantly speaking to me of her health, her past, and the impact of war. She reminds me again and again that bad things have happened both to her and to her mother during those war years, and that she so wishes she was closer to her mother and that she asked her mother more. "We did not get along at all. Children never appreciate their mother until she's gone," she reminds me and I remain at a loss as to what to say or how I can help her redress her loss of childhood and its effects.

She and my father move into my brother's holiday home during his relocation abroad and then, on his return, into a converted stable next door. In addition to the financial support we now provide our parents, my brother pays my mother additional money to clean because she says she'd like to work and it's the only job she's equipped to do and his house could use it. At the end of a cookout at my sister's place during a family reunion, I go back to his house to change the sheets as he's hosting so many of us in his house. I arrive to find my mother already there, having left the cookout over an hour before. She is in one of the bathrooms. In her fist is a toothbrush, the bristles split and worn. Her feet are bare with manicured toes, her hair just set. A bead of sweat hangs precariously from her nose. Her clothing is worn.

"This bathroom has so far taken me almost an hour," she says. She is in gray sweatpants, pulled taut around her waist, and a tattered T-shirt with "Dartmouth" splayed across her breast. "And I already did the sheets."

I tell her that she does not need to clean. She tells me that she does. It's her job.

"Not right now, though," I say.

"It has to get done," she responds.

My niece appears. Ten years old and fresh-faced, she asks my mother to please come downstairs.

"I have too much to do," my mother says, exhaling while balancing herself on the edge of the sink. "I have to get this done."

"I know, Gran," my niece says, gently putting her arm around her grandmother. "But please come down. Take a rest."

"That is sweet of you. But not yet," she replies, removing her granddaughter's arm before kissing her on the forehead.

My mother turns to me. "You are lucky you don't have to do this." She climbs atop the toilet lid to swipe the top of the mirror frame for dust. "I never should have sold the flat," she continues from above us, "or lent your father that ten thousand pounds. It was all that my father left me. A mistake," she says.

"Gran," my niece says. "Come down."

My mother pauses, looks at herself in the mirror, and tucks a stray hair behind her left ear with a yellow-gloved hand.

"Gran," my niece repeats.

"I would do it differently," my mother responds, now wiping the mirror hard, trying to make it shine.

"Excuse me?" my niece asks.

She steps down. "All I'm saying is that it's a man's world. My mother, my grandmother, and I were all casualties of it." She turns to face my niece. "You, as my granddaughter, can do so much more. You are smart and capable. You are receiving a good education. I've raised strong children, good parents. You and your parents, your aunts, and your uncles can stand on your own two feet. You have a good mind. The world's your oyster. Don't forget that."

"Okay," my niece gently replies. "Now come downstairs?"

"Not yet," she says, despite how tired she appears. "You go. I have more to do," she insists, kissing her granddaughter on the cheek and shooing me away before dropping to one knee to scrub the sliver of floor behind the toilet with her toothbrush.

I do not try to stop my mother. She will finish this bathroom today at a standard that no one else maintains. She will show us how clean she can make a bathroom, and she will continue to make her perspective known, even if she thinks we have stopped listening, even if she thinks we cannot appreciate how deserving she is for having raised seven children and successfully provided us a secure and loving home, even if she thinks we do not appreciate the fact that she was separated from her mother when she was only aged three years and three months, packed onto a train with her one-and-a-half-year-old brother with a backpack and a number hanging around her neck to be fostered by a stranger. When one day I will tell her that the name of the program that the British government implemented at the outbreak of World War II was Operation Pied Piper, she will laugh at what the fable portended: the whistle of a train like the flute of the Pied Piper taking millions of children out of London and away. With such a name, how could the British government not have been aware that so many children risked being traumatized so, their identities taken away?

My mother comes downstairs in search of Ajax. Two of my brothers, a sister, and I have gathered in the kitchen around the island. We are talking about lunch, drinking tea.

"I've got much more to do," my mother announces, rag waving in her hand. "And Elizabeth, don't forget about my history. You need to write it," she says.

"Yes, Mom," I say.

"Join us for some tea," my sister says.

"I can't. Too much to do," she says.

The next day, I go to my mother. At forty years old and with children of my own, I continue to believe the best way I can help her is to make her story heard. I know I could provide more, as so many of my siblings do, siblings who are quicker to kiss her, to lend an arm or a shoulder when she needs physical support. Among the seven siblings, we all have different roles. But I decide I am to my mother the *ashik*, the bard, the *pingshu*, the minstrel, even if I have not yet realized that role.

I find my mother in my parents' converted stable sitting at her mother's desk, looking at two pictures she has laid out. The first picture is the one with Anna's thin, grave lips pursed, her tied-back hair receding at the beginning of that forgotten part. The other is an overexposed black-and-white picture of four people seated at a corner table. I have never seen that one. I ask her about it.

"A good one, don't you think?" she asks, handing it to me.

On the back of the picture, Neville has labeled two of the people "Mother and Father." They are a young George and Violet. Due to poor light, the other two are old and harder to discern. Behind a fluorescent tablecloth, their faces are ghostlike, their features indiscernible, their bodies fading silhouettes. I assume they are Anna and Louis, but I do not know.

"I do not know why my mother never told us that she was illegitimate and that she had relatives in Canada. Why, when I was growing up, did she withhold so much from me?"

"I do not know," I say.

"Well, I have always tried to share with you. I do not understand why you will not visit Jack's gravesite in Canada with me, or the schools I attended, or the places where I lived. I don't know why you will not come with me."

"I'm busy, Mom," I say. "I have three kids, a family of my own."

She sighs, then takes her picture back.

"Well, never mind. You should know that Neville has sent me a few other things as well. Telegrams. Not sure where they are right now. I'll have Dad send them to you though. They're very interesting. I'm expecting you to be the keeper of them."

"Yeah, I know."

"Yes. Say *yes*. It's important. Don't forget. *Yes*."

"Yes." I say, then tell her I'm going outside to join my kids. They're waiting for me to play a family game of capture the flag. I ask her to join us. She says she cannot.

Two weeks later, my father sends me two telegrams sent between Violet and George. They read as if the two of them are happy, as if there is no war, as if everyone is on the mend. A woman named Ida who is referenced and I do not know who she is. Violet says she has been to visit her, perhaps suggesting that she has done something pleasant with her, like having tea with a friend. But then I think that perhaps the suggestion is something else entirely. A plan for an escape from occupied Holland? A woman with whom she once accused my grandfather of having an affair and now is indicating that she is forgiving him? I cannot know; I can only imagine. Unlike my mother who speaks of her past all the time, my grandmother never shared. I am no longer sure which is the better course: When we talk about our past so frequently, do we keep its flame too alive in us? And what of those who absorb those tales, who live in their wake and feel their reverberations? What impact does it have on us? I read the telegrams.

RED CROSS TELEGRAM TO GEORGE CUSWORTH

11 MARCH, 1942

I AM WELL AND HAVE BEEN TO SEE IDA. I THINK ABOUT YOU CONSTANTLY. KISS THE CHILDREN. ALL LOVE VIOLET.

RED CROSS TELEGRAM TO VIOLET CROSS CUSWORTH

13 JULY, 1942

VERY RELIEVED TO GET YOUR MESSAGE. CHILDREN BOTH WELL AND HAPPY. THANKFUL THAT YOUR HEALTH IMPROVES. LOVE AND KISSES FROM US ALL. GEORGE BARBARA AND NEVILLE.

I think of my family, my siblings, and my own children. I think how grateful I am to be present in this life with them. Such a simple thing, to have a family beside you, and I have that. I think about George, sending his wife Red Cross telegrams during her internment. I imagine him not allowing himself to give in to romantic thought of her, the way she might have folded a telegram or squeezed a piece of fruit. He was a rational man, and he prided himself on his ability to use facts to find solutions. I think that most the time, he must have thought that he did what was right, that he made the right choice. But sometimes in the kitchen, squeezing a rare piece of fruit, perhaps he did not. And when he did question, perhaps he reminded himself that his primary responsibility as a father was to provide his children with a safe home and that he had delivered on that for several months, despite the risks, despite the doodlebugs whirring down onto London. Never mind that as a man, George knew little about raising children and keeping a home. He did what he could given the situation at hand, as Violet would have wished.

In the end, though, George sent his children to Wales, as the government had advised. All the young women had joined the war by that point, and as George had to return to work, no one was left to care for them. Because London was unsafe, George sent Barbara Christine and Neville out of London like all the other children in Operation Pied Piper, young though they both were. They had each other, George may have reminded himself. He no doubt trusted they would be okay. Yes, the situation was not ideal, but the dangers of war were far worse. That was what the government said. And when George received that letter from the townsperson expressing concern for the children, a letter that hinted of abuse, George picked them up right away and found a better place for them and then found two more places after that, when those did not work out. He did all he could, as he had no doubt promised to his wife. No, I suspect he had not wanted to let his children go, to sacrifice their early years with the remaining parent they had, but at least this way they would survive.

VIOLET

WASSENAR, HOLLAND, 1942

It was 1942. The occupation was now two years in and each day, Sister Meike came into Violet's room. She was most definitely pretty and George, if he were beside her, would have remarked on that. George had an eye for women like her. Her face was bleached of color, an absence that would be hard to achieve with only a pencil at hand, but if Violet's movement had returned to her arm, she would have tried. She always had liked to draw and Sister Meike's profile reminded Violet of the carved black gypsy doll that had once sat propped on the wooden high chair in her daughter's room. The doll's nose was an isosceles triangle, its side pasted to her face and the base slightly upturned. Looking at Sister Meike's profile, Violet thought how delicate such faces were, the nose liable to snap off with the slightest of blows, the face crack with the cold, the pencil tip break. So fragile they all were.

On her visits, Sister Meike often talked, so Violet indulged her in it. She was once like that. Not now. During these years in which Violet was interned in Rotterdam in that small convent room, she preferred not to speak too much. She would lie in her bed and listen as Sister Meike sat beside the window that overlooked the park. The girl seemed to prefer windows, bathing in a light that caressed her delicate face. Sister Meike was only twenty-three—a child, Violet realized now, a daughter to someone else. Violet sometimes wondered if the nun's mother knew she was alive.

Since the occupation, Sister Meike seemed to like to tell tales and Violet usually gave her the audience she sought, even if it was only an audience of one. She recognized the nun's need to speak even if she opted not to speak much herself. In the beginning the girl had been tentative with Violet, but prodded by even a single word, Sister Meike chirped on. During those early days of the occupation, Sister Meike spoke of a country that had been overrun by squadrons, of the parachutes that streamed down, of

German soldiers taking control of the streets. Violet listened as Sister Meike recounted how the Dutch crates of ammunition had been filled with sand and gravel, placed there by people employed by the Germans before the invasion. Sister Meike told Violet that being confined to her bed at that time with her paralyzed side had been a blessing in some sense, that she had been better off not having seen or having had to bear witness to a country destroyed by the Germans, to bombs that whirled and whistled as if enjoying their ride down, to diseases, destruction, every d-word the nun could conjure up. She recounted to Violet how the young officers had come into the Catholic hospital afterward, their unlined faces burned and mangled. She told Violet that she hated the war. It ruined everything, she said, and Violet agreed. She knew better than to take the nun's coping mechanism from her, to deny her what she saw. In some ways, Sister Meike had saved her, even if she had told her that her children had died only later to inform her that they were alive. She now knew that they had made the difficult passage out of Holland into England and were living in the countryside. As long as Hitler did not invade England, her children would be fine. In the evenings, she would lie in bed and picture her daughter, ribbons in her thick, blond hair, and her sweet, placid son, toddling around. Hitler could starve her of food but he would never be able to deprive her of her thoughts of her children that to her were as tangible as jewels and much more meaningful, stitched beneath her skin.

That's not to say that Violet did not worry. She knew that the situation for the Jews seemed to worsen by the day and she feared for them and for the state of the world. But trapped in occupied Holland, there was still nothing she could do and with nothing hopeful to see or to do, she preferred not to speak of anything at all. Not so Sister Meike. She talked a great deal of all that befell Holland, and Violet did her best to listen, aware that it was Sister Meike's way to cope and in some way, in her passivity, now hers as well. Until one day, Sister Meike told her that a rumor had surfaced that Jews could be exiled under the Nazi regime, and that all these Jews had shown up at the town hall with bandages on their wrists and necks, having stopped their suicides mid-slit in the hope they could get out. Then on arrival at the town hall their names had been taken and they were released. The Jews had been tricked, no doubt soon to be rounded up. The news made Violet sick. "Please don't tell me such things," she asked. "I can't bear it. Don't talk to me of this." Sister Meike's stories changed after that. Staring out the window, the nun spoke thereafter only of more innocuous things: a new leaf maybe, or a still-surviving tree, and Violet welcomed such talk. It was better that way.

Life under German occupation was not easy for any of them and they had their struggles, even if small compared to those of the Jews who were being sent away to camps. Violet did not know the fate of her own Jewish stepfather back in Germany. She hoped he was safe, but she tried not to think about him. The fate of no one was assured in times like this. It was enough to think of her children, to try to will them to survive, to hope that Hitler and his forces did not get to them.

While Violet did little in the day, on some late evenings, when she had gone particularly long without food, she would sneak out of her room at night and forage for scraps in the streets. Her arm was still paralyzed but she was able to walk. She never left long. She would visit the cluster of garbage cans just across the street and beyond them, a wheat field. Such trips carried risks but so did starvation. When she went, she always shared on her return the food she had scavenged with Sister Meike, who was never happy that Violet had snuck out and inevitably scolded her for such trips. But Sister Meikie was unfailingly appreciative of the offering too. Such exchanges were inherent to their relationship now. Only a few months into her internment, Sister Meike had somehow tracked down Violet's dog, Jeannie, and surprised her with it. On another occasion, Sister Meike had arranged a visit to Violet's young housekeeper, Ida, who lived fifteen minutes away. Violet had not wanted to go but she had gone because Sister Meike had been so excited about it. The trip had been exhausting and risky. The Jews were wearing their Star of David badges that the Catholic Church had so vehemently condemned. Violet preferred not to look. It was a trip she would never do again.

Sister Meike struggled, too, and as the occupation continued, Violet could see that Sister Meike had to work harder to hold on. In German-occupied Holland, it was sometimes hard to maintain the will to live. Violet knew that she herself at least had the thought of her children to hold onto, their memory and a hoped future with them. Sister Meike, on the other hand, had no such buoy. Violet sensed that even faith for Sister Meike sometimes might not have been enough and so she used imagination as well. Violet for the most part knew better than to deflate such supports, even if Sister's Meike's imagination had begun to err toward presenting fantasy as fact. Only a few months into the occupation, Sister Meike had stopped mentioning the marching Germans who sometimes crossed the park, their feet in polished jackboots kicking empty air. When Sister Meike came into Violet's room and took her spot by the window overlooking the park, she instead would tell Violet that she saw lovers lounging on the grass, the women with tight skirts wrinkling at the waist, the men discovering the women's hands, their knees, and their pouting lips. So discreet, Sister Meike said, there under the big trees, behind the arrowed iron rails, down beneath the tulips, but not too discreet enough for Sister Meike, it seemed. No, not her. "Wet grass and sultry kisses," Sister Meike told Violet with a wistful smile, and although Violet recognized a certain subversion in what the nun said and how she spoke, she did not remark on it. She instead let Sister Meike speak of these things, just as she once might have done, for in Sister Meike she saw a little of her old self.

"I see a man with a woman," Sister Meike told her one evening. "The woman is pulled so tightly to his side that I see four legs and one body."

It was midsummer, the daylight now extended deep into the night and the hours of darkness were few.

"Her hair is long," the nun continued in her reverie, her voice whimsical, capricious even, and her head turned with its delicate profile held in the window light. "They're happy. He's combing her hair with his hand. He's telling her how lovely she looks."

Impossible, Violet knew. The Germans had their rules. Curfews were set. Shades were pulled. Other rules were strictly enforced now too: identity cards and a ban against listening to the BBC, an action punishable by death. Still, Violet let the nun speak, let her dream. Violet knew the importance of concentrating on the small things, the beautiful incidentals of life even if you needed to invent.

"Really?" Violet said.

"Yes, there's a small blue window on the top floor of an old building," Sister Meike continued. "And another window with light slipping out beneath a closed shade. I can't quite see what lies behind it. But maybe, if I look harder . . ." She strained and then paused. "Do you want to know what else I see?"

The room was hot, but Sister Meike seemed not to notice. She continued before Violet could even respond.

"I see a German soldier. He's flashing a light at me," Sister Meike said.

Violet jumped. What had she just said? "A light?" What was the girl saying?

"A light," Sister Meike repeated, smiling. "At me."

"What are you saying? Move away!"

"He's smiling," the nun said.

"Move away," Violet commanded, her voice quaking, her body tense. "Get down!"

"But he's smiling," the nun repeated.

"Stupid girl," Violet yelled. "Get down!"

Violet started to get out of bed, preparing to throw the nun down with her crippled arm and weak legs and bones.

Stunned, Sister Meike stepped away from the window. She moved toward Violet, contrite.

"Was a soldier really there?" Violet demanded.

Sister Meike did not reply.

"Answer me," Violet demanded.

"It's late. Past curfew. The people are shut away, afraid, like us," Sister Meike offered. She adjusted her habit, cowering in her seat.

Violet, sensing that the girl was about to cry, relocated her gentleness, rebuked herself for her harshness. She had gone so long without losing her patience, but her anger seemed to move into her even faster now, like a morning mist that came out of the night, encompassing her. Admittedly, if she inhaled deeply and slowly exhaled, the mist cleared, but it took such strength and sometimes now she felt she was no match for it, steeped as it was in deep-seated fear that she had carried for so long, a part of her DNA.

"We'll be alright," Violet said, despite how she felt, despite what the flushed pallor of her face belied.

"We might be," Sister Meike said.

"We *will* be," Violet said, no longer believing herself.

CHAPTER 12

WESTON, MASSACHUSETTS — 2008

There are advantages to using diagnostic labels. They describe what's happening. . . . They allow for efficient communication between everyone involved in someone's care, including the person herself. Use them for what they are—tools for communication and improvement. Just don't let them become a term for who you are.[43]

"Great news" are the first words I hear when I answer my mother's call.

Over the last year, my mother's health has deteriorated further still. Her coterie of doctors now includes a psychologist, a neurologist, a dermatologist, an allergist, and a pulmonologist. Her medical expenses are exorbitant.

"What news?" I ask, noting cautiously that my mother's voice has temporarily returned.

"I've been recommended to go down to the NIH in Virginia to participate in a study of people who have suffered like me. It's very hard to be invited, but somehow I qualified. Such exciting news!" she exclaims, her voice undeniably and incontestably strong.

"That's good, Mom," I say, guardedly heartened.

"There's hope at last," she continues, excitedly driving home her point. "I'm a very special case. People want to study me. Isn't that wonderful? So few are asked. The NIH is apparently conducting some new study that is very cutting edge, and I was recommended for it. They say they might be able to figure out my voice," she adds, her voice faltering at the end, as if to remind me what her challenge is all about.

"Encouraging," I respond, measured but trying to sound supportive as well.

"Just incredible," she counters.

"Yes, it's good," I repeat, reaffirming as best I can.

"Can you take me? I can't afford the flight." Her voice falls.

"When?" I ask, not remarking on the change in tone.

"One week's time in Virginia," she forces out, in a voice that once again has turned into both a whisper and a scream, a voice that belongs in all caps, like Owen Meany's in that book by John Irving. "Can you drive?" she goes on, screaming her whisper now. She has stopped driving completely on account of her debilitating fear of bridges due to her mother driving her off a bridge.

"I'm sorry, I can't. Too much to do with the kids. Can someone else take you?" I add, continuing in my attempt to sound supportive.

"I'll see," she says curtly, and hangs up.

My mother does eventually go, my sister and sister-in-law having offered to drive her, and she returns home ecstatic from the trip. She recounts to all of us children how interesting and informative the experience has been. She explains that when she arrived at the facility, she was issued a pass and the researchers asked her to sit in a room. They posed lots of questions and requested that she sing a song, despite the fact that she could never carry a tune. "It was all so silly," she recounts. She is clearly tone deaf, and she warned them of that, but the researchers insisted. She sang "Happy Birthday" and felt like a real dummy and laughed at the inanity of it, but they didn't think it funny at all. They did not even crack a smile. So serious they were. I have not heard my mother sound this happy since London.

My mother goes on to explain that she told the doctors all about her childhood, about the places she lived and some of the experiences she had. She was not able to remember all of her experiences, but they told her that was fine. A whole team was in the room analyzing her. It was really quite incredible, she says. So fascinating. They wanted to hear what she had to say about her youth. They were so interested in little old her. They wanted to hear about her mother and their relationship, and she told them about her too. She is so glad, so happy she went. She is going to be part of a study of children who were evacuated in Operation Pied Piper during the war. And what was most interesting was that they did all sorts of tests on her voice and told her she did not have dysphonia at all!

"And guess what? I have something called PTSD," she announces. She asks if I have ever heard of it. "It stands for Post Traumatic Stress Disorder. P-T-S-D. A lot of veterans have it. Look it up. The PTSD is due to my war experiences, they said. My lost voice apparently stems from the war and is due to my early separation from my mother, to those years I lived in foster care and to what happened to me then. Not at all good. I did not form attachment or something like that and then I experienced trauma on top of all that. My financial stress apparently triggered my PTSD. It all has to do with the brain and an involuntary response to trauma based on what already has been wired into my brain. I actually cannot control it. Very complicated," she continues. "With work though, they say, I might be able to learn to retrain my brain a bit. Isn't that wonderful, Elizabeth?" she asks.

I say it is.

"I'm so thrilled. I might even be able to drive again one day. And one of the doctors is going to refer to me in a speech he's giving on PTSD in adults who as children were separated from their parents in the war! He said I could attend."

"That's great, Mom," I say.

We are silent.

"Well, okay?" I at last ask.

"Fine," she says abruptly, and hangs up.

My mother begins to see a specialist who, she says, is very well recognized in the field. He sort of hypnotizes her, my mother explains a few weeks later. He does all sorts of other things with her too. My mother cannot remember all her experiences in detail, especially the ones where she was abused as a little girl, but the doctor tells her he can help her remember more if she wants, but she has decided she would rather not relive all of it again.[44] Didn't

I agree? He said it was her choice, but it made sense not to go there if she didn't want to. Of course, she dreams about those experiences, but she never can remember her dreams, and that is just as well because they are not good dreams. The doctor also has recommended that she begin writing about her experiences and those of her mother, as they are so interrelated. He tells her writing can help. She tells him that long ago she asked her daughter to do exactly the same thing and she also has been keeping notes here and there and her brother has been collecting material and writing as well so she is not sure if there's a need. But you can write them, too, the doctor apparently told her. It will serve you well. She tells him she is not very good at writing on account of not having had much of an education.

"So do you still want to write the story?" she asks me.

I say I do but that I agree with the doctor that she can write it too.

"We'll see," she responds. "But I also have to tell you that something else has happened as well," she continues. "I met this woman at a party who is a writer, and I told her about my family history and my PTSD, and this woman said she could write the story and it could become a film. Amazing, don't you think?"

"It is amazing," I say.

"So, if you don't want to write it, I can give it to this woman instead."

I hesitate.

"Elizabeth? Really, you don't have to write it. I can get this woman to do it instead."

"No, I will. I'd like to," I say.

"Really, you don't have to. I can give it to this lady. Your father agreed."

"I'll do it," I say, more forcefully.

"Well, keep working on it then. You're the aspiring writer in the family. You can do it. If it's something you want to do, you have to persevere. I always told you that, didn't I? Shall I send you more documents? Neville recently sent me a packet that looks very interesting."

"Yes, that would be great."

"My life is fascinating. That's what this woman says."

"Yes," I say.

Within a few days, a package arrives at my home in Massachusetts with a note from my father. I might as well get this done, I tell myself, even if I do not know how I will find the time. I am working part-time and commuting nearly an hour to work if I include dropping my boys at their schools. I am not the writer I dreamed I would be as a small girl, nor am I the journalist I was on my way to becoming when I lived in Hong Kong. I am instead a content producer for a large website.

When I call to thank my father for sending the material along, he tells me that my mother is very pleased that I have agreed to help get this story done. It is important, he explains. Her doctors have told her that. Your mother is a great mother, he continues, and she has had a very difficult childhood. She has worked very hard for all you children her entire life. She has done the best she can to raise you. Do I understand? I tell him I do.

For a while, things get better. With her PTSD diagnosis, my mother's spirits continue to improve. She and my father move into a condominium that my two sisters have bought for them. She seems in a more secure place. Her voice is back. She is feeling good. She really likes the people at the gym where each day she still works out for three hours at a time. The people there are much younger than she is, but they consider her a friend. They think she is amazing, she tells me with pride. She seems to me as happy as she has been in a long time. She is talking about her mother freely with me.

"Keep writing about my story!" she says.

I don't tell her that I am having difficulty finding the time to write while raising my children or that I'm not sure I can even write this story as I think it needs to be told. I have not yet read research into the life course of World War II children who have been separated from parents and subjected to adverse conditions. I do not yet know that this trauma can seriously affect their development, from learning and behavior to their ability to function socially in the world.[45]

BARBARA

IN HER OWN WORDS, 1939 - 1943[46]

We duly arrived in England, at Ramsgate, in Kent, wearing only the clothes on our backs, which were not ours. We then travelled by train to Hull in Yorkshire and arrived at Paragon Station, where we were met by my grandmother. At first, my father thought of taking us to live in Devon. He quickly realized he had to find a job first. On being offered work in London, by his old firm Price Waterhouse (he had no possessions and no home), he decided to go and accept the job in spite of the danger of bombing. His office was located on Old Jewry Lane, EC4. He managed to rent a house in the Park, Middlesex. The house had been built by an Indian civil servant and was designed on his house in India. It had some porches in the front, a comfortable downstairs with a bedroom and tiny rooms on the first floor. It looked onto the Moor Gate Golf Course, and on the back it looked onto the grounds of Merchant Taylor School (a public school). It had a large orchard in the back that was completely overgrown, but my brother and I loved it. At first, we were looked after by a series of nannies, but they soon became bored and wanted to join the war effort. Help was impossible to find, and so my father had to send us away. We stayed with one foster home and then another. We were very unhappy at both of them, as they were very unkind to us, especially to me. All I really remember is having my hands tied behind my back every night, and so I found it very difficult to sleep.

My father eventually took us away from those homes and sent us to a boarding school in Wales, at a place called Llandbedr, which is situated on the coast just below Harlech. Again, we were ill-treated. When I was in Wales, among the things I remember is being locked in a room, with just bread and water to eat and drink. Also being in a toilet and thinking a bear was coming through the window.

The local villagers were so upset by our treatment that they managed to get my father's address and write to him and say we had to be taken away from there, and that a local farmer and his wife were willing to look after us. We went to stay with them for a year. They had one son about our age, and the family only spoke Welsh. I presume we soon picked it up. There was no electricity and no running water. To wash, there was a pitcher next to a china bowl. Once we tried going down to the beach, only to find barbed wire all along it, with mines on the sand to prevent the enemy from landing. In the summer, we helped with the hay raking and were then given a ride in the back of the hay wagon. Another time I helped to churn the butter. One time I was walking home and some man pulled up beside me and offered me sweets if I would get in the car. I ran like mad to get away from him. Once we were chased across the field by a bull, and we ran as fast as we could, being absolutely terrified that he would get to us. Once, walking into the village, we had to wait by two snakes lying on the path while the farmer's wife went back to the farm for something. I kept my eyes glued to them, as I did not know whether they were alive or dead. Ever since then, I have been terrified of snakes, and all my nightmares have been about them. During that time and from our arrival in England, I was my brother's mother and protected him as best I could. I always took any blame that was directed at him, hence I think I was always in trouble.

Throughout, my father was travelling to London every day, by train and then switching to the Tube. At first, during the Blitz, they would all rush to get to the shelters when the sirens went off, but gradually they ceased bothering as they were not getting any work done. In August 1940, after the Home Guard was formed, to help protect Britain in the event of invasion, my father signed up to join. Every night, on returning home from work, he would report for duty. They were all issued tin helmets and revolvers, but no bullets, as there were none to be had! Apart from patrolling around the neighborhoods for German invaders, they would also check to make sure blackouts were done properly.

I do not remember going to any kind of school. After a year in Wales, my father sent us to a boarding school in Mitcheldean,

Gloucestershire, situated at the end of the Forest of Dean. I have no idea how we travelled there. The school was called Fredville Park School for Girls—now called Bradford Court—but as it was wartime, they were taking in boys as well as girls. I was five and a half years old; my brother was four years old. The headmistress was Miss Hardy, a descendent of Nelson—"Kiss Me Hardy." She had Hardy's sword hanging up in the entrance hall, and her assistant was also Miss Hardy, a niece. I have no idea how old she was, but as a small child I thought she seemed very old. My father said she loved children but disliked men. I loved it there, and it became my home. I learnt to ride there, and we would go hacking in the Forest of Dean, which was wonderful. Whenever the horses' shoes needed replacing, we would ride the horses into the village to the village blacksmith—now a thing of the past. I became horse-mad, but my brother never cared for them. Whenever we were poorly, we would be sent to sleep with the mistress. She wore a nightcap and nightdress, and we slept in a four-poster bed with her. I found it all quite terrifying. The house was in a state of poor repair, and so whenever it rained we had to run around with buckets to try and catch the water. My father would come and visit us on our birthdays and bring presents. The countryside around Mitcheldon was very beautiful. Once while riding we came across an old Elizabethan House, where supposedly Queen Elizabeth I had spent the night. In the spring, there would be primroses and bluebells everywhere. I found it all so beautiful.

One weekend in the autumn of 1943, three and a half years after I had last seen my mother, my brother and I were told we were going to meet her in a local hotel. My father introduced us, and my brother immediately said, "Is that my real Mummy?" I, however, just stared at her.

CHAPTER 13

WESTON, MASSACHUSETTS — 2009

It is not rare to see clients with PTSD who have taken on the iden-tity of the victim or survivor to the exclusion of pursuing future goals. Examples of this include . . . a childhood abuse survivor who continues to define him or herself as the caretaker of his or her adult siblings whom he or she protected from the abuse.[47]

It is no surprise to me that Neville's stroke devastates my mother. Before his stroke, my mother often told me that because she cared so well for him, when she was old, Neville would care for her. After his stroke, her hope is dashed. She tells me that her one family member is, for all intents and purposes, gone and she is alone. I decide not to point out that my mother still has a husband and seven children. I know she would reply that is not the point, that her brother can no longer share anything with her anymore— past reminiscences, his knowledge, their youth. He can only smile and say "yes." It is like talking to a shell or, worse yet, a dunce, she tells me. He is no longer the bright man he once was. She looked after him when they were young, they were very close, and now he is not going to be able to look after her.

"You don't understand," she says when I tell her that at least her brother still seems happy, even after his stroke. "It is very hard for me."

We talk of my mother's past and the stories grow worse. My mother speaks of her hands tied behind her back at night. "So

I didn't play with myself, I suppose." She speaks of a bear she imagined trying to come into the window when she hid by the toilet. She speaks of being left to stand alone all day by two snakes and how frightening it all was. She speaks of a man who tried to lure her into a car with sweets and of frequently being locked in a room with bread and water alone. "I suppose that's why, when your father and I would get in an argument," she tells me, "I'd lock myself in a closet and refuse to come out." My mother's early childhood, I realize, is one long sequence of terrifying events.

My father, meanwhile, continues to forward me information, most of it from Neville when he was well and able to research. "I hope this is of interest to you and Elizabeth," Neville wrote to my mother, signing his notes "with much love." I decide that we are all writing this story together. I tell myself that it will all come together. I recognize that Neville's research introduces facts into the narrative, facts that sometimes are at odds with what I imagined or my mother has long believed. But the facts give me markers to proceed.

Neville has a very different vantage point than my mother. He was close to his mother. His sister was not. Perhaps had I asked before his stroke, he would have explained to me why. Our nanny, Dorothy, who knew my grandmother well because she worked for her in Germany before she came to the States, once told me that Violet and my mother were not at all alike. Violet, she said, loved to sit and drink coffee and laugh. Not like my mother was the suggestion in what she said. Perhaps had I asked Neville before his stroke, he might have elaborated on that single detail. Based on that single piece of information Dorothy provided me, I liked to imagine what he might have said. He might have told me that Violet could pull a pastry out of a bag, paying no heed to the crumbs that fell on her skirt, or that while eating that pastry she could drink a coffee without insisting on cleaning the grounds from the filter first. Perhaps he could have told me that as she sipped, Violet would not remark on what the coffee cost or the effort it took to carry the pastry from the shop. Perhaps he would have said that Violet simply could enjoy the way the pastry dissolved in her mouth, savoring the bitterness of the coffee that washed the pastry down without having to preoccupy herself with all that. Perhaps he would have said that Violet had learned at some point to refuse to have her pleasures compromised by unnecessary reflection on circumstance. Perhaps he would have said that Violet relished each moment and that for her, how one lived was a conscious and deliberate act. Perhaps he would have said that Violet took pleasure where she could and refused to have that pleasure taken away from her. Perhaps he would have told me that Violet, because she had been through so much, chose to live a life unfettered, to exist in a space in which she could find what was pretty and put all her attention toward that. Perhaps he would have said that for all these reasons and more, Violet was unlike my mother and much more like him. It might have explained a lot.

But while helpful, that knowledge still does not fully explain to me why some can handle trauma and some cannot. If we are a combination of genetics and experience, how much is attributable to each? Is a giraffe's neck long because they out-survived those giraffes with shorter necks when food was scarce and the longer necks could reach the taller trees? Or did short-necked giraffes simply begin to stretch their necks because scarcity of food resulted in some giraffes making use of some until-then-dormant ability in them? Did experience trigger the dormant expression of these traits or was it a simple case of natural selection? I have a tendency toward anxiety like my mother. Is there some benefit to it? Can I overcome my anxiety as I like to imagine Violet tried to do by focusing on what is innocuous in the present? Am I more or less anxious than she was? Why am I more anxious than my siblings if we carry the same genetic material? If depression is steeped in one's past and my past was secure, can secure early attachment mitigate concern about my future as well? Is how genetic traits display in any way a choice? I think about these questions when my high school freshman daughter worries whether her decision to drop soccer will be a decision that irrevocably changes the trajectory of her high school experience for the worse. When she second-guesses and questions herself like this, I wonder if I have attached to her in the right way or too much. And is her neck long or short and how much is that length attributable to me? I think again about my mother's relationship with Violet, what it looked like, and how much was out of her control. How much better equipped to deal with life's struggle am I, are we, the next generation of women, than these women who preceded us, and how much of that is choice?

NEVILLE

In his own words, 1943[48]

By 1943, VHC (Violet Helene Cross) was well enough to travel, and she applied to the Red Cross to be repatriated to England in exchange for injured German civilians in England who wanted to be repatriated to Germany. The Red Cross agreed to make the necessary arrangements, and so, with her little dog, Jeannie, she travelled to Switzerland and from there to Lisbon, in Portugal, where she arrived in September 1943. On 13 September, the Irish legation in Lisbon issued her with a visa to enter the Irish Republic. All three countries, Switzerland, Portugal and the Republic of Ireland, were neutral during the war, and that is why VHC was able to travel through there, even though Britain and Germany were at war. She landed at Shannon Airport in Ireland on 12 October 1943 and immediately left for England, landing at Poole in Dorset on the same day.

As soon as GEC (George E. Cusworth) had met VHC at Poole Airport, he brought her down to Fredville Park School in Gloucestershire to meet the children. They had not seen her for three and a half years, and the younger child, Neville, had completely forgotten her. He can remember the meeting as though it were yesterday. His first words were: 'Is that my real Mummy?'

Although the reunion was a happy one for GEC, VHC and the children, it was not without a residual sadness for VHC. Her dog, Jeannie, (whom she had somehow kept throughout her internment) had to be placed in kennels on arrival back in England for a six-month period of quarantine. While there, it took sick and died, as VHC would often say, 'of a broken heart.' Furthermore, she was never able to see her mother, Anna Bracker, again. Anna, being a German national, had remained in Germany during the war and died of typhoid fever before VHC was able to return to Germany to see her.

CHAPTER 14

WESTON, MASSACHUSETTS — 2009

An adult with poor self-regulation skills may lack self-confidence and self-esteem and have trouble handling stress and frustration. Often, this might be expressed in terms of anger or anxiety, and in more severe cases, may be diagnosed as a mental disorder.[49]

As I research, I learn more about Violet and the details of her past. I learn about the repeated trauma that Violet experienced well into adulthood, and I begin to understand why her relationship with my mother was so difficult.

"Why didn't you live with your mother when she returned?" I ask my mother one day.

"She was still recovering," she says.

"Did you see your mother on weekends then, after her return? That must have been so hard."

"I don't remember seeing her much. The truth is I really did not care that much at the time. The few times I did see my mother, she always wanted me to share my confidences with her. I was always reluctant because, when I did, I would regret sharing them with her. The next day, she would tell everyone what I said. It got me so mad. I could not trust her at all. Sometimes, I would be asleep and I would wake up and find her just staring at me. I had no idea how long she had been there. I hated that. I just wanted her to get away."

"So then you went to boarding school and you still did not see your mother much at all?"

"No."

"That must have been hard for your mother. Were at least she and your father close?"

"I'm not sure. My mother was changed from the war. And we had that woman living with us after the war. We always seemed to have women living with us at different times."

"Were they mistresses?"

"I don't know. It was very strange. But I really never thought about it at all. That woman was younger but kind, and I could not relate to my mother at all."

"Why not?"

"She was changed and lost her temper so fast. And I was not the little girl she left."

When I ask her about this time, I hear the same theme again and again, the little girl left. When I share my mother's story with my friend Beth, the psychologist, she tells me that my mother could have ended up much worse. My mother was fortunate to marry someone who was patient, who intuitively knew the importance of secure attachment, and who could provide support, which I later learn is all the more important for youth who have self-regulation difficulties due to adverse childhood experiences.[50] I think about my mother and how even a broken clock that she does not have the budget to fix can set her off, leaving her shaking and flushed.

"Your mother must have had to work extra hard to provide all you children the attachment she never had, to be consistently loving and supportive. And she must have understood that you needed your father and she did not get in the way of that. You were lucky," she says. "But so in her adult life is she."

BARBARA

IN HER OWN WORDS, 1944 – 1947[51]

Around 1944, the school moved to another house outside Winchester, due to the first building's appalling condition. There the house was smaller, with fewer students. Riding was not as enjoyable, but nevertheless I loved the countryside too. Every Saturday morning, we would walk to the sweet shop to pick up our weekly sweet allowance. I always chose the gobstoppers.

My parents moved to a small, third floor flat in Ealing Village, Ealing. My brother was sent to St. Benedict's School as a day boy, where he received an excellent education. He was delighted. I remained at boarding school. In May 1945, I remember being called into the headmistress's drawing room to listen to Winston Churchill declare on the radio that the war was over. The next term (summer term), I was taken away from that boarding school and sent to a posh day school instead, where we had uniforms and had to wear white gloves. The only reason I was accepted was that the headmistress was from Yorkshire, like my father. I dreaded that I would hate the school even before I got there, and I made life so miserable for everyone that the next term I was sent back to my beloved boarding school. I was eight years old.

During the Christmas holiday of 1945, my father came home and told my mother he had been asked by the Government to go back to Germany and help put the iron and steel industry on its feet. He did not want to go, as he had vowed never to go back. My mother talked him into accepting the job, as she hated living in England, with all the gloomy conditions. Everything was rationed; there was limited food and no help. My mother missed the Continental way of life. In Moor Park, the pipes had frozen every winter and then burst! In Germany, we would be living in Düsseldorf, my parents' old hometown, and he would be number two in the hierarchy, with the rank of Brigadier. He would wear military uniform and have a car and driver.

My mother stayed in England, though, with my brother at day school and myself at Fredville Park School. That Christmas, my mother did not have any presents for us, but on Christmas Eve, after Neville and I had gone to bed, she received a telephone call to say she could come and meet someone at a certain place to pick up presents that my father had sent for us. Not being able to leave us alone in the flat, she woke us up and we all had to take the Underground to go and pick up the presents. The next morning, Neville and I found a pillowcase of presents for us at the ends of our beds! What joy!

Sometime around then, my grandmother—my mother's mother—was coming to England by train from Hamburg, where she had survived the war. Sadly, there was an outbreak of typhoid on the train. My grandmother caught it and died. She was taken off the train and buried, and my mother never knew where she had been laid to rest. I remember her getting the telegram and crying and crying. I did not really understand what it was all about or why she was so sad.

After Christmas the following year, before I went back to school, I was told I would be leaving there after the spring term and going out to Germany. I was devastated.

On the 1st of April 1947, we set out to Germany, leaving Tilbury Docks in London, on an army troop ship.

CHAPTER 15

OLD SAYBROOK, CONNECTICUT — 2012

During early and mid- adolescence (i.e., 11-15 years), brain systems that seek rewards and process emotions are more developed than cognitive control systems responsible for good decision-making and future planning. This means that self-regulation is developmentally "out of balance" at this age . . . Given that poor decisions during adolescence can have long-term negative consequences, self-regulation supports during this developmental period are critical. This is especially important for youth with a history of adverse childhood experiences.[52]

My parents are descending into financial hardship again, which I have learned is not uncommon among those who suffer from PTSD.[53] My father's health is worse, his heart is growing weaker, and he rarely leaves the house. My mother tells us that we children need to alternate visits to them as caring for him and the house is very draining. She is cleaning on manic tears. Her medications have increased to the point where she sometimes cannot walk a straight line. I call her psychologist to tell him that her prescription is too strong if she is going to drive. He tells me: "Sweetheart, she will be fine, and which daughter by the way are you?" I am furious with her doctor for his dismissiveness and apparent lack of attention to her care. At the same time, I am at a loss as to how we children can further help. We are providing financial support, but it seems never to be enough. When I call, she tells me that my father is not the same as he once was. She tells me that he no longer walks the dog they so love, a Sealyham terrier like the one her mother owned. He has no energy and is short-tempered, she says. They did not enjoy an evening cocktail together on the porch all summer, and she is so tired of being the one to do all the chores. She tells me that the condominium is too much, too big to clean without help, and that there is too much garden to put to bed, and she is too old to carry the patio furniture on her own into the garage. That garage is such a long way. It is all so exhausting for her, caring for our father, for the house, and for everything else. She tells me that she does not have a moment to rest and that she is eating only bread and cheese for lunch, as money is so tight. She tells me she is not sure how much longer she can go on like this.

A week before Christmas, I visit my parents and my father asks that I drive my mother to help her do her chores. I drive her to the bank where she deposits a check, then to the drug store to buy more medication, then to a shop across town to buy a half-liter bottle of $25 extra virgin olive oil, then to the dermatologist so he can zap a tiny burst capillary that she thinks is too conspicuous on her face but that as hard as I look, I cannot see. "Elizabeth, you're blind. When did you last have your eyes checked?"

She is wearing Ugg Boots and a new, long, designer coat, the price of which I surreptitiously look up on my phone while she goes into the doctor's office.

"Mom, that coat costs $900," I say, reprimanding her when she comes out. "How can you spend that much when money is so tight?"

She looks at me then looks away. She is shaking. Furious. I have triggered her anger, anger that has always seemed to me akin to a flash of heat lightning, striking when the unstable air is hot and thick. It does not take much to sense its impending onset. Of course, if I were to wait it out, to let the ensuing rain fall, to briefly seek shelter, or better yet to provide her shelter as well, through words, through touch, through an expression of love, the sky would eventually clear, the day restore. She would self-regulate. But today I lack both the patience and the will. I do not think about why. I do not address that in me. I trigger her anger and choose not to apologize to her, but then nor does she apologize to me. We are silent. I drop her home and leave.

I go on holiday to Canada with my family and she sends me a livid email that I delete rather than read. We have not spoken for two weeks.

My father calls me when I return home from our Christmas trip. "Your mother is still very upset," he explains. "Life is hard for her. She is struggling. She deserves a few nice things. She has lost her voice. She is not well."

I do not respond. I ask after him.

"It is your mother you should be worried about," he says, clearly impatient with me. "I love you, but you need to try to understand."

I call one of my sisters. My sister can talk on the phone for hours. When she was twelve, our parents installed her own phone line in our house. They said it was the children's line, but it was hers, as it sat on the night table beside her bed. She now lives in a nearby town to my parents and visits them most every day. My mother often calls her and her husband to help with small tasks and fix things around the house. My sister can joke with my mother in a way that I cannot.

"Just forget it," she urges me, having listened to my story of our falling out. "That's just the way she is."

"I know," I say. "It's just so frustrating."

"Believe me, I know," she replies.

Then she reminds me of the story of the end of Violet's life. After our grandfather George had died, Violet came to visit our mother. Our mother had five children at that point. Our Swiss German nanny Dorothy knew and loved Violet as Dorothy had cared for her and George in Germany before Violet recommended she come to the U.S. to help my mother care for us. ("Don't ever tell me there's no such thing as the American Dream," Dorothy always told us growing up. "I came here with a dollar in my pocket, and now look at me.")

"You know when Mom's mother was visiting, that time she abruptly left?" asks my sister.

"Yeah," I reply.

"It was right before she died. She must have been sick with cancer then. She was partially paralyzed from the war and very frail."

"Yeah," I say.

"Well, you know how Mom always said she could not do much to help her mother as she was raising all of us and looking after the house and the garden and how her mother always wanted to sit and chat but she did not have the time and so her mother left?"

"Yeah."

"Well, Dorothy helped care for Mom's mom on that visit and she told me that very hurtful things were said between them and our grandmother left prematurely, on terrible terms. I don't think she and Mom ever spoke again. Mom cannot handle stonewalling, you know. It is too much, Elizabeth."

"Okay," I say and decide to start talking to my mother again.

When I call, my father answers. "Elizabeth, hello!" He invites my mother onto the line, as if nothing has transpired between us. She says hello.

"How are you?" he asks.

I tell him I am well.

"Well, tell us about your trip. Your mother and I would love to hear."

And so I do. I tell them about Canada and how the houses line the byways North as if the road itself constitutes a view. My mother expresses disbelief. As close to the road as that, she asks, our argument now forgotten, long passed. Yes, I say. Quite incredible, she says. I then tell them about how much my daughter and my youngest son love to cross-country ski and how they skied for miles each day beneath iced branches on countless groomed trails. I tell them how my older son went dog sledding with eight large huskies and how much he loves dogs. A dog person like her, my mother says, but not at all like me. I continue to talk about Canada and the cold and the condition of the snow, explaining in detail all we did until my mother says that my children sound happy and healthy and that she is glad that we enjoyed our holidays so much. When I in turn ask my parents how their holiday was, my father says great and my mother responds that she has to get back to all that needs to be done and hangs up. And I remember that unlike my children and me, my mother had little parental guidance and support. That insecure attachment in early childhood, which research says is such a robust predictor of PTSD and which may impede the development of effective strategies for regulating affect and coping with stress, particularly for those older adults exposed to a broad range of traumas,[54] had no opportunity to be redressed in adolescence for her.

VIOLET

EALING TO DÜSSELDORF, 1947

Violet wanted to go back to Germany, but she would not admit to it. She said she was leaving England because of the plumbing, the damp, the way the London air covered you like cold wet dirt, so that you felt as if you were being suffocated beneath shoveled earth. Her focus was the leaving, she always maintained, not the moving toward. The distinction was important: a transitioning from an experienced past rather than toward an envisioned future. She had lived long enough to know that one had to persevere, divorced from false promises or the expectation that came with hope.

In Holland, during the war, there had been plenty of times when she had nearly given up—mornings, evenings. Especially evenings. But somehow she had gone on. Sometimes she was grateful for the physical pain; it distracted her from committing that one final hurt as she lay restless in the night. Had anyone asked, she could not say why she had not killed herself after she was told the boat on which her family had tried to escape Rotterdam during Hitler's Blitz had been torpedoed, leaving her children dead. Maybe she just did not have the wherewithal to tie a noose around her neck or find a gun to put inside her mouth, but once she had learned they were alive, she had found reason to live, to go foraging in the fields for seeds, to pick through a German officer's garbage in the dark, to open her eyes each day as she lay at the Dutch convent where she had been interned. When she knew her children had made it to Britain from the port at Ymuiden, she willed herself to remain.

Not that she had provided her children much since. Well, not her daughter anyway. It had not turned out as she had envisioned during her internment. They were with her now. Barbara Christine, ten, and Neville, eight, on a train heading toward a converted troop ship, once an ocean liner, the *Empire Halladale*. They were en route to Germany, her daughter forlorn and silently defiant on her seat, staring out the train window back toward England, and her son accepting, sitting between them, jumping a rubber elephant up and down on his sweet little knobble knee.

She and her two children had awoken early, locked the front door of their flat in Ealing one last time, and taken a cab to the station for the London Tilbury Southend Line. It was a forty-five minute ride from Fenchurch Street Station to the Tilbury Docks. Her son was excited, her daughter recalcitrant, as she so often was.

The Tilbury Docks were on the north shore of the river Thames, downstream of Tower Bridge, at a point where the river looped and narrowed, meandering through a marsh. The train traveled east and Violet was glad to be departing from sunless England, heartened to be at last on her way. The Bank of England, which stood so self-importantly at the country's heart, had so far been ineffectual in its efforts to beat life back into the Empire, and she was not sure it ever would. As the train swayed its way toward the coast, rocking them back and forth to the measured click of the wheels on the track, Violet felt a familiar and palpable sense of relief that they were at last getting out.

Violet knew that the liberation she felt in leaving a victorious London for a defeated Germany would make no sense to most. The first years of her life in England had been such happy years before moving aged six to Bethnal Green, where as the daughter of a German national, she and her family had been unceremoniously thrown out after Germany torpedoed the *Lusitania* and World War I broke out. Germany, of course, was no better with its food shortages and lack of coal, but at least with so many men at war, her mother got to work. And later, after the war, after Violet had grown up and found a job she loved in Hamburg and given birth to children of her own, life was better for a time. Better until war struck again and they fled to England and then to Rotterdam, from which once again they had to escape.

She laughed knowingly. Germany was always the impetus behind the leave, Germany always upending her life. Violet should have resented Germany but she did not.

"I don't want to be on this train," Barbara was telling the window. "I don't want to go to Germany."

Violet thought about responding but then did not. What was there to say? She was herself glad to be on the train with her daughter and her son heading toward the *Empire Halladale* to go back. She was glad the time had come. She was grateful for it. That night eighteen months ago when the war was over and Violet had resettled in England, the possibility of leaving England which her husband had half-heartedly proposed had been a welcome prospect. It was fall and although the war had ended, the children were at boarding school because Violet still was not entirely well. One evening, George had walked into their home, where in the winter the pipes always froze, and he told her the CCG had approached him to help rebuild Germany's iron and steel industry. Life together with George had not been what it had been before the war. Food had been rationed, and the prospect of recovery bleak. George often returned home late, having stopped at the pub for a lager, joining crowds of men drinking frothy-headed beers out of thick glass mugs, smoking cigarettes and chewing pipes while their housewives waited at home, having stood in long lines for a slab of meat or a family ration of bread. It was not like Düsseldorf before the war with a newborn boy and a girl who happily called her Mum. Germany would be a welcome change, she had told herself. A chance for a fresh start.

On the train to Tilbury Docks with her two children by her side, Violet replayed in her head the conversation in which George first brought up his employer's offer to move back to Germany again.

"Of course, I won't accept," George had said before Violet could respond, dislodging her momentary gladness as soon as it had taken hold.

"Might not leaving be a nice change for us?" she had asked, knowing she had to be careful. 'They had been through so much in this short time. George initially had moved to Moor Park because of her, because it was such a short distance to her early childhood home in Rickmansworth where she had lived so happily with her two spinster aunts before her mother adopted her back into that tenement in London's East End Jewish slums. Never mind those aunts had passed away. So many had. Louis too. In a concentration camp. The Germans, not the Brits, killed him in the end. Still, she did not like Britain.

"Tell me more," Violet had insisted, and George had told her that they wanted him to be deputy controller, which, he had explained with some pride, would be the most important practical administration post.

"That's exceptional," Violet had said, knowing that, like all men, he liked to have his ego fed. She had asked him to tell her more.

"I'll be working for Percy Mills, the industrialist," he had continued, as if she would know who that was.

"Oh yes, oh yes," Violet had said, nodding.

"And I know the business of Vereinigte Stahlwerke well, which is a very important business in Germany right now, and they need someone fluent in German."

"Of course, of course. That's quite something."

She then had reminded him that he spoke some French as well. Violet herself was bilingual in German and English, and she spoke French and Dutch, too, but there had been no need to remind him of that.

"Yes," he had replied hesitantly. He wasn't a stupid man. He likely had known what she was aiming for.

Their relationship had been formal since her repatriation from Holland, both of them changed by what had befallen them, neither wanting to voice blame, each pressing on, as everyone did. They had lived together for only four years before being separated by the Second World War. She often reminded herself that it was on her insistence that she and the children had joined him in Rotterdam after they had fled Düsseldorf, too late some might have thought, but Violet had so cherished their life together that she did not want to give that up. Admittedly, George had not wanted his family to join him in Holland because he feared what Hitler had in store for it, and he turned out to be right, as he so often was. And during the first attempt at escape, he had decided to remain with her, his infirmed wife. He had given her that.

"I don't want to go to Germany," Barbara said to her mother again now from the seat on the train. "I want to stay here."

"Well, we're going," Violet replied, and her daughter turned her back to her, went silent as she so often did.

George had said the same. That first night after he came home with the offer to go back he had said, "It's Germany. Why go back to that? After everything we've been through, after what Germany has done to us, to our family, to Britain, to everyone else?"

It was a good question. But returning was not just about going back to Germany, it was going back to being a family once again, to taking up where so many years ago they had left off.

"But Hitler is gone," she had reminded George. "It will be different now." She had seen that he was growing impatient, so she had dismissed herself, poured him another drink, giving him a moment to collect himself. Then she had sat beside him on the couch.

"It will be worse than England," he had protested. "A real mess. A flattened city of rubble. Rationing will be much worse than it is here. I can't do it, go back to that."

George had taken another sip of his drink then, swirling it in circles in his glass, and in his swirling silence, he had sipped again. George always had a tendency to eat and drink too much. When Violet had finally returned from Holland, she had been struck by the fact that he was still overweight, while there she was, skin and bones. But she never mentioned his girth. She kept quiet on so much.

She also at first had resisted telling him how provincial Moor Park felt, how claustrophobic her life was as a housewife, how much freedom the men possessed, going to work and coming home at their whim. Until she had not and they had begun to argue more. That night, however, when he had come with the possibility of returning to Germany, she had restrained herself from speaking of such things. Instead, she had reminded him that Germany, without Hitler, had the capacity to revive itself, that the Germans were an industrious people, that they had come back before and could do it again. She herself had been witness to it in Hamburg after World War I, as eventually had he. Forget Hitler and what Germany had been. To go to Germany now was a great opportunity to start again, and he could fill the role as no one else could. She had not raised her voice. "Just think about it, please," she had suggested before letting the issue drop.

They had not discussed the move again, but the discussion had replayed itself in the pauses of their conversation at dinner and in the silences before they went to sleep, on opposite sides of the bed. The conversation still replayed itself now, almost two years after he had left, when she and the children were on their way to Düsseldorf to join him. She told herself it would be better with him than it had been.

Violet sighed. The train was pulling into the station, the conductor announcing their imminent arrival, the train horn signaling, the brakes screeching so loudly that little Neville covered his ears. He was such a sweet little boy, Violet thought. The train stopped with a jolt, and Neville clutched her arm with a laugh, as Barbara Christine quietly held the side of her chair. Barbara had argued over the window seat with Neville when they first embarked, and Neville, faced with her obstinacy, had relented right away. "You take it. That's fine," he had said, and Violet was grateful that he had averted a scene. It was too early in the journey to be mediating children's arguments.

"We're here," she told them, and Barbara Christine immediately stood up. Violet followed her daughter's lead. "Come on, children. Lots to do," she cheerily said.

She led Neville by his hand, with Barbara at his side, down the passenger car. They inched along the line of passengers disembarking from the train—expectant and impatient like them. It was early, only 8:45. They took the passenger causeway to the hall that housed the baggage and the waiting and the immigration areas. The hall was enormous, two stories of brick. As they entered that capacious space, a porter trailing behind them, Neville kept his head turned up, captivated by the height of the ceilings and the enormous cupola. Violet thought the building would have seemed more like a cathedral than a station were it not for the large clock that presided over it.

"Pay attention," she reminded Neville, pulling him along. "Lots to do."

"You said that already," Barbara Christine remarked, and Violet gave her a rebuking glare. Barbara Christine marched on, paying little attention to what her mother said.

After confirming her family's passage to Cuxhaven and registering their luggage with the help of the porter, keeping only one small overnight bag for themselves, Violet found a spot on a cold wooden bench. The *Empire Halladale* had already arrived, but departure was a few hours hence. Barbara Christine asked why they had arrived so early if the ship was not departing for such a long time, and Violet reminded her that the train schedule gave them no option but to arrive a bit early, and anyway it was better not to be rushed and to be prepared.

"Why didn't we just take a cab?" Barbara asked, and Violet told her that cabs were for first-class passengers, not for them; they were an unnecessary extravagance. Barbara said she wished she was a first-class passenger, and Violet said that would be nice but they weren't.

Neville pulled his rubber elephant out of his pocket and began jumping it along the top of the bench, while Violet and Barbara watched a crowd of Germans navigate the hall, collecting their baggage and lining up for immigration. Violet explained to her children that the Germans likely were from the British Zone and had probably come to work as cooks, canteen hands, and waitresses until their country got back on its feet.

"Why are we going there if they are coming here?" Barbara asked.

"To be with your father," Violet said, and that seemed to placate her daughter for a bit, she so idolized him. Then Violet reminded the children that her own mother, their grandmother, had been a German cook and had come to London on a ship, just like the Germans in this hall.

Her daughter did not respond.

"There are probably German brides here too," Violet continued, appealing to her daughter's romantic side. "See all those pretty young women hugging and holding hands with the men? I bet they're brides."

"You think so?" said Barbara, her interest piqued.

"Most definitely," Violet replied.

"How many are there?"

"I don't know. Let's see how many we can find."

For the next ten minutes, she and her daughter passed the time by speculating on who the brides were in the crowd of Germans. Bouquets, they decided, were a dead giveaway—those and clasped hands, both of which made them easier to count—and Violet had fun playing with her girl.

Such games with her daughter were rare, try as Violet did. Reuniting with her children after the war had been a stilted affair, and her relationship with her daughter remained, in many respects, as awkward as it was at their first reunion. That first meeting following her repatriation through the Red Cross to Great Britain, Violet met both her children in a hotel lobby outside London. The meeting was painful to recall. After their separation during the bombing of Rotterdam, when Barbara was only three, she had been Neville's keeper, both sent out of London on a train with numbers round their necks and placed in foster homes. It was not a good time for anyone then.

That first reunion remained with Violet though. Sitting on the red hotel couch, she had hoped her daughter would be excited to see her, even if she herself felt insecure and displaced. She was expectant as her daughter appeared, distant but curious, her head bowed. Seeing his daughter's discomfort, George had beckoned Barbara Christine to come to Violet, but Barbara had refused, resolutely standing her ground. With her one good arm, Violet had

weakly reached out, embarrassingly awkward and stiff, calling to
her children with a trembling voice. "It's me, your Mummy," she
had said, ashamed of her weakness, of her hollowed cheeks and
buckled posture, of how old and frightening she appeared, even
to herself. Her son—how much he had grown!—barely had hesitated. "Is this my real Mummy?" he had asked his father, George.
Neville was clearly bright, and Violet had interjected before her
husband could reply, buoyed by her son's quick acceptance of her:
"Yes. Yes! It's me. Your Mummy," she had said. Looking at her
one extended arm, she had self-consciously drawn it in, but her
son had not seemed to care about her arm or her wiry hair or
any of it. He had come to her, this battered old woman unrecognizable to those she knew before the war. He had run to her, in
fact, his flicker of hesitation discarded, his question answered,
his real mother certified and found. She, in turn, had not cried
when he had pressed himself to her. Instead she had concentrated
on absorbing his pliable and fleshy warmth, a sensation she had
dreamed for so long. After she had kissed him, on his head and
face and all down his tiny neck, she had looked up at her daughter
and, despite the shame she felt about her thinness and bone-white
pallor, she had stretched out her one good arm again. Her daughter, however, had remained fixed, head bowed, large blue eyes
turned askance, refusing to engage. "Barbara Christine," Violet
had said, but her daughter had taken a step further away, length-
ening the distance from her mother. And in that step, Violet's
long-held fear had begun to transform into truth: the time for
her daughter to come to her had been lost perhaps, never to be
found again. She had looked at her husband, who had raised his
shoulders as if to say there was nothing to be done, and resignedly
she had turned back to her son, finding solace in this child who
had decided he had nothing to forgive, who through his body was
slowly restoring life into her.

The hall clock struck 10:00.

"Time to board?" Neville asked.

"Not yet, my sweet," Violet said. "Sit tight just a little bit more.
Are you excited?"

"Yes. So excited!" Neville said.

"Me too," Violet replied. "Are you a little excited too?" she tentatively asked Barbara Christine.

Barbara did not reply.

Violet asked the question more playfully: "Maybe just a teeny, tiny bit, like a very small crumb for a mouse?"

"Maybe a little," Barbara said, rolling her eyes.

Late that morning, after Violet had fed her children with drinks and snacks from the concession stand, she gathered them together and moved toward the landing stage, a floating platform secured to the riverbank by hinged steel beams that allowed the platform to rise and fall with the tide. The stage was an impressive feat of engineering, Violet pointed out to her children as they stepped onto it from one of five bridges that extended from the two-story passenger hall. The entire area seemed to Violet a mass of wires and nylon ropes, and as they walked, she reminded the children to watch their step and their heads. Above them, bags were being loaded onto the ship in enormous nets that hung from rotating cranes but somehow did not spin. The crew worked diligently before them, making adjustments, turning winches, tying ropes, and affixing chains on hooks. Neville couldn't keep his eyes away from them.

Together they walked up the gangway, Violet again reminding her children to watch their step and Barbara Christine replying that she was ten and could walk just fine. As they stepped onto the ship, a steward asked for their ticket and offered to show them to their bunks. The children stood behind Violet as she rustled through her purse. She had held the ticket only a few minutes before and had tucked it away to be safe, but she feared that she had dropped it along the way. "It's somewhere," she said, feeling stupid and ill prepared. "Oh, here it is," she laughed, as her daughter looked away.

They followed the steward through a labyrinth of passageways until they reached a six-bunk cabin. The children claimed two beds on top and Violet one below. Then Violet asked if the children wanted to find a spot on the ship's deck with a view of the Thames and the docks. Barbara Christine said fine, and Neville said he'd like that very much.

Tilbury lay almost equidistant between England's East Coast and the heart of London itself, and they waited at their perch, watching passengers scurry across the landing stage to their ship like mice. Violet, seeing two lone German immigrants on the quay being sprayed by river mist, felt affirmed in the decision she had made. Those Germans had not an inkling of what awaited them in England, but she was here with her children, en route to a place that she was now trusting would be better for all of them.

At 2:00 pm they left, and as the ship's horn sounded, a tug pulling them out from the docks toward the North Sea, Violet watched the distance grow between herself and London. The ship navigated past the Royal Navy towers, built on squat concrete pillars and narrow stilts, and soon Violet was unable to discern where the open water stopped and the inlet began. Essex and Kent were behind them and Germany ahead, and Violet felt better than she had in a long time.

When the North Sea air grew cold and windy, Violet took the children indoors and found seats for them.

Barbara Christine sat by a porthole, with Violet beside her and Neville to her right. Pressed against the ship, she began to sulk. "Why do we have to go?" Barbara Christine asked, as much to the river bank as to Violet herself.

Violet again ignored that question, pretending that it was not directed at her. For two years, she had tried to be patient, to wait until her daughter came around. She knew how long it had taken her own six-year-old self to accept her mother Anna when Anna had readopted her into her home in London's East End. Anna had been so patient with her, endured her derision and refusal to call her Mother, so attached was she to those two spinster aunts who had raised her illegitimate self, born of a German house cook and British man who had fled England and whom she had never met once and never would. But her mother Anna had waited, and eventually Violet had come around, learning to love her mother, to appreciate her stalwart forbearance and stoic perseverance. They had eventually even grown close. When her mother died of a typhoid epidemic en route to London, Violet had been devastated, crying for days on end. And as Violet had cried over that loss of her mother, so complete, her daughter Barbara had just looked at her, unable to understand why she grieved. That had almost been as devastating as the loss itself, seeing her own daughter so unsympathetic to what losing a mother could mean.

Still, Violet had not given up. Not yet. She was well practiced in waiting, and sitting beside her daughter on the ship now, she continued to try. They had lost so much time during the war, and what little time they had had together since her return had always been so strained. But if she could send her daughter to day school in Düsseldorf and establish a daily routine, become a consistent presence for Barbara Christine, maybe gradually their relationship could be restored. Admittedly, it had not happened yet. On her return from Holland, she had accepted George's insistence that she needed to recover, to get well, before she could live with her children again. After they reunited, she had acquiesced to her daughter's wish to return to boarding school and to look after her daughter only during holidays. Her arm paralyzed, her body prematurely arthritic, she had attended to her daughter with everything she had. During those holidays she had brushed her hair in the morning and tucked her into bed at night. She had told her daughter that she loved her frequently. She had sat by her bed as she slept, and she had often been there, at her daughter's side, when her daughter woke. Although Barbara often had complained that she was babying her, Violet had vowed to continue, so that her daughter could come to understand that her mother was present for her. She waited, just as her own mother had done with her.

Neville tugged at her, asking for a drink from the galley. Where had he learned that term? He was a bright boy for eight years old.

"No, not yet, dear," Violet said, and Neville said, "Alright."

Barbara Christine looked at him and rolled her eyes, as if to say what a stupid remark from a child it was. "How long is this journey?" she asked, reaching out from the island of isolation on which she stranded herself.

"Two days, as I said," Violet replied. "One night, in the bunks. You saw the bunks. Looks like fun, don't you think?"

"Do we get dinner here?" Barbara Christine asked.

"Of course."

"What will they be serving?"

"I don't know. But we shall see, won't we?"

"I guess."

"Isn't this trip fun?" Violet continued, then regretted the question for the negativity it would inevitably draw.

"No," Barbara said, and turned back toward the window again.

Violet reached toward Neville, patted his leg. Patience, she reminded herself. "Is Elephant liking this trip?" she asked Neville.

"Yes, Mummy. He's loving it," he said, and Violet thought how thankful she was for her boy and for the way he had taken to his new life and to her. His embrace at the hotel had been repeated again and again, countless times, and it meant so much to her. Maybe she'd get there with Barbara Christine yet. Violet wasn't perfect, she knew. Perhaps she was too desperate in her attempt to get close. Perhaps she tried too hard to make up for lost time. And yes, sometimes she asked her daughter to share her secrets, and yes, sometimes she discussed those secrets with her friends, but that was what all normal mothers did. They sat and chatted and laughed, and so she did the same, knowing what a rare privilege being a mother was. She only wanted to get close, to be a mother again. And that's what she still wanted now.

At 6:00 P.M., dinner was served. They had sailed all day across the North Sea, drifting through minefields, engines cut to stop vibrations from the ship. They sailed toward the children's father and that boarder who now lived with him, whatever her name was. The ship's crew served pudding, and Barbara Christine was delighted by it. Violet smiled. Nothing compared to being a witness to your child's joy.

They went to bed early, though Violet did not sleep much. She spent most of the night listening to her children's breathing. After Barbara Christine's premature birth, Violet had been sick and was forced to remain in the hospital long after her baby had been sent home. Once Violet had been released from the hospital, George had thought her ridiculous for how often in the night she went to her sleeping baby girl, put her ear to the baby's mouth, and listened to her breathing, but he did not know what it was to carry a child for nine months, then to be separated from her. Frequently at night, when her daughter was home, she lay awake still, not because she feared the breathing would stop but because she took such pleasure in it.

The next day they arrived at Cuxhaven as scheduled, having sailed toward the large, wooden, rocket-shaped lighthouse on the mouth of the Elbe that marked the boundary between the river and the North Sea. The ship docked with a jolt. Violet gathered her children, and they made their way off the *Empire Halladale*. Transit with young children was such a challenging affair—keeping her children close and collecting their bags and finding a porter and a cab for the short trip to the station. Although the children spoke no German, Neville had somehow picked up the word *wunderbar* and repeated it to everyone and everything he encountered. His sweet little British voice was endearing at first, but, like her daughter, Violet soon found his repetition trying.

When they at last found their seats on the train to Düsseldorf and Barbara told him impatiently to stop—"You're driving me mad, and have you even looked around?"—Violet had to agree with her daughter. The landscape was devastating; there was absolutely nothing *wunderbar* about it. "Shocking" was not a strong enough word for the destruction the war had wrought. "Carpet-bombing," while in some respects apt given the sense of entirety the term evoked, suggested a smooth landscape. What lay before them was a junkyard of debris and deprivation. George, of course, had warned her about the decimation of land and lives—55,000 women and children killed in Bremerhaven alone, the first city through which their train went—but she could find no words to describe what she saw. The destruction in London had been terrible, but this—this was far worse. Violet felt sickened by it, by what people did in war.

"And I thought London was bad," Barbara said after thirty minutes on the train.

"Crushing" was all Violet could say.

Once they made it through Bremenville, Violet was struck that Dortmund seemed almost as bad, though she realized that comparing levels of destruction between cities was as pointless as comparing which of two murdered victims was more dead. In Dortmund, the train passed through industrial and residential districts with almost everything flattened beyond recognition, leaving behind a trail of broken remains and toppled wooden frames. Like her daughter, Violet was silenced by what she saw and began counting the minutes before their ride would end.

On the train, whenever her son spoke, Violet felt overly conscious of his British accent and what it suggested of her. She knew as both a German and a British national she could be perceived as either the aggressor or the victim, and her accent rendered it hard to distinguish which was more accurate of her. When asked, she said that she was "Continental European," a term that blurred distinctions. Before the war, she had refused to Heil Hitler, an offense punishable by imprisonment and even concentration camp, but still, she had remained in Germany until 1939, hoping to hold onto what she at last had gained: a home, a family, a legitimacy that as a bastard child she never had been able to claim. In hindsight, some might claim that being content to remain was her sin, if one believed in that sort of thing. What those people did not acknowledge was that history made it easy to cast blame. Had they been in her shoes, what would they have done differently to stop what came? What crime of humanity would history one day tell them they had not fought hard enough against? What were they unwilling to risk, to sacrifice, in the face of their powerlessness? Whose life? Their children's? She doubted it.

George stood waiting for them when they arrived at the terminal at Düsseldorf. He was dressed in his army uniform, and on seeing him, Barbara Christine ran straight into his arms, with Neville close behind. "Daddy!" she yelled. Their separation had been close to two years, and still she ran to him.

"Babs," he responded, using his now pet name for her. "How was the trip?" he asked, kissing his daughter on her forehead.

"Just fine."

"You look well, and so grown up."

"Thank you," Barbara coyly replied.

"And you too," he told Neville as an afterthought.

"Thank you," Neville replied.

When George turned to his wife, she wondered what he thought. She had put her hair up in pins and pressed her wrinkled clothing with her hands before getting off the train, so she presumed she looked respectable enough. But they hadn't seen one another for so long.

"Hello, dear," he said. "You look well." He kissed her on the cheek, and she could not tell if he meant it or not. When he kissed her, she noticed that he smelled of ironed shirts, as he always did, and she could not help but wonder who had been ironing for him. He had put on a few pounds. He must be eating well, too, Violet thought. He was clearly being looked after well.

George introduced his driver, Hans, who was slight, with a big nose and skinny fingers. He was deferential to George, whom he seemed to treat as a superior, the way a lower-ranking soldier might. *So this is how it will be,* Violet thought as George took both his children's hands and walked them toward the car—two porters in tow and Hans leading them toward the car.

The train ride and even the descriptions in George's letters left Violet ill-prepared for what she saw in Düsseldorf on the way to their new home. To see places that had been so familiar razed was heart-wrenching, despite her vow to steel herself. Violet knew the country was without infrastructure, housing, or coal, but she wasn't prepared to see so many undernourished people. They walked the streets dazed, as if the war were still on. Old women carried sawn-up logs for fuel and children appeared out of cellars that were all that remained of their homes. As they drove, Violet wondered whom among them she had known. Was that the local butcher, or that the once-jolly conductor from the tram? They passed so quickly that she could not discern them, swiveling her head here and there, wondering if she, too, would also appear unrecognizable to them.

George sat in the front, narrating as they went. He explained that the British were slowly but surely restoring stability, basic services, and a rule of law. They were having some success in taking over German enterprises as well, and in the current economic recovery plan. He spoke with pride about the responsibility they had for more than twenty million people in the British Zone, and how much improvement there had been.

The house was a welcome surprise. Their former housekeeper, Ilse, greeted them with ruddy cheeks and gave Violet an enormous hug. Ilse had prepared a mountain of teacakes in a sunroom that was light and clean, and Violet felt overwhelmed with appreciation and relief. When Barbara Christine entered the room, she, too, was nearly paralyzed with awe. "For us?" she asked, and Violet exclaimed, "Yes!"

Before they sat down, they finished the house tour, then walked behind the house in a lovely garden with rose bushes and a fish pond. "Behind us lives a little German girl—you're sure to become fast friends with her," George said to Barbara, who said she would like that. He then took them all upstairs, showing the children their rooms and passing quickly by a room he described as belonging to a boarder, whom they would meet "at some point." Violet was glad he had been sensitive enough to ask the boarder to make herself scarce. She was not sure she would have had the strength to maintain her composure just then.

The children remained in Düsseldorf, attending the British army school, for one year. Violet never regretted her decision to come back. Although living in Germany was difficult in many ways, she was relieved to have her family together in one place, untraditional as their arrangement was. Female boarders came and went, and neither Violet nor George explained the women's presence to the children. Housing was so difficult and their home so large that it made sense. They had to live side by side with the Germans, they explained. It was for his ties and for German friendships that George had been employed by the CCG. Still, the rifts created by the war and deepened during the occupation were often hard to bridge. The children rode in open-backed trucks to their school, and German children frequently threw stones at them, so resentful were they of the occupation and all the privileges the British enjoyed—food without restriction, cars with drivers, homes that were fully furnished. Theft was rampant. George slept with a revolver under his pillow, and they triple-locked their doors at night.

George and Violet continued to face challenges, which Violet preferred not to discuss. She recognized that life was better than it had been in a long time, and that they were much more fortunate than most. Her relationship with her daughter had its challenges as well. While Violet still maintained that one had to live in the present and not focus on what had occurred in the past, she remained acutely aware that there was something in her daughter's past that Barbara might never be able to overcome. She was not sure exactly what had happened, but there were things Barbara did and said that did not seem quite right, behavior that vacillated between flagrant disregard for boundaries and deep-seated fear. At home, Barbara would sometimes lock herself in the closet for hours on end when scolded, reappear completely composed, and strike out at her father or mother with a lacerating comment that would send her straight back to her room. Outside the home, Barbara had no compunction about stealing the plumber's bike and riding willy-nilly through town, ringing neighbors' doorbells, making mischief wherever she liked.

Violet did her best to disregard such behavior. *It will pass,* she told herself. *It must.* But sometimes, after a particularly trying day, Violet could not help feeling the guilt of accountability for who her daughter was becoming. When she shared such thoughts with George, he told her she was being absurd. There was nothing they could have done. Their hands had been forced. Still, sometimes, as hard she tried, she began to find that she no longer could keep the "if onlys" at bay. If only she had not insisted that the family join George in Rotterdam. If only she had not gone out to lunch that day. If only she had seen the charabanc before they came to the viaduct so that she had not got into an accident and been infirmed when they had attempted to escape. If only she had insisted that George keep the children with him in London during the war so they were not put on trains and placed in foster homes with people who did not care about them. If only she had gotten out of Holland, somehow. And once the "if onlys" started, Violet found them nearly impossible to stop, for at their source was the knowledge that no matter what she did, she could not make reparations for failing her daughter in the most fundamental way. Ensuring that one's child was safe and secure was the most basic responsibility a mother had. Her daughter, no doubt, would never forgive Violet for her betrayal of that fundamental truth. And Violet was not able to forgive herself either.

What her daughter did not recognize was that Violet understood this. She understood that Neville could accept his mother because Barbara had stood in as mother when Violet herself was interned. She understood that Barbara, only a little girl, had been forced to fulfill a mother's role, by instinct or by default, it did not matter which, when she and her little brother were carted from one foster home to the next. She understood how difficult that role was to relinquish, let alone to one's own mother. And while Violet never explained that she understood—what could one say—she tried her hardest to close the distance and make her feelings felt. She continually told Barbara that she loved her. She told her that she was a great sister. She put her in charge of her brother, as she once had been, despite the trouble she knew they would find, despite the fact that such overtures did not seem to bridge the distance with her daughter, who was still distrustful of her.

By the time Barbara was at the end of her tenth year, the very age when she herself had gone to Germany at the outbreak of World War I, Violet found herself having to accept that the space her absence had created would always remain. Her own mother, now deceased, had closed that gap with her, but for whatever reason Violet had not succeeded in doing the same with Barbara— and she realized with great sadness that she probably never would. So, with resignation, Violet sent Barbara back to boarding school and she remained in Germany without her daughter, despite her long-held wish of at last being with her.

CHAPTER 16

OLD SAYBROOK, CONNECTICUT — 2013

For some clients, the task of recounting the trauma memory is so daunting due to intense emotions such as fear, guilt, and shame that they may engage in hard to identify forms of avoidance to prevent emotionally connecting with the experience. In some cases, avoidance of the memory may include omission of specific details about the traumatic experience. A final common clinical issue that often arises with individuals with PTSD is their thoughts are so focused on the past that they cannot see or experience the future, and thus are, in many respects, stuck in the past. When the trauma itself becomes the core of the person's identity, to the exclusion of other character traits and life experiences, then it can become problematic for the individual to lead a balanced life in which he or she can integrate his or her past traumatic experience with his or her current roles (e.g., friend, parent, career) in life.[55]

"You have to come down here to see how I've put this all together. You need to know," my mother is telling me. It is late summer. My mother is putting the last touches on her personal history, as her doctors recommended. She wants to get it done. She still has her voice, but she can never be certain for how long. Her chronic ailments have returned: eczema, sarcoidosis, infections of the bladder, asthma, bronchitis, and shortness of breath. It is likely only a matter of time before Dr. Love increases her Xanax prescription again.

We children try to help. We increase our parents' financial support. We find a hairdresser and therapists nearby, so my mother does not have to travel into New York City, but she says she cannot switch because the good therapists who know how to address her unique needs are all in New York. We suggest yoga to calm her mind and restore her faltering balance, but she tells us she has no interest in that. We encourage her to join a PTSD support group, but she claims to have nothing in common with the vets. The cause of her PTSD is so different, and anyway, the vets are American, not English like her, and she cannot relate to them at all.

We want her so much to get well and be self-sufficient, but we are coming to see how unrealistic that hope is. An awareness of the effects of her childhood trauma and loss do, to some extent, now explain what I long did not understand. From a distance, I use her PTSD to put a label on behavior that would otherwise be inexplicable. Up close, however, to see and hear and feel the effect of that trauma remains inherently challenging for me.

As my mother struggles to put order to her story, I do too. I have reluctantly come to realize that this story is not going to have the ending I hoped. I wanted to believe that recreating the story might suffice for both of us, that through it we might satisfy a need to air this maternal narrative. But it all seemed so simple in the beginning, like laying tracks cut to fit together on a line. At forty-six, I realize the story is not linear at all.

My mother, however, is not giving up. She still wants to see the story through. She still believes that with her input, we can succeed in getting this story laid out.

On my arrival to see my ill father, he exclaims in his characteristic way, "Elizabeth, hello!" from his favorite chair. The chair is striped in muted pink and moss green, with a supportive back that allows him to get in and out of it more easily.

I give my father a kiss hello while my mother remains crouched beneath the red Georgian mahogany couch, wiping dust from the just-polished wooden floor.

On her hands and knees, my mother tells me that she has not stopped all day, and I reply that she must be exhausted and that it is nice to be there with them.

Head and shoulders obscured by the couch, she responds, "Of course I'm exhausted. I've been going all day," and my father asks my mother to please stop cleaning now that their youngest daughter is here. My mother, in turn, tells him from beneath the couch not to tell her what to do. Backing out from beneath the couch on all fours, she navigates between the coffee table and her small dog that waits loyally by her side. I watch as she uses the edge of the couch to rise to her knees and to her feet. She sets down her rag on the coffee table, scans the room, and exhales in an attempt to manage her breath. I release a barely discernible but deep exhale, steeling myself to persist.

"I have more writing to show you," she announces. She wears her gray sweatpants, another tattered T-shirt, and predictably bright yellow shoes. A skewed picture above the couch catches her eye, and she straightens it.

"Hello, Mom," I reply. I approach her and rest a hand on her shoulder, brushing my cheek to my mother's lips as she reprimands me, asking why after all these years I still kiss like that.

I apologize and tell her that the house looks great.

"Well, I've been working like a Trojan all day. Come on, Phantom," she replies.

Her small white terrier shakes its combed white coat and trails behind her into her bedroom.

I turn to my father, whose health has deteriorated significantly. He is dressed today in his favorite blue blazer and one of his few remaining pairs of pants that is not too big. His face is pale with broken capillaries around his nose. Folds of khaki are bunched beneath his tightened belt, in which he has tucked a pinstriped, baby blue shirt. I worry, as I have so many times, that my father will soon die.

"So wonderful to see you, Elizabeth. How was your drive?" he asks, brushing back his thinning hair with his now consistently shaking palm.

"The drive was easy," I say, as enthusiastically as he asked. "How are you doing?"

"Great," he says.

"Great," I echo, in lockstep, maintaining his charade that everything is fine.

My mother reemerges, announcing her arrival with a fistful of pages and a declaration that she has more writing for me to review, and what a lot of work it has been.

"Barbara, can't you let her put her things away first?"

"Hush, Stephen. I have to get through this." She moves to my side, handing me the pages one by one, releasing them from her arthritic clutch.

"How about you give me the whole pile, Mom," I gently suggest, trying to be patient, kind, and attuned.

"Fine," my mother says, dropping the pages into my hands as if letting go of a great big weight.

Feeling both of my parents gazing at me, I take the pages and set them down on the dining room table. Bending over, I scan them as my parents wait expectantly. The pages are out of order, some in duplicate, some typed, and some in my mother's barely legible combination of cursive and print. On each page, sentences have been inserted and others crossed out. Pages of Neville's writing also have been included, and in the margins of his pages are his sister's edits, correcting her brother on dates and personal details. I wonder whether I will ever be able to make sense of what she has given to me.

"I know it's a bit of a mess," my mother remarks. "Your father has given up." She glances at my father.

He laughs from his chair. "It's so complicated."

"Still, you could try. I've been working very hard on it."

"She hasn't even put away her bag, Barbara."

"Quiet, Stephen. I need someone to go through this." She sits down again and deeply inhales, then exhales a long, slow breath.

I remain standing, wondering what to do next. I attempt to arrange the pages in a semblance of order. I place a numbered insert beside a passage with the corresponding numbered mark.

"That's not the right one," my mother interjects, and, reaching over, she thumbs through the pile and pulls out what appears to be a typed version of the written insertion I have found. "Your father typed some of these. They're easier to read. But he hasn't got through all of them, and he doesn't always get it right."

"I'm trying," my father says.

"He's trying," I repeat in his defense, flipping through the pile, realizing that pages and even whole sections are missing. "Is this all of them?" I ask.

"I have more in my room. I just have to go through them."

The grandfather clock chimes seven.

"Oh, damn it. The salmon," she says.

"Your mother's made an absolutely delicious dinner," my father tells me as my mother darts away.

"Your father always says that," she retorts from behind the Chinese painted screen that separates the small kitchen from the living room.

"Why don't you go and put your things away?" he suggests. "Then we'll eat. You can do this later for your mother. She has a lot to do on it," he adds quietly.

"I heard that. I'm here," my mother says from behind the screen.

I drop my bag in the guest room, and when I emerge I find my father trying to get up. I offer to help, but he insists that he is fine. He slowly rises and, reaching for the cane behind him, makes his way to the kitchen where the small round table has been set. Phantom trails behind him as he shuffles through the living room, which we children have told our mother contains far too many pieces of furniture, making it hard for him to navigate. Many of the pieces are ones my father's mother handed down, pieces from her trip to East Asia when he was young, before his father died. His mother was very wealthy, and he grew up with a silver spoon in his mouth, our mother often told us. His mother never had to learn to drive and had a chauffeur her entire life—unlike her, my mother said. For years, my mother carted around seven children and a succession of Great Danes, Saint Bernards, Irish Wolfhounds and even a Bullmastiff. She loves big dogs and babies. Only in her later years did she turn to Sealyham terriers, like her mum.

Over a dinner of salmon, salad, and French bread, my father asks about his grandchildren. Is our daughter excited about college, has our son decided where he will be going to college, and is our youngest still planning on rowing in high school?

"My father was a rower," my mother interjects. "Stephen, you eat so quickly. Slow down. Elizabeth, get that picture on the coffee table there, the one of my father."

I get up and return with the picture of my grandfather with his large stomach and enormous grin. I hand it to my mother, who glances at the picture before setting it down. "My father was a rower. My brother was a coxswain at Oxford. Your children come from a long line of rowers."

"I know," I say.

"My father was a very bright man. We had a woman, Hilda, who lived with us then. I remember coming back from boarding school to Germany sometime after the war, and Hilda was there. I never could ascertain what she did or why she lived at our house. She wasn't a governess. My mother didn't seem to mind, though. Different times."

"Different times," I say.

"Yes," my mother repeats. She says it is late and time to clear, and I thank her for the delicious meal and help her clean up.

After dinner, she calls me into her bedroom. My father is in the bathroom, carrying out his ablutions before bed.

"I need to speak with you," she says. I walk into the yellow room. Yellow is my mother's favorite interior color—so cheerful, she says.

"When I die, I want you to have this writing desk of my mother's," she begins. "You know I have nothing of my mother's but it. And that fur coat that I got from my sister-in-law of course."

"Yes," I say. "Thank you. It's beautiful."

She points to the pile of writing on the desk. "That's everything so far. I've taken it back from the dining table and put it all together again. I have a little more to do, I admit. I was hoping you could help me sort out what's left."

"Okay," I say.

"I'll do the last bits, but then I'd like you to put it all together and share it with your siblings. You can add what you've got to my writing, if that's better for you. How's your writing going, anyway?"

"Fine," I say.

"Are you actually writing?"

"A bit."

"Well, keep working, and I'll finish my part, and your father can send it all to you, and you can figure it out."

"Sounds good," I say.

"Promise me."

"I will."

My mother is quiet. I know she wants more. She wants me to talk, to share, to hug—but it is late.

"It's all very difficult," my mother remarks.

"Yes."

"Yes," my mother repeats, stroking her own arm. "War is damaging," she adds as my father turns the knob on the bathroom door. "That's what my doctor says. I don't think I'll ever get over it. I'll always have this PTSD. I just have to manage it." She rubs her arm hard, no longer stroking it, and lays it gently across her lap. "This eczema is terrible. I hope you don't inherit it."

"I hope so, too, Mom," I say as my father shuffles slowly into the room. I brush her cheek with my lips and kiss my father's forehead. "Sleep tight," I tell them.

"Don't let the bed bugs bite," my father replies, "and if they do, squeeze them tight and save their blood for another night." My mother has already turned out the light.

I walk to the adjacent room and get into my parents' guest bed, wondering if, when I was young and my mother brushed my soft blond hair into a small spout atop my head, she envisioned a different future with her daughter, with all of us. I wonder if that future included long chats and long walks as we aged and discussions of the most intimate of topics. I wonder if she envisioned us laughing and sipping Earl Grey Tea, our feet resting together on a beautiful ottoman, expensive and hand-stitched, from somewhere far away like the Orient, where my father's mother went and came back with so much. I wonder, when she sits in her home beside a sun-drenched sill with the afternoon light catching the dust in its rays, whether she holds onto the memory of a baby at her breast, suckling, while knowing that time has long passed, and whether she still feels the baby drawing from her. I wonder if, like me, she looks at our feet and remembers the time when her children's feet were so small and delicate that she caressed them in tender disbelief that something so beautiful and unblemished could one day become so cracked, hard, and worn. I wonder whether she too looks forward to us circling back for years to come like kittens brushing up against her skin, taking succor from her warmth as she takes succor from us. I wonder whether my mother's picture is at odds with who we became.

A few weeks later, the finished pages arrive, out of order and still partly in duplicate. I assemble the pages as best I can, sitting on the window seat in my living room and making my way through them. As I read, I am reminded of the graphic novel *Maus* that I read in college by Art Spiegelman, in which the cartoonist interviews his father about his experiences as a Polish Jew and a Holocaust survivor. Spiegelman inserts himself and his relationship with his father into the narrative. I always admired how he did that, seamlessly. I knew I couldn't do it like that. My mother was not a Jew, nor was my grandmother. They were not sent to a concentration camp, even though my step great-grandfather was. Plus I have never been able to draw. But in thinking about that story, I am reminded that the traumas that stem from war are evident in all of us who follow. I think about my own children and how I parent them. My siblings tell me I am anxious about my children, that I worry too much, that I am far too involved in the ups and downs of their lives, carrying their disappointment as if my own. My children also tell me that I am too quickly moved by all that surrounds me and especially by them, even if I never kiss properly and hugging me is like hugging a metal post and I call myself a cold fish. I tell myself that I have to think about how I handle my mother in a different way. I have learned through my work that even a single stable, reliable person in one's life—whether a parent, a teacher, or a neighbor—can help promote resilience, processing trauma, and even with seeking out help.[56] I resolve to be more responsive, more understanding, and more kind. I have to take a little of what I strive to do for my children and do it for my mother as well. I have to accept that if there ever was a proverbial 'elephant in the room,' it is the trauma memory itself, and that research shows that approaching the topic in a sensitive, nonjudgmental, non-dismissive way is the best approach for someone with PTSD.[57]

A few days later my father sends me all that my mother has written, including her adolescence in Germany after the war, how she tore around the city, and how difficult her relationship with her mother remained. He encloses a note. "I thought you might like this," he writes. "Great talking the other day. We love you very much, xoxo Mom and Dad."

BARBARA

IN HER OWN WORDS, 1947 - 1959[58]

Going to school in Düsseldorf was an adventure. We were sent in open-backed army trucks to that army day school. The German children used to wait around corners to throw stones at us. We all became quite proficient at throwing stones back, and we taught ourselves to ride bicycles. I would borrow the boiler man's bike, and, as it was a man's bike, the only way I could get off it was to fall off. Eventually, I succeeded in mastering the technique. How my brother succeeded in learning to ride I do not remember. Soon afterwards, my parents bought us each our own bicycle. I am sure the boiler man must have complained to my father about my using his bike. Once we had our bikes, Neville and I took off at every opportunity to cycle all over Düsseldorf. I do not think my mother knew where we were half the time, and it is surprising we did not get lost. Everything had been completely bombed flat. We thought it great fun to cycle no-handed and to go down all the steps at the British Leave Centers, where there were shopping areas. My brother and I also used to play ring and run—ringing someone's doorbell and running away, until one day we were caught and never did it again. My mother never knew and did not know what we got up to. We had complete freedom and ran wild. My father wore an army uniform, as did everyone in the CCG (the Control Commission for Germany). I am not sure what his rank was then, but he was eventually promoted to Brigadier.

Neville and I stayed at the day school in Düsseldorf for a year. Then, Neville was sent back to Colet Court in London, a prep school. I was deeply envious. I was instead pushed off to a British Military boarding school in the north of Germany in a place called Plön, Schleswig-Holstein, near Kiel. It had just been formed and was called King Alfred School. We slept in dorms of six per room in army cots. Up until then I had not really been taught anything except riding, ballet, French, piano, posture (which was walking with books on my head), and how to be a young lady. Wartime in England did not have much time to worry about education, dentistry, etc., as long as we were safe and away from the bombing. My father was horrified at my lack of education.

I had been devastated to leave England and my beloved school, and I would cry myself to sleep each night. At King Alfred School, we were never allowed to leave during the term time except to go out to lunch or supper, if our parents visited. We had three holidays a year: four weeks at Christmas and Easter and six weeks in the summer. Our headmaster was Mr. Spencer Chapman, an army war hero who had written the book *The Jungle is Neutral* about his escape from the Japanese in Malaysia and how he survived until he was rescued. The teachers were all ex-army, and the school was run on military lines. We were taken back and forth to school at the beginning and end of term in a military train that snaked its way around the British Sector, from Aachen on the Dutch border until it reached Plön, in Schleswig-Holstein (near Kiel). Hamburg was the last stop before Plön. It took all day from Düsseldorf to Plön.

There were six forms, and the first form for eleven-year-olds went from A to G, A being the top. I started in G, but gradually I was moved up a class each term, until I finally ended up in the A class. Life was difficult because the average stay of both teachers and students was two terms, and so one constantly had to make new friends and adjust to new teachers. In the beginning, the teachers were the same. I loved my geography teacher, who was also my riding teacher. He swore like a trooper and treated us all as if we were his troops. Then there was my history teacher, whom I loved too. They both inspired me and had great faith in me.

When I was half-weary through studying for my O levels, the British Government took over running the school from the British Army. As a result, the headmaster left and so too did all the ex-army teachers. I was devastated. I hated my new Geography and Biology teachers and immediately dropped Geography, as he completely changed the syllabus. Then I came down with what was thought to be meningitis and spent three weeks in a German hospital, all on my own, never seeing my parents. As a result, I had to divide my O levels into two different terms. I failed my Biology O level because I hated my teacher, but took it again the next term with a different teacher and passed with flying colors. I remember, the first time I failed, the teacher coming up to me afterwards and saying I had failed on purpose, because she knew I did not like her! I had no answer because it was true.

The school was big on sports, everyone had to play. I was no good at hand-eye sports but was on the house team for track, high jump, riding and breaststroke in swimming. I tried the crawl, but my instructor told me I looked like a battered windmill, and so that was the end of that! I did receive my house colors in riding and was on the reserve team for the school breaststroke!

We lived in Düsseldorf until I was fifteen years old. We had moved to a larger house as my father's rank went up. I was always an outspoken little girl as regards my brother. On one occasion at lunchtime, my brother did something wrong and was told to go to his room without pudding. I immediately spoke up—I was eleven years old—and said to my father, who was overweight, that it seemed to me if anyone should go without their pudding it should be him. He was stunned, but needless to say then sent me to my room too. Many years later, he loved to repeat the story, so I never forgot the incident.

By the time I was taking my A levels, I was the only person left in the school of six hundred who had been there since the age of eleven, and I was tired of having to make new friends all the time, so I left before completing my exams. In retrospect, a big mistake. My father should have made me stay on, especially as I had been told I would have been head girl.

We eventually moved to Hamburg, as the CCG was disbanded and my father went back to his old firm, Price Waterhouse, and this time was sent to Hamburg because of his fluency in German. Hamburg was quite an adjustment, as we were now completely living on the German economy, as opposed to the Army. After leaving King Alfred School, Plön, I took a Berlitz course in French. I learnt to get around the public transport system on my own and had to use my German all the time too. I learnt to enjoy living in Hamburg. I would go to the YWCA once a week, where they had Scottish dancing. Everyone was about my age or older, up to twenty-two. It was great fun. It was a very cosmopolitan society, and my father was a member of the Cosmopolitan Club. I loved going there for meals and social events. It was in a beautiful building overlooking the Ulster. Whenever we had come home for the holidays from school, my father would take us there for lunch. My favorite pudding was Peach Melba. In those days, raspberries were not sprayed and so it was quite usual to find little white worms in them! As my mother had worked in Hamburg before the war, she had numerous German friends whom we would visit.

After I returned from British Army boarding school, I was eventually sent to a finishing school in Arosa, Switzerland. I was seventeen years of age by that point. My father took me to the train, which was a silver bullet and boarded in the evening. My father had booked me a first-class ticket with my own sleeping compartment. Arosa did not allow any cars, so on arriving there, I was met by a horse and sleigh driver, sent by the school, to be taken up to Belri, the name of the school. Arosa is a magnificent resort in the Swiss Alps.

Belri was a one-year-long finishing school for seventeen- to eighteen-year-olds. It was open to all nationalities, and you could speak any language as long as it was not your native one. Every night they would have a roll call, and as your name was called you had to say whether or not you had spoken more than ten words in your native tongue. You either said *non* or *beaucoup*, meaning more than ten words. If that was the case, you could have one privilege taken away, such as being able to ski the next day or going to the cinema the next time they had an outing. The school accepted about fifty girls. Our classes consisted of languages, dressmaking, and cooking, plus skiing lessons in the afternoon. The cooking meant helping the French chef prepare meals and taking down all the recipes on the day. We had classes in the morning and evening, with skiing classes in the afternoon. Initially, I avoided trying French as I found German easier. After a short time, I was told I could only speak French. I enjoyed French, and by the end of the year my teacher wanted me to go on to the Sorbonne, but my father had other ideas. The school was run by an English woman and a Swiss woman. Later I learned that they were gay, but they certainly never bothered us. We were strictly monitored and never allowed to speak to any males.

In the late spring, we travelled to the south of France, to Menton, via Lugano in the Italian part of Switzerland. To me, Lugano was the most beautiful city, situated as it is on Lake Lugano. Palm trees were everywhere. There were open-air cafés and restaurants. We stayed in a youth hostel before moving on by train to Menton. There the school took over a small family hotel overlooking the Mediterranean. There was a road between the hotel and the beach. When it was our day to help the chef, we would get up early to go to the food market, to be with the chef while he bought fresh produce. I used to love those mornings. We spent three months in Menton, studying the history of art, all in French. In the afternoons, we would walk along the coast to Monte Carlo. The coast was breathtaking, completely free of buildings. Other times, we would go to Nice or up into the mountains. It was a wonderful three months.

At the end of the time, we were taken to Italy to visit Florence, Rome, and Venice and to see all the art we had been studying in

Menton. We travelled by train and stayed in hotels. We walked everywhere in crocodiles. One teacher walked at the front of the line with a rolled-up newspaper, and one walked at the end with another rolled-up newspaper. Whenever any Italian approached us, they would use the rolled-up newspapers to swat them. We found it all hilarious, as I am sure the men did too. The Italians found all these seventeen- and eighteen-year-olds irresistible. When we travelled by train, girls would have to take it in turns to keep their feet up on the carriage doors to keep them closed and therefore prevent the men from coming in. The trains all had separate compartments along a corridor. For lunch, we would be taken to a little bistro and had the choice of minestrone or gelato. That was it for lunch. In the evening, we ate at our hotel. After the tour, we all went home. The only holiday we had was at Christmas.

After finishing school, my father sent me to St. James Secretarial School in London. To begin with, I lived in a YWCA, but after a while I had to move and so found another hostel, before I settled in a house owned by one of the owners of the school. It was on Gloucester Rd., where she rented out rooms to students. I made some good friends and loved living in London. At first I found bookkeeping and shorthand impossible, but eventually I conquered it and did very well. It was a nine-month course, although, while there, I had to take a break of a few weeks to get my gallbladder removed, at nineteen years old, in Bath, Somerset. I spent three weeks in the nursing home and two weeks at home in Frankfurt (where my father had been transferred from Hamburg). I then went back to St. James, where I finished the course.

After completing it, I did some temporary work in London before deciding that I should try living at home for a while, as I had always been at boarding school. I was offered a job at IBM in Frankfurt when it was just starting off, but turned it down. I then worked for about six weeks for the minister of the American Episcopal Church. It was not a happy period. I did not like my boss. I was then offered a job at the British Consulate General, which I accepted. I began working in a secretarial pool, but then moved up to be secretary to two men in the commercial division. I was twenty years old. I enjoyed working there and made some very good friends, particularly with a secretary named Althea, ten years older than me. Althea and I did everything together. I started leading a very social life.

I never developed a close relationship with my mother. I would sometimes wake up in the morning and find her sitting next to my bed, asking me to give her a kiss. I found this truly irritating. Sadly, she always wanted to find the little girl she had been parted from all those years ago, but that little girl was no more. Life had changed me, as I had learnt to survive on my own and no longer related to her. It was sad for both of us.

During my time at the Consulate, I met my future husband, Stephen, who was in the US Army doing his two years' service. I met him at twenty years old, and he came to my twenty-first birthday party. In August of that third year, he asked me to marry him, but I was not ready and turned him down. After I told my mother that I had turned Stephen down, she became very upset. Later she tried to commit suicide with an overdose of pills. Our German G.P. was called, and she was saved. After this incident, the G.P. called me to his office. Then he told me in no uncertain terms that he did not care whether I married the man or not, but if I decided not to I could never live at home again and had to leave. I was twenty-one years old and was stunned. I thought about it and was determined it would not influence me in my eventual decision. This, however, was the last straw in my relationship with my mother.

I really did not want to marry an American and leave Europe. Stephen returned to the U.S. in September. After he left, he arranged to have flowers delivered to me every Saturday. At first I thought it was a one-time thing, but then, every Saturday, they kept coming. He wrote me every day, and I wrote back. In December, I gave up working and took the S.S. *United States* to New York City to see him and meet his family. While there, we became engaged. Then I returned to Europe.

We were married in April 1959 at the Episcopal Church in Frankfurt and had our civil ceremony at the British Consulate General. We spent our honeymoon in Portugal and returned to Hartford to begin married life together.

CHAPTER 17

OLD SAYBROOK, CONNECTICUT — 2015

Whether you witnessed or experienced violence as a child or your caretakers emotionally or physically neglected you, when you grow up in a traumatizing environment you are likely to still show signs of that trauma as an adult. Children make meaning out of the events they witness and the things that happen to them, and they create an internal map of how the world is. This meaning-making helps them cope. But if children don't create a new internal map as they grow up, their old way of interpreting the world can damage their ability to function as adults.[59]

The doctor has told my father unequivocally that he will soon die of heart disease. He does not want to go. He is leaving my mother with nothing, save a $10,000 death benefit, which my brother has somehow procured for him. When he thinks no one is looking, he winces in a way I have never before seen. He is attached to an oxygen tank and will uncharacteristically curse when the cord gets caught at corners and on carpets. He says he hates being confined to the house. In the middle of the night, I find him, still attached to his tank, at the kitchen table, flipping through bills, endlessly combing back his hair with his frail hand, his breathing labored, his body frail.

"You okay?" I ask.

"Fine. Just figuring a few things out," he says.

I am forty-eight years old. We children have been alternating visits in the last few months of his life. My mother, near eighty, looks surprisingly well, younger than her years, particularly compared to my father.

Up until this point, I have always seen my father as the selfless one, the calm one, the one without a temper, the spouse who does everything to meet the other spouse's needs. But during this time, when my father cannot care for himself, I see a different mother and a different wife, one without concern for herself who is dedicated solely to meeting her husband's needs and who is placid and calm with us. When I visit, my mother does not mention her past or her lack of money or that it is spring and she needs to buy annuals for her beds. She has no apparent need of doctors or new clothes. She drives herself to the pharmacy to get my father's medications. She cooks food for him when he says he is hungry and removes his plate when he says he cannot eat. She walks a straight line, is even-tempered, and her voice is consistently strong. She remains always near him. She shows no signs of her PTSD.

In contrast, my father loses his temper with me for the third time in my life. I have opened one of his bills without permission to see what money he owes and whether we children might have to pay. In a raised voice, he tells me that opening his mail is not my right. I apologize and go to the hardware store to buy him a new pad for a cane that he will never get to use. On my return, he apologizes to me.

"I'm sorry, Elizabeth," he says, as we sit on the sun porch, the closest he has come to sitting outside in half a year. "It's just hard as an optimist to accept things, especially death."

"We all have to," my mother replies. "And you will too."

Obstinately, he looks away.

The fact is that as an eternal optimist, my father is having a hard time accepting death. In the past, my father has always, against the odds, found a way. Despite his succession of life-threatening illnesses and ever-growing financial strain, he has survived. When he underwent treatment for testicular cancer and was told he would be sterile, he impregnated his wife and she gave birth to me. When his heart first started to falter and he had a pacemaker inserted, his heart again became strong despite his lack of fitness. When his aortic valve failed and that pig's valve did not take, his

mechanical valve proved a good substitute. When his heart weak-
ened further still and he received a bypass, he again recovered.
When he was diagnosed with pancreatic cancer, stage three, he
became one of the single-digit percentage of people who survive
more than five years. Throughout, he persevered, through remov-
als of melanomas with blood that was too thick and, once medicated, too thin. We children always said he had more lives than
a cat, and he always laughed in response, telling us that life was
great, our mother was fantastic, and he was a very fortunate man.
He always told us that he loved us very much. But what buoyed
him most was always our mother. Whenever he was recovering in
his hospital bed from a surgery, it was enough for him to see her
arrive in an unfamiliar hat placed delicately aslant, a new designer
pantsuit, and a pair of half-inch heels that he had never before
seen. "Hello, Toots!" he would say, smiling despite the exhaustion from the chemo or the searing incision across his stomach or
chest. My brother will one day share with me that as he lay dying
in his bed, my mother will enter his room shirtless with only her
bra and shimmy for him. He will laugh and lovingly repeat her
name, even though he has not spoken and been unresponsive for
some time. "I thought you needed that," she will say.

Those final few days of his life, my father refuses death. He
holds his lips tight so that the hospice nurse is not able to feed
him his morphine. He tells my mother that morphine is an acceptance of death and he will not agree to it. My mother replies that
when the time comes, she will have to give it to him. He does
not respond. His face is a skull, his skin a thin, yellowed sheath
pulled taut over his head like a suffocating plastic bag. His sunken
eyes are too small for their sockets. His thin lips are parched. He
says his room is filled with spirit animals beckoning to him. He
has long ago lost his faith when, during his second open-heart
surgery, his heart stopped and he saw black. "No light, no heaven,
just darkness," he told my mother, his wife. Toward the end of
his life, he has started to go to church again but he still does not
believe in God in the traditional sense. When I ask him why he
has returned, he tells me that God to him is family and that,
at church, he finds a way to connect through thoughts of us to

something bigger than himself. He still does not believe in the afterlife. He says that when he dies he will join the earth as dust, and that will be the end for him.

Just before he dies, we children gather at our parents' condo, slipping noiselessly in and out of his room. Though his eyes are closed, each time one of us enters his room he knows. The corners of his lips rise, and he harnesses all of his energy in greeting us. When we all arrive that last time, he asks for celebratory champagne in his room. Although he cannot drink, he raises his glass shakily and gives a toast, finding joy in us.

Just a few minutes earlier, his nails began to turn black and the hospice nurse declared that he was dying at last. But with his toast, his nails reveal pink flesh still living beneath them. "You must stay out of his room," the hospice nurse chides us. "He won't accept death as long as he has you."

It is at that point that I decide I have to let go. I reenter his room one last time and lean down to hug him, to tell him I love him, to say goodbye one last time, knowing my long-held fear has come, that death will soon take him from me.

In response, my father tries to rise. "I love you. Don't go. I'll drive you," he says.

"You can't, Dad," I say.

"I will drive you," he insists, with the little strength he has left.

I tell him goodbye, repeat "I love you," and, crying in my car, I leave.

But over the years, the image that remains most pronounced for me remains that of my mother, lying next to my father in his small hospice bed. The nurse has told her that she has to stop going into his room to rest beside him. The children are difficult enough, but her presence makes it impossible for him to die. Still my mother goes to my father, and over the remaining weeks of her husband's life, I will often find her lying beside him in his room. During that time, she carries water to him when he asks, and just as assuredly she takes it back when he tells her he cannot drink. She raises his bed when he requests and lowers it when he asks her why she is raising it. She wears gray sweatpants and lies barefoot beside him for hours at a time, stroking the thinned hair on his head and saying it will be okay. She tries to close the already shut windows tighter when he says the outside air is trying to get in, and she opens the windows when he says he has to get the stale inside air out. When the need for morphine comes, when he is struggling too hard to breathe, she syringes him with morphine because he will not acquiesce to the nurse, only to her. She says she loves him over and over again, and he replies, "You are the love of my life," over and over again, and when she finally agrees to the nurse's demand that she stop entering his room, he dies.

For the year after his death, my mother does not cry. "I'll be fine. I'm a survivor," she says. But eventually she begins to fall into the familiar spiral of debt, and we children increase our financial support in a futile attempt to put a stop to it. When her dog Phantom dies, my mother grows worse. She cries as we children have never before seen her cry. She complains of her health, of her PTSD, of being left destitute. She loses her balance completely. "It's all too difficult," she tells her children. "This childhood PTSD." When she gets a new Sealyham terrier, she shows improvement at last. She calls me right away. "I have someone to care for again," she says. "His name is Romeo. Romeo, Romeo, wherefore art thou, Romeo? He makes me laugh so." Her psychologist issues her a letter, explaining to whom it may concern that he has worked with this patient for many years and this emotional support dog is necessary for her on all forms of public transportation because of her mental health diagnosis that includes anxiety and PTSD. She reads the letter to me. Isn't this wonderful, she says.

I finish the history. I realize that aside from the writing desk and the fur coat, the details of her youth are all that she thinks she has left to share with me. But despite what her mother and the mothers before her have endured, I know that she and my father have given me and my siblings so much more. My parents together have succeeded in raising seven children who attended good colleges, earn decent livings, are resilient, and have confidence in themselves. My father may have believed my mother always looked after him, even if to us children, it always looked to be him looking after her, but I will at last understand that both were always true, in different ways and at different times. And between a negative and a positive charge, what really matters is the force of the attachment they together give.

My children have done okay. My daughter has graduated with an Ivy League degree in government and psychology. She is the granddaughter of a woman without a college degree, the great-granddaughter of an illegitimate wartime survivor, the great-great-granddaughter of a German house servant. When I tell her I'm depressed, she tells me that I've used the wrong term. "You worry about the future, Mom. You are anxious, not depressed. I have a tendency to be anxious too," she says. "But we will be okay."

As I age, I, like my mother, will sometimes struggle. In the dark, I will sometimes wonder about the purpose of my life and why I carry on. *For my children*, I will tell myself.

And I will come to see in my mother both courage and strength. I will see that she has never been afraid to have her nakedness exposed. I will recognize that while she has always wanted me to listen to her stories, she also has given them to me to write, despite how she might be perceived, for she always has believed in their power and her strength as a mother. I was given these stories and so much else from her. I read a passage by the National Child Traumatic Stress Network about families and caregivers.

> Parents and caregivers play an essential role in helping children and teenagers recover from traumatic events. . . . The more caregivers learn about how traumatic events affect their children, the more they understand the reasons for their children's behaviors and emotions, and the better prepared they are to help them cope. When children know that caring adults are working to keep them safe and support them in understanding their reactions to trauma, most can recover and go on to live healthy and productive lives.[60]

I think about the fact that perhaps, if I swap the words parents and caregivers with children, the reverse also holds true: children can help their parents recover. It is complicated. It is hard. But with this approach, maybe I can begin to understand my mother more and in so doing, help her.

And so I reimagine my mother when I was twenty-four, before I knew what it was to love and raise children, before I could begin to imagine what it was to be a mother to children when you were never parented yourself.

BARBARA CHRISTINE

LONDON, ENGLAND, 1991

Barbara Christine's favorite restaurant front was marine blue with gold trim and an ivory awning that mechanically opened by draping steel-link chains. The restaurant's hand-painted oval sign hung from a narrow wrought iron bar with an arrowhead at the tip. The restaurant was located on Walton Street in Chelsea, an area that had once been billed as the Victorian artists' colony but had long since become a draw for the well-heeled. Bookended by Harrods and The Conran Shop, the street was an enclave of antique shops, art galleries, and home interior stores that included a store specializing in English lamps and another that sold mono-grammed linens. Barbara liked English lamps and cream-colored, bell-shaped, silk shades. Her interior sense was characteristically English. She also liked chintz and was not afraid of color or mixing patterns. Her husband, Stephen, had often observed that she was talented in decorating. No one could make a home as nice as theirs, but then no wife was as beautiful as his, no mother could run a family the way she did, and no woman was as well-read or well-informed. No dessert was better than the one she had just served.

Tony was the maître d'. When Barbara entered in her blue Armani jacket and pencil-line skirt for dinner with her daughter and her daughter's boyfriend, Tony kissed her on both cheeks. Her husband, Stephen, followed behind. "Mrs. Wilcox, *buonasera*." "*Buonasera*, Tony."

Stephen had now sold the flat, and Elizabeth had moved into her boyfriend's place. The boyfriend had first met her husband at this same bar the year prior, without a tie and with a drink already poured. Stephen had been reserved with Elizabeth's boyfriend, whom she actually quite liked. Barbara later explained to Elizabeth that her father had seen her elder sister's charismatic ex-fiancé in him, the one who had postponed the wedding and wanted her to convert to Catholicism for him. Big mistake that would have been. The Catholic Church was so patriarchal. The Church of England was so much better. Not so male. Anyway, she had decided her daughter Elizabeth should know why Stephen was reserved with this boyfriend of hers. It all had to do with sexual mores, which Stephen also had been funny about until he met her. "But don't worry what your father thinks," Barbara had assured her daughter. "He's a Puritan at heart. He'll come around."

The four of them sat tonight at one of the round tables on the perimeter of the yellow room, near the Picasso prints on the wall. Tony knew the seat that *Signora* liked, the one from which she could watch the entering patrons and what they wore. He also knew both the dish she preferred and the one that, on a whim, she would order instead.

"The escargot tonight or the *sogliola alla griglia?*"

"I think I'll do the escargot. *Grazie*, Tony."

"*Grazie*," he returned.

"I'm not quite with it," she explained to no one in particular. "Adjusting to the time change. And I haven't slept well the last two nights. The Overseas Club is not the same, not the same as having your own place." She looked away from her husband, who sat on the opposing side of the linen tablecloth that the waiter had just de-crumbed with a few swipes of a polished metal blade.

Barbara was finding it difficult to be in London without the flat. The sale had happened so fast. She had not been prepared for it. She had loved that flat, which was in Knightsbridge and overlooked a garden square to which all residents were given a key. The garden had white pebble paths, immaculately maintained flowerbeds, a tennis court, and a closely shorn lawn with a sign that said "No Playing with Balls." The location was really ideal. Hyde Park was within walking distance, and Sloane Street ran parallel to them. Harrods was two blocks away, with its enormous food halls and pulsating clothing floors. Around the corner was a well-stocked grocery store that sold smoked salmon and fresh bread daily. Delicious.

"Elizabeth, you liked playing tennis there, didn't you?"

"Where? What?" Elizabeth asked.

"At the flat."

"Oh yeah," Elizabeth said. "It was nice."

Barbara was still upset about having to sell. It was a leasehold, and there had been only seventeen years left on the lease, so her husband had claimed that keeping it made no sense, as the brick Dutch Victorian would soon revert to the Cadogan family and be valueless to them. But that was beside the point, Barbara had explained to both her husband and her children. Their father had promised her a flat, a place she could call her own in England, and now he had rescinded on that. She was not an American and never would be. Her children knew that.

"They kept it up so well," she observed.

"Yeah," Elizabeth said.

Barbara often reminded her children that living in London had been the most contented time in her life, and she would tell her children that same thing for years to come, blaming the sale for the start of what turned out to be a steady decline. Prior to living in the flat, when she and their father had rented a three-story townhouse on Camden Square, they had eaten out frequently and driven each weekend to a small cottage in Derbyshire. The thatched-roof cottage was on the edge of a vale near the Chatsworth estate, and in the evenings they lit fires and sipped white wine beneath exposed beams. The local shop sold fresh Bakewell tarts, and Barbara had been so happy then that sometimes she even thought she'd cry in delight.

When the flat had come up for sale in Cadogan Square and she and Stephen decided they would buy, Barbara had been happier still. So excited was she that, when Stephen wavered, Barbara had told him that he could use the ten thousand pounds her father had left her to purchase it. Admittedly the flat cost much more than ten thousand pounds, and arguably the capital had already been spent, but over time the interest the capital accrued would have gone some way toward the purchase. Anyway, the point was that she had made what little contribution she could, with what little money she had, the only money that had ever been her own, and now it had been taken from her and she was finding it extremely difficult to accept. It had been her dream. She was not afraid to share that fact with her children. With the sale of the flat, her dream had been taken away.

"Fizzy or still?" the waiter asked.

"Fizzy, please," Barbara said.

No, she had not wanted to leave. While she still loved coming back to London, returning was hard. She liked the choices one had in Europe, which she missed in the States. One always had the options of still or fizzy, and still water did not automatically come with ice.

"It always takes a few days to adjust," Elizabeth's boyfriend was assuring her now.

"Yes," she agreed. "But I do love coming back. Life was good here."

Then she thought, *Well, until Bob took over and squeezed Stephen out.* But she refrained from sharing that with her daughter and her daughter's boyfriend. Her husband would not appreciate her mentioning that fact or the fact that, having been relocated in order to set up a permanent London office only six years back, he had succeeded in generating more revenue for the company than the home office ever had and yet still he was pushed out. A travesty. Of course, her husband had not fought the decision or tried to stage a coup. He never did. A peach of a fellow, too kind, too quick to accept his fate. She had known at the time that it was the wrong decision. But when he took the money his deceased mother had willed him and proposed moving back to the small place they owned in Vermont, to set up his own business there, she did not feel she could say no. He wanted it so much. Though her children thought she was tough on him, she actually was far more supportive than they realized. She did not get involved in his financial decisions at all.

"Well, you've arrived to terrible weather," the boyfriend noted.

"Yes, dreary," Barbara affirmed. She wanted a pleasant evening, like everyone else. "My mother hated it here. She hated English plumbing and English weather. I do love England, though." She quoted, "'Oh to be in England, now that April's there.' That's Robert Browning. I could recite you more."

"She knows so many poems," Stephen said.

"I didn't have much of an education, but I know my poems. And I do miss England."

"But you get to visit quite a lot," the boyfriend pointed out. "And Vermont is so beautiful."

"It is," her husband said.

Barbara refrained from saying that Vermont had always been her husband's dream, not hers. In making his argument to move there, he had explained that he'd had enough of city life, that he wanted to listen to the peepers at dusk and to walk at night beneath the bright starlit Vermont sky, to slow down life a bit. He was so sentimental, and she had indulged him in his dream. In exchange, though, he had promised that she could keep the flat and visit a few times every year, to see her brother and her friends and to get her hair highlighted by Jean Michael. It was one of many barters they had made. "I do this, and in time you will get that." She had always wanted to believe that those trades would pay off. She had always wanted to find that all she had given up had been replaced by something better, that she had made the sacrifice for him and still in the end had benefited as well. But she was finding it hard to have confidence in future outcomes anymore.

"Tell me about the new house, Barbara," the boyfriend was continuing. "Elizabeth says you've done a beautiful job. I hope to get there soon."

"It's been a lot of work," Barbara said.

"It's fantastic," her husband said.

"It's been a lot of work," she repeated. "But thank you. It's getting there."

Since moving into the big house, the smaller house had been partitioned off and sold to friends, who in relocating the pond had buried Barbara's Rock. A sadness that Elizabeth got particularly upset about, but as she often told her children, you just had to get on with life. Barbara was a realist at heart. The new pond was being stocked with trout; beneath the spot for the clay tennis court was an apple tree, under which one could spot the tracks of an occasional bear; the porch was going to have much better views of Bromley Mountain to the west; and there was so much space now for the children and grandchildren to stay. In the summer, Stephen was going to keep the grass long on the approaching hill, with the exception of a meandering path he would mow so the grandchildren could feel lost in it. It was the right decision to build the new house, despite what Elizabeth said. The children and grandchildren would love it when they came home. So much better for all of them.

Her husband nodded to the departing waiter to refill his wine. He had lost weight since relocating back to the States. His jowls had lessened a bit, and his combed-back hair was thinning and dark, with only a hint of gray at the temples. He was wearing his favorite navy blue, pinstripe suit, having met some former colleagues that day. Those colleagues had asked him to join their new business years back, but he had declined, not wanting to betray his employer. He now agreed with her that he should have joined them when he had the chance. He was loyal to the end, and for that loyalty he had received nothing but a knife in his back. It angered Barbara, thinking about it. She had no place for his optimism. She had lived long enough to know that, should she anticipate too much, disappointment would inevitably win out.

"This wine is delicious," Stephen said.

"Yes, quite good," the boyfriend agreed.

Her husband was incapable of thinking that his business would not be a success, that the fax and the phone would not hide the fact that his office sat in an abandoned train station on a long-defunct Vermont track in an almost-abandoned, rural town. Though beautiful in its way, Vermont was such a provincial place. Had he been able to listen, she could have warned him, instead of allowing him to invest so much in it.

"It must be good to be back in the States," the boyfriend was saying. "You get to see your children and your grandchildren as well. There must be a lot of snow there right now."

She appreciated that he was trying hard to make her see the positive, jollying her along. No doubt he had been cued by Elizabeth as to her feelings about the move and the selling of the flat and the precariousness of it all, but Barbara didn't want to be persuaded by him or by anyone else. She would come to terms on her own time, at her own pace. So be it.

"It's been so cold and rainy here," he continued.

"Yes, it is wonderful in Vermont," Stephen offered. "Really wonderful up there. There's no sky with brighter stars, and there are no city lights. Our grandchildren have already visited twice. Barbara is skiing all the time."

"Not all the time. You exaggerate," she said. "The house requires a lot of time."

"Yes, yes, it does. You've done a fantastic job. Elizabeth's mother is spending a lot of time on the house. This winter, she skied with her friend Ann from next door, maybe three times a week? Is that right?" he asked.

"Twice. In the mornings. I got a special Vermont rate. It saves money. Your father has decided he can't ski anymore."

"I couldn't keep up. She is so good now. You should see her shoot down the mountain. No one can keep up."

She smiled, appreciating his remarks. He did try.

"I didn't start skiing until I was twenty-one," she said. She might as well share a bit with them. "I practiced every weekend when the children were young. We took them up every weekend to Vermont, and I learned as they did. It was a lot of work. Not many people learn as adults. I, of course, didn't have the opportunity to learn to ski when I was young, like you children." She motioned toward her daughter. Together, she and Stephen had tried to give their children the best childhood they could. They had always agreed on that.

"Elizabeth's mother is very determined," Stephen observed.

"I set my mind to things and do it," she said. "I am very determined, aren't I, Elizabeth?"

"Yes, you are," Elizabeth said.

"That's your mum," Barbara said about herself.

Stephen gave her an affirming look. Barbara took a sip of her fizzy water and cleared her throat.

"That must be fun for you. Being able to ski, living in Vermont," Elizabeth's boyfriend observed. "I'm sure it's beautiful."

He had drifted into hyperbole, and she decided to correct him. "The builder has done a cheap job on our house, though. I wouldn't use him again."

"It's a fantastic house," Stephen said.

"And winter is a very cold time of year," Barbara countered. Her husband liked to sugarcoat everything.

"But the days are getting longer now. Winter solstice has passed. It's almost full-fledged spring," he said.

"Your father always says that," she replied, looking at Elizabeth again.

"I know. That's what we love about him," Elizabeth responded, and her father smiled at her. They had always had that special little bond.

Barbara looked out toward Walton Street. It was dark outside, but the street was well lit. Stephen had been trying to get the business going for eighteen months. He had promised that he would give it no more than three years, and Barbara really was doing her best to be patient, not to let her resentment grow. He had three people working for him, but he still could not pay himself. Her daughter had no idea. The children never did. When the children were growing up, she had assumed the role of disciplinarian, allowing him to take the place of the favored one if that's what her children needed, which some of them did.

"It sounds lovely. I hope to see Vermont sometime," the boyfriend said.

"We hope you do too," Barbara said politely.

The food arrived. Stephen remarked on how delicious it looked and ordered another bottle of wine.

"Is the business going okay?" the boyfriend asked after the entrées had been served.

Barbara waited to see how her husband would reply.

"Coming along," Stephen replied. "Coming along."

Barbara sighed. His prospects did not seem to be improving, but she kept her views to herself. She had a limited knowledge of what her husband did, not because she could not grasp it but because business did not interest her much at all. She preferred to discuss history and current events and the books she read. She knew her husband's business provided services to so-called "American Names" who were investors in syndicates that were part of the insurer of insurers, Lloyd's of London. It was all so boring. Stephen had explained to her on several occasions that he secured for these Names the necessary documentation of their wealth and managed the Lloyd's relationship for them. In Britain, Names were extremely rich. They weren't her set, though she wouldn't have minded if they were, or even if her American husband had been British and one of those rich Names. As it was, though, when he had launched the business, she'd had her reservations about providing services to them—about all of this, in fact.

Stephen had his reservations now too. She could see that. He would not directly express his worry to her, but after more than thirty years of marriage he did not have to speak. She could read him through his level of restlessness. He never could sit still long, always jingling the change in his pocket or pulling out his hanky to blow his nose. That drove her crazy. In the mornings, she could hear him blowing his nose from the bedroom. He had a deviated septum. He should have had his nose fixed as a child, but he never bothered with self-improvement like that. He hadn't been allowed to be a pilot in the army because of that nose. He'd had to be a sharpshooter and a decoder instead. He'd hated being a sharpshooter. It wasn't a talent he wanted. He was concerned now though. She could tell. He was getting up from meals before she was done, visiting the post office even when he'd already checked the mail that day. She was trying her best to persevere, as she always did, but she was getting worried about their future too. She'd always felt rootless as a child, and she was beginning to feel untethered again.

"It must take a while," the boyfriend was saying. "Any business requires a few years' investment." The boyfriend was young and in finance. He was a stockbroker, as her husband had been. He was only twenty-five, had been only three years in the workforce. One thought one knew so much then.

"You're right," Stephen said. "Precisely." His eyes crinkled into a smile, exchanging a knowing glance with his wife as if to say, *They are young, aren't they?*

Barbara held her silence in respect for her daughter. Three years. Did her husband remember the promise he had made? Less than eighteen months left. He had never told her that he wouldn't be paid during that time. In setting up the business, he had said it could be big, make a lot of money for them. He had assured her that the only way the business wouldn't work was if some big catastrophe hit, and even then they weren't investing in Lloyd's, only helping those who did. The risk was limited, he said. But no income? He had never told her that. Still, for all Lloyd's history, the Names had more or less been fine, their assets safe. He had assured her of that, so Barbara had reluctantly agreed. What else could she do? What choice did she have? It was what her husband wanted to do. Lloyd's did seem to offer easy money for its Names. In serving them, perhaps there would be easy money for them as well. Money begetting money, as big money so often did. It had always seemed so unfair to her—the rich getting richer—but that was the way it was. Why not reap rewards from it? She wanted to keep living the way she did, continue returning to London, even if the flat had now been sold. Business was Stephen's affair, not hers. But she had never anticipated all the money that would be required, the drain that in eighteen short months the business had become. He hadn't warned her of that. She just wanted to feel secure. She deserved that.

"And that Long Tail at Lloyd's that everyone is talking about?" the boyfriend was asking now.

The Long Tail was some term that Stephen and now Elizabeth and apparently even the boyfriend used that had to do with insurance risk that just went on and on and on and that could be hard to stop. She wasn't really interested in it. She wished the boyfriend would stop. She liked him—he was charming and kind, and he loved her daughter, she had seen that from the start, in the way they held hands in front of her on the street the first time they'd gone out. "I can see you're keen on one another," she had remarked to her daughter when they returned to the flat. Elizabeth had blushed, and Barbara had known then that the affair was not short-term. Mothers have a sense for that. They do. She had decided that he was the type of man she'd pick for her daughter. Quick to forgive, at ease, and able to make her daughter laugh. Her daughter had a tendency toward morose detachment. Her daughter could be insensitive and cold, but she accepted her children for what they were.

"That business will get sorted out," the boyfriend was continuing.

Her daughter was looking at him, besotted, proud. They were living together now. Despite his initial reservations, Stephen had decided that he liked the boyfriend, too, but he was not supportive of Elizabeth living with him. He had never told this to Elizabeth, but it was the reason he had never visited the boyfriend's flat. He could not condone his daughter living with him. That Puritan in him again. To be fair, she also was only twenty-three, and he didn't want to see her hurt. He was a great father, though. Barbara had always told her children that. So often, though, she'd had to convince him to permit the children to be free. Parenting to her had to be a gradual letting go, a slow push from the nest. He had always wanted to keep them close, but she was a firm believer in fostering independence so that they could learn to stand on their own two feet. It helped them grow. She knew that, even if they did not.

"Lloyd's has been around for so many years." The boyfriend was offering his views. "An institution like that doesn't just collapse. These syndicates reinsuring one another and then reinsuring themselves to create not just a Long Tail but a spiral of risk. That shouldn't have happened."

Stephen was silent, letting him talk.

Then Elizabeth began to interject, showing her father what she knew. "The asbestosis claims are just getting worse. And the Superfund sites. They need regulations in place. It's a spiral of catastrophic risk, and reserves aren't meeting claims. Some Names are getting hit so hard."

Elizabeth was a reinsurance journalist now in London. Her father was proud of that, but he was proud of all his children. They were fantastic to him. Barbara was finding all this talk of business incredibly boring. She'd just bought a new Armani jacket. Armani was so talented. No one matched him.

"What do you think, Stephen?" the boyfriend asked.

Stephen bristled at the boyfriend's use of his first name. He still was not comfortable with the familiarity. "Lloyd's will get sorted out," he said.

Barbara watched as a woman entered the restaurant wearing a fur coat. She had taken hers out of storage but decided not to bring it to London on this trip. Maybe she should have. In the summers, it was important to keep fur protected from the heat and humidity. Maybe she would bequeath hers to her daughter. It had been her mother's, one of the few things she had from her mother; Neville's wife had given it to her. That and the writing desk. Maybe she'd give her youngest daughter both. She needed to ask Elizabeth how her history was going. She was a little apprehensive about what she would produce. Elizabeth always wrote such depressing work. It was as if she were trying to make her parents cry. Her husband always cried when he read her work. Barbara was much tougher than that, on account of her childhood and what she had endured. She wondered if her daughter would like the fur coat. She probably wouldn't look after it. Her daughter wasn't attentive to things like that.

Barbara took another bite as Elizabeth spoke of the damn Long Tail again. Barbara was quite bored by this conversation. It was almost putting her to sleep. "I don't see how it's going to get sorted out," Elizabeth said. "All the asbestosis and those Superfund sites." Business talk. Honestly, Barbara could add nothing to the conversation. It was stultifying, really. She had no insights, so why get involved? She just wanted not to go broke. Was that too much to ask?

"How many syndicates are affected? Over a dozen now?" her daughter asked, answering her own question to show her father how knowledgeable she was.

Stephen was putting butter on the tip of his long, Italian bread-stick. It was not good for his cholesterol levels, but he never liked his wife commenting on his health. He would eat what he chose. Although her children wouldn't agree, she did keep her mouth shut about many decisions that her husband made. Not when it came to the house or the children, but in business matters she was unquestionably restrained. And if she did question his decisions in this realm, quite innocuously, he inevitably grew short-tempered with her.

Just a few weeks prior, she had asked why he had not antici-pated that the business might not take off. An innocent enough question. Her husband had responded by saying that he wasn't a clairvoyant, that no one had anticipated the asbestosis claims and the liabilities and the lawsuits against everyone remotely involved. "Lawsuits?" she had asked. "Forget it," he had replied. Her chil-dren, of course, never saw the short temper that he sometimes showed with her. Both she and her husband had their shortcom-ings and their roles. Their children's generation didn't understand this division of labor. He was the provider, and she managed the home. Marriage wasn't easy, but she had never strayed. She loved him, even though he drove her crazier and crazier each year.

"It should sort itself out," Elizabeth's boyfriend was saying now, sensing at last that the conversation needed to change.

Thank you, boyfriend, Barbara thought. Yes, her daughter wasn't as sensitive as he was. When Elizabeth had been young, she had often gone hours without speaking to her mother. At a young age, she had been aware of how stonewalling affected her mother. Children could be so cruel. Barbara had often been cruel to her own mother, she saw that now.

"Yes, it will be fine," her husband affirmed, as much to the chil-dren as to his wife. "Now, who is going to want dessert?"

"Not me," Barbara said.

She thought how funny it was, her daughter always trying to define herself against her mother, and now here she was with a boyfriend so much like her father, both optimists, both kind. She wondered if Elizabeth and her boyfriend had good sex. It wasn't something you asked your child, but it was important, sometimes the only thread that kept a marriage in place. Never say no to your husband. Her mother had taught her that. Had she shared with her daughter that piece of advice? She couldn't recall. Next time she had a moment with her daughter, she would bring that issue up, as well as the writing desk and the fur coat. She'd make a note when she got home to put them in the will for her. She and her daughter were much more alike than her daughter would concede. But Elizabeth had parts of her grandmother as well. The sloppiness, for one. The hot and cold nature. Everything was genetics. Her daughter had not learned that yet, but she would when she had children of her own. Elizabeth wasn't actually all that interested in her mother's story at the moment; she was too caught up in her own life and so had left her heritage to rest. But Barbara could bring up the writing desk at least.

The waiter began clearing the plates. Barbara suddenly felt depleted. She wanted to get back to the Overseas Club and go to bed. She had a lot on her mind. It was time to leave. She nodded to her husband to get the bill. He had drunk too much, so she had to nod at him several times. Eventually, when she had nodded a million more times, he understood. "Waiter," he said.

He paid the bill, and they got up and left her favorite restaurant. Tony kissed her on both cheeks and called her *belissima*. She thanked him as her husband held her coat.

"Sleep well," Barbara said, kissing her daughter goodbye outside the restaurant. "You both look very well."

"We loved seeing you," Stephen said.

"Me too," Elizabeth replied. "Thank you for dinner," she told her father.

"It was delicious," her boyfriend added.

"Enjoy the next few days," Elizabeth added. Taking her boyfriend's hand, she walked away.

As Elizabeth departed, Barbara thought how gratifying it was for her daughter to be young. She imagined what her own mother would have thought, watching her and Stephen walk away buoyed by the infinite possibility of young love. Her mother had loved Stephen so much, as had her father. A peach of a fellow. Stephen and she had succeeded in giving their children a secure and happy childhood. Their offspring had been fortunate, unlike her mother, unlike her, unlike so many children unstitched by war—rag dolls torn and floating and adrift. Watching Elizabeth go, she felt an acute awareness that with her and all her other children went threads of herself that she had laboriously and self-preservingly re-stitched.

She turned to her husband. "Should we go?"

He said, "Yes, beautiful," and she took his arm as she always did, knowing that his business would fail and that her life was slowly but inevitably coming unthread once again, splitting apart like the two strands of the double helix at her core.

CHAPTER 18

FAIRLEE, VERMONT — 2018

The challenge with raising a baby when you have unresolved trauma is really huge. . . . Research shows that if you don't pause and reflect in terms of what you remember and how you draw meaning from what you remember, your kids, whether you want to or not, will receive the kind of negative things that you received, that you hadn't made sense of. But the research is also clear that if negative things happened to you and you understand the impact of them, you can actually have what's called earned security, where you can learn how to develop what I call an integrated way of being. When kids are securely attached, they end up having a wonderful way they can balance their emotions. They have a way of understanding themselves. They can pause before acting on an impulse. They can approach stresses with resilience. They can take on all sorts of challenges without withdrawing from them. There are all sorts of amazing and important developmental things that happen with secure attachment.[61]

My eighty-year-old mother is walking toward the car with her rubber-capped cane, my six-foot, four-inch son guiding her across the flagstone path. I have changed my mother's sheets and placed her luggage by our door. I have said nothing in response to her remark that she has decided I do not like her very much.

Her complaints of her health concerns, lack of food, and US policies still reverberate with me. I know she has lived through Hitler, that she has seen the consequences of incendiary politics,

237

that she fears another war. I have listened to her stories of being placed on a train to Wales under Operation Pied Piper, of being picked up by a stranger from a train platform with a number hanging around her neck, of becoming a mother at age three, of spending her childhood in a succession of foster homes and boarding schools, of being abused, of having no childhood at all.

I know that she is not alone in the adverse childhood experiences she has endured, that her trauma was complex, that my grandmother Violet experienced the same and that they both suffered the physical and mental health effects of trauma in later life. I am aware of the inheritability of trauma with its long tail, and how the parenting she and my father provided mitigated its effects.

And yet I do not walk my mother to the car or apologize to her as she sits erect in the front seat of our car, eyes fixed on the green trellis that we have not yet fixed, patiently waiting for her daughter to drive her home. Instead, I go to my husband and share with him what she said about me not liking her very much.

"Tell her you're sorry, that you're stressed out, that the house has been full, that you did not mean to be short. Say something, Elizabeth. If you don't, you will regret it."

So reluctantly I do. I apologize to her and she tells me not to worry, that she is fine, that she understands all about stress. She tells me she loves me.

After I have taken her home, I return to Vermont. I sit with my husband and my grown children on our screened porch, overlooking the lake. A red air balloon rises in the distance then dips below a crenellated tree line as together we eat the risotto I made with asparagus, sausage, and onions that I picked up from our local farm, the one where each morning I write the stories of Violet and my mother. As we eat, I listen to the peepers by our pond make their peeper calls, the air leaving their lungs and passing over their vocal cords into their vocal sacs, loud and strong, and I think how grateful I am for my children, my husband, my siblings, my deceased father, and my mother, and how fortunate I am as well.

BARBARA

IN HER OWN WORDS, 1960[62]

Once I was married, I did have my parents over to the U.S. to stay. When I was twenty-nine years old, my father died of colon cancer. Three years later my mother died from the same disease.

When my mother's will was read, I discovered that she had completely cut me out of the will and that all was left to my brother. I was stunned, but I suppose not too surprised. Several years later, I woke up one night and heard my mother talking to me. I was sure she was right there. She said, "Please forgive me, I love you," and I said, "I love you too." With that she vanished, and I went back to sleep.

Now, at this time in my life, I have forgiven her and only wish our relationship could have been different. She and my brother had a much more loving and easygoing relationship. He lived in England while I lived in the U.S. Deep down, I think I always resented her for having abandoned me as a child, leaving me to fend for myself and become my brother's mother and survive without her. I had been such a spoilt, adored little girl, and I am sure the suddenness of the parting left me feeling confused. At the time, I did not realize this. Today I miss her, several years later. I still think of her often and have photographs of her around the house. Someday, I think I would like to have some of my ashes scattered with hers on the Sussex downs.

VIOLET

George was not happy with me for taking the pills. But he could not know what it was to feel as I did. I had grown so tired. I never slept. I looked in the mirror each morning at the dark circles beneath my eyes and my wiry gray hair and thought what use was

I? I was so worried for her but she would not listen to me. She never had. After the war, she never responded to me in a way that other children responded to their mothers. She never touched me or hugged me or gave me a kiss. I was so useless to her. Invisible like a ghost. I had seen too much. Endured too much pain. I only wanted to be heard. To be seen. For her to recognize that I was there, that I was still flesh. My act was the last power I had. Not since Barbara Christine was three years old had she let me be her mother. Pushing her in that laced carriage along the cobble sidewalk. Her big blue eyes. That Hapsburg chin. My joy. How lucky I had been to have a daughter and a son of my own. There is nothing comparable to the privilege of loving a child and nothing as devastating as that love withheld. A mother's role is to be present for her child, and if that child does not want her to be present, does not return that love, what choice does a mother have but to do whatever is required to ensure that someone else will be present for the child instead, to love her unconditionally as her parent does, whether she knows that or not? Stephen, I knew, could be that person for her in adulthood. I did what I had to. My daughter married him, so was that so bad in the end? He married her and they had seven children and those children would one day have children whom they would love unconditionally as well.

I forgive my daughter. We mothers do. Even when our children are mothers, they are still our children. We love them as much as we possibly can. We are not perfect. There is so much we do wrong. I never should have cut her out of my will. I never should have done or said so little and also so much. We can only hope that one day on reflection, our children will come to understand that our intentions came from a place of love and that they see us for who we wanted to be, despite what preceded, despite who we became. We can hope that they forgive us and that when they have children of their own, they do better than we did. We can hope that they will realize what they can control and what they cannot, that they will find a way to cope, that they will love and be loved, and that they will take one day at a time, one step, one breath, and go on, creating and finding joy in their present life and forging on as best they can.

POSTSCRIPT

"While trauma researchers have made great strides in understanding and treating single-episode present-life trauma, they are just beginning to explore the impact of intergenerational trauma and its expression, says APA Div. 56 (Trauma Psychology) President Diane Castillo, PhD, a former Texas A&M University associate professor of psychology who has studied and treated combat-related post-traumatic stress disorder (PTSD) for 30 years. . . . Continuing to explore intergenerational effects can help the field better understand and treat psychological pain at its roots," —Yael Danieli, PhD, co-founder and director of the Group Project for Holocaust Survivors and Their Children in New York.[63]

ACKNOWLEDGMENTS
AND GRATITUDE

I am grateful first to my mother for believing in the importance of this story, despite what it revealed, for her patience with me, for her love, and for always striving to be the best parent she could be. I am grateful to my siblings and their spouses for their ability to set differences aside in support of our mother and one another, and especially to my sister Carolyn for her help in getting this story heard and to her and Julia both for bearing so much. I am grateful to my husband for his love and his reservoir of emotional competence that I sometimes lack, and to his parents, especially his mother, in nurturing that competence in him. I am grateful to my children, Zoe, Ben, and Oliver, and for their joy, love, and support that so inform this work. I am grateful to my friend Beth who subtly but skillfully helps me reframe when I am struggling and who did so throughout the writing of this book. I am grateful to Emily and Rebecca for their valuable input on the early versions of this work and for their enduring friendship. I am grateful to Cathy for her perceptive reading, to Steph for her candor, to Paula for her early belief in this work, to Jackie for her publishing acumen, and to my cousin Nicholas for his unconditional support. I am grateful to Linda for always listening as we run. I am grateful to The Lionheart Foundation for the work they do in serving the most disadvantaged and for Housman Institute for their work in early childhood training and education. I am grateful to my copyeditor, Sarah Ellis for her attention to detail; to the editor, Rose Alexandre-Leach for her invaluable work; and to my publisher, Dede Cummings for believing in the importance of getting this story heard and who signs every email with the words of Naomi Klein: "To change everything, we need everyone." I am grateful to all those who read chapters of my work and encouraged me to write more. I am grateful to my publicist, Stephanie Barko for pushing me to persist. I am grateful to the psychologists, psychiatrists, and other professionals, including and especially Emma and Conor, who do the valuable work of helping youth and adults to develop strategies to address trauma and its deleterious effects.

ENDNOTES

1. "What is long-tail liability?" (March 30, 2020) Retrieved from: https://www.superlawyers.com/new-jersey/article/what-is-long-tail-liability/76faa6f4-32dd-467e-9deb-16e2b47c9e91.html

2. 28. Rusby J, Tasker F. Long-term effects of the British evacuation of children during World War 2 on their adult mental health. Aging Mental Health (2009) 13(3):391–404.10.1080/1360786090286775.

3. Online Assessment Measures, DSM-5, American Psychiatric Association. https://www.psychiatry.org/psychiatrists/practice/dsm/educational-resources/assessment-measures

4. Murray, D. W., Rosanbalm, K., & Christopoulos, C. (2016). Self-regulation and toxic stress report 3: A comprehensive review of self-regulation interventions from birth through young adulthood (Report #2016-34). Washington DC: Office of Planning, Research and Evaluation, Administration of Children and Families, US Department of Health and Human Services.

5. Rosanbalm, K.D., & Murray, D.W. (2017). Promoting Self-Regulation in Early Childhood: A Practice Brief. OPRE Brief #2017-79. Washington, DC: Office of Planning, Research, and Evaluation,Administration for Children and Families, US. Department of Health and Human Services.

6. Housman, D.K. (2017). The importance of emotional competence and self-regulation from birth: a case for the evidence-based emotional cognitive social early learning approach. ICEP 11, 13 (2017). https://doi.org/10.1186/s40723-017-0038-6

7. Schalinski, I., Teicher, M. H., Nischk, D., Hinderer, E., Müller, O., & Rockstroh, B. (2016). Type and timing of adverse childhood experiences differentially affect severity of PTSD, dissociative and depressive symptoms in adult inpatients. BMC psychiatry, 16, 295. doi:10.1186/s12888-016-1004-5

8. National Comorbidity Survey Replication. Retrieved from: https://www.ptsd.va.gov/professional/treat/specific/ptsd_research_women.asp

9. Duncan, L., Ratanatharathorn, A., Aiello, A. et al. Largest GWAS of PTSD (N=20 070) yields genetic overlap with schizophrenia and sex differences in heritability. Mol Psychiatry 23, 666–673 (2018) doi:10.1038/mp.2017.77

10. Ryan J, Chaudieu I, Ancelin ML, Saffery R (September 30, 2016). Biological underpinnings of trauma and post-traumatic stress disorder: focusing on genetics and epigenetics. Epigenomics, Vol 8, No. 11. https://doi.org/10.2217/epi-2016-0083.

11. What Is A Vestigial Tail in Humans?, Healthline. Retrieved from: https://www.healthline.com/health/vestigial-tail#causes

12. Colin, Virginia L,, Nancy Low & Associates, Inc, (June 28, 1991). Infant Attachment: What We Know Now, US Department of Health and Human services. Retrieved from: https://aspe.hhs.gov/basic-report/infant-attachment-what-we-know-now.

13. Bowlby, J. (1988). A secure base: Parent-child attachment and healthy human development. New York, NY, US: Basic Books.

14. Hofer, M. A. (2006). Psychobiological Roots of Early Attachment. Current Directions in Psychological Science, 15(2), 84–88. doi:10.1111/j.0963-7214.2006.00412.x as referenced in "How Mother-Child Separation Causes Neurobiological Vulnerability Into Adulthood," Association for Psychological Science. Retrieved from: https://www.psychologicalscience.org/publications/observer/obsonline/how-mother-child-separation-causes-neurobiological-vulnerability-into-adulthood.html.

15. Dörfel D., Lamke J. P., Hummel F., et al. (2014): Common and differential neural networks of emotion regulation by detachment, reinterpretation, distraction, and expressive suppression: a comparative fMRI investigation. Neuroimage, 101:298–309.

16. Scott, E. (October 27, 2018). Avoidance coping and why it creates additional stress. Retrieved from: https://www.verywellmind.com/avoidance-coping-and-stress-4137836.

17.18. Coé S. M., Boivin M., Nagin D. S., et al. (2017). The Role of Maternal Education and Nonmaternal Care Services in the Prevention of Children's Physical Aggression Problems. Arch Gen Psychiatry; 64(11):1305–1312. doi:10.1001/archpsyc.64.11.1305.

19. "About Child Trauma" The National Child Traumatic Stress Network. Retrieved from: https://www.nctsn.org/what-is-child-trauma/about-child-trauma

20. Bowlby, J., Ainsworth, M., Boston, M., & Rosenbluth, D. (1956). The effects of mother-child separation: A follow-up study. British Journal of Medical Psychology, 29(3-4). 211-247. doi: 10.1111/j.2044-8341.1956.tb00915.x.

21 Murray, D. W. & Rosanbalm, K. (2017). Promoting Self-Regulation in Adolescents and Young Adults: A Practice Brief. OPRE Report #2015-82. Washington, DC: Office of Planning, Research, and Evaluation, Administration for Children and Families, US Department of Health and Human Services.

22 Bousalham, R., Benazzouz, B., Hessni, A., Ouichou, A. & Mesfioui, A. (2013). Maternal separation affects mothers' affective and reproductive behaviors as well as second offspring's emotionality. Journal of Behavioral and Brain Science, 3(5), 409-414. doi: 10.4236/jbbs.2013.35042.

23 Casarjian, B. (2019). EQ2: Empowering Direct Care Staff to Build Trauma-Informed Communities for Youth. Lionheart Foundation.

24 Casarjian, (2019).

25 Honeycutt, J. A., Demaestri, C., Peterzell, S., Silveri, M. M., Cai, X.,Kulkarni, P., Cunningham, M. G., Ferris, C. F., & Brenhouse, H. C. (2020). Altered corticolimbic connectivity reveals sex-specific adolescent outcomes in a rat model of early life adversity. ELife, 9, e52651. https://doi.org/10.7554/eLife.52651

26 Br Med J (1931); 2:239.

27 Copeland, W.E., Shanahan, L., Hinesley, J., Chan, C.F., Aberg, K.A., Fairbank, J.A....Costello, J.(2018). Association of childhood trauma exposure with adult psychiatric disorders and functional outcomes. JAMA Netw Open, 1(7). doi:10.1001/jamanetworkopen.2018.4493.

28 Copeland, W.E et al.(2018).

29 Adams, J. (2008) Obesity, epigenetics, and gene regulation. Nature Education 1(1):128

30 Epigenetic regulation of the glucocorticoid receptor in human brain associates with childhood abuse (Mar, 2009). McGowan PO, Sasaki A, D'Alessio AC, Dymov S, Labonté B, Szyf M, Turecki G, Meaney MJ Nat Neurosci; 12(3):342-8 as referenced in Kathryn Gudsnuk, Frances A. Champagne (Dec 2012) Epigenetic Influence of Stress and the Social Environment ILAR J.; 53(3-4): 279–288. doi: 10.1093/ilar.53.3-4.279.

31 Coé S.M. et al. (2017).

32 "About Child Trauma" The National Child Traumatic Stress Network. Retrieved from: https://www.nctsn.org/what-is-child-trauma/aboutchild- trauma.

33 Benware, J.P. (2013). Predictors of father-child and mother-child attachment in two-parent families (Master's Thesis, Utah State University); iii. Retrieved from https://digitalcommons.usu.edu/cgi/viewcontent.cgi?article=

2731&context=etd.

34 Center for Substance Abuse Treatment (US). Trauma-Informed Care in Behavioral Health Services. Rockville (MD): Substance Abuse and Mental Health Services Administration (US); 2014. (Treatment Improvement Protocol (TIP) Series, No. 57.) Chapter 3, Understanding the Impact of Trauma. Retrieved from: https://www.ncbi.nlm.nih.gov/books/NBK207191/.

35 Casarjian (2019).

36 Scott, E. (October 27, 2018). Avoidance coping and why it creates additional stress. Retrieved from: https://www.verywellmind.com/avoidance- coping-and-stress-4137836.

37 Cuncic, A. (Mar 15, 2019). How to Practice Self-Regulation. Verywell Mind. Retrieved from: https://www.verywellmind.com/how-you-canpractice-self-regulation-4163536.

38 *The Hull Daily Mail* (April 2, 1940) "Hull Family in Dutch Road Smash; Car Down 15-Foot Bank: Mother and Daughter Injured".

39 Tully, E.C. & Donohue, M.R. (2017). Empathic responses to mother's emotions predict internalizing problems in children of depressed mothers. Child Psychiatry and Human Development, 48(1), 94-106. doi: 10.1007/ s10578-016-0656-1.

40 *The Hull Daily Mail* (14 May, 1940) "Hull Man Was in Mined Ship Now in England—But Wife Left in Holland".

41 Rees, C. (2007). Childhood attachment. British Journal of General Practice, 57(544), 920–922. doi: 10.3399/096016407782317955.

42 Dube S.R., Anda R.F., Felitti V.J., Chapman D.P, Williamson D.F., Giles W.H. (2001) Childhood Abuse, Household Dysfunction, and the Risk of Attempted Suicide Throughout the Life Span: Findings From the Adverse Childhood Experiences Study. JAMA.286(24):3089–3096. doi:https://doi.org/10.1001/jama.286.24.3089.

43 Peterson, T. J. (n.d.). Are mental health diagnostic labels a good idea? Retrieved from https://www.healthyplace.com/other-info/mental- health-newsletter/are-mental-illness-diagnostic-labels-a-good-idea.

44 "There is a consensus among memory researchers and clinicians that most people who were sexually abused as children remember all or part of what happened to them although they may not fully understand or disclose it." American Psychological Association (n.d.). Memories of childhood abuse. Retrieved from https://www.apa.org/topics/trauma/memories.aspx.

45 Koplewicz, H. S. (2018). Separating families and creating trauma.Ret rieved from https://childmind.org/blog/separating-families- and-creating-trauma/.

46 Wilcox, B. (circa 2013). Untitled and unpublished but given the title "In Her Own Words". Shared with her daughter Elizabeth Wilcox over the course of many years.

47 Zoellner, L. A.,Feeny, N. C.,Bittinger, J. N.,Bedard-Gilligan, M. A.,Slagle, D. M.,Post, Loren M.,Chen, J. A. (Sep 2011) Teaching trauma-focused exposure therapy for PTSD: Critical clinical lessons for novice exposure therapists. Psychological Trauma: Theory, Research, Practice, and Policy, Vol 3(3), 300-308 doi: 10.1037/a0024642

48 Cusworth, N. (2010) "Is That My Real Mummy", a reprinted excerpt from his written family history, circa 2010. Cusworth, N. (2010) "Is That My Real Mummy", a reprinted excerpt from his written family history, circa 2010.

49 Cuncic (2019).

50 Murray, D. W. & Rosanbalm, K. (2017)

51 Wilcox, B. (circa 2013).

52 Murray, D. W. & Rosanbalm, K. (2017,) p.1.

53 Post-Traumatic Stress Disorder: The Management of PTSD in Adults and Children in Primary and Secondary Care (2005). NICE Clinical Guidelines, No. 26.National Collaborating Centre for Mental Health (UK). Leicester (UK): Gaskell. Retrieved from: https://www.ncbi.nlm. nih.gov/books/NBK56506/.

54 Ogle, C. M., Rubin, D. C., & Siegler, I. C. (2015). The relation between insecure attachment and posttraumatic stress: Early life versus adulthood traumas. Psychological trauma : theory, research, practice and policy, 7(4), 324–332. doi:10.1037/tra0000015

55 Zoellner, L.A.,et. al. (2011).

56 Disease Control and Prevention principal deputy director, Dr. Anne Schuchat as quoted by Chatterjee, Rhittu (November 5, 2019), CDC: Childhood Trauma Is A Public Health Issue And We Can Do More To Prevent It, NPR, retrieved from https://www.npr.org/sections/health-shots/2019/11/05/776550377/cdc-

childhood-trauma-is-a-public-health-issue-and-we-can-do-more-prevent-it?
on publication of Preventing Adverse Childhood Experiences (ACEs): Leveraging the Best Available Evidence 2019 Division of Violence Prevention National Center for In-jury Prevention and Control Centers for Disease Control and Prevention Atlanta, Georgia available at: https://www.cdc.gov/violenceprevention/pdf/preventingACES-508.pdf

57 Zoellner, L. A.,et al, (2011).

58 Wilcox, B. (circa 2013).

59 Brandt, A. (2017). Four ways that childhood trauma impacts adults. Retrieved from https://www.psychologytoday.com/us/blog/mindful-an-ger/201706/4-ways-childhood-trauma-impacts-adults.

60 The National Child Traumatic Stress Network (n.d.). Families and caregivers. Retrieved from https://www.nctsn.org/audiences/fami-lies-and-caregivers.

61 Siegel, D. (September 15, 2014) The Challenge for Parents with Unre-solved Trauma [Video File]. Retrieved from https://www.youtube.com/watch?v=nzMd-B4Z5dxw.

62 Wilcox, B. (circa 2013).

63 DeAngelis, T. (February 2019) The Legacy of Trauma, Vol 50, No. 2. Retrieved from: https://www.apa.org/monitor/2019/02/legacy-trauma

ABOUT THE AUTHOR

ELIZABETH WILCOX is the fifth of seven children, born to an English mother and American father. She has worked as a journalist, editor, and producer in London, Hong Kong, and the United States in print, radio, television and on the web. She lives in Vermont with her husband and the occasional visit of her three grown children. She invites readers to her website at www.elizabethwilcox.net to learn more about her writing.